Naked at the Interview

Tips and Quizzes to Prepare You for Your First, Real Job

Burton Jay Nadler

John Wiley & Sons, Inc.

New York • Chichester • Brisbane • Toronto • Singapore

ClickArt Business Cartoons
Courtesy of T/Maker Company. Used with permission

This text is printed on acid-free paper.

This publication is designed to provide accurate and authoritative
information in regard to the subject matter covered. It is sold
with the understanding that the publisher is not engaged in
rendering professional services. If legal, accounting, medical,
psychological, or any other expert assistance is requried, the
services of a competent professional person should be sought.
ADAPTED FROM A DECLARATION OF PRINCIPLES OF A JOINT COMMITTEE OF
THE AMERICAN BAR ASSOCIATION AND PUBLISHERS.

Library of Congress Cataloging in Publication Data:

Nadler, Burton Jay, 1953–
    Naked at the Interview: tips and quizzes to prepare you for
  your first real job / by Burton Jay Nadler.
      p.   cm.
  Includes bibliographical references.
  ISBN 0-471-59449-0 (paper)
    1. Job hunting. 2. Vocational guidance. 3. College graduates-
-Employment.   I. Title.
  HF5382.7.N33   1994
  650.14—dc20   93-23780

Printed in the United States of America

10 9 8 7 6 5 4 3 2 1

This book is dedicated to:
Family

Teri, Jordan, and Justin: You've tested me for many years and I hope Poppy has passed the exams to date. Our course is far from over.

Those from New Jersey to California to Texas: I've tested you over the years, and vice versa. Everyone seems to be doing quite nicely. Thanks for supporting my years of formal and personal education.

Grandpa David: I'm sorry you didn't read this one, but I thought of you while it was being written. We shared some of the same experiences at Penn and may have sat in the same seats when taking exams. We all miss you.

Uncle Zum: You didn't read this one either, but at least you knew it was being written. Your tests were some of the most challenging I've ever experienced and I hope I passed a few. Yes, you were a good teacher. We all miss you too.

Friends

Jud and Shelly: I most definitely have failed a few tests of time, but my feelings have never diminished, nor have my memories faded. I hope friendship will be judged by quality of time and thoughts, not quantity of time spent together.

Professional Colleagues and Co-workers: I've passed a few and I've failed a few, but we've always learned from our tests together. Thanks for listening. Thanks for learning. Most sincerely, thanks for teaching. Mary, Skip, and Terry, special thanks to you!

Special Students

Thanks to all of you who worked with me over the years I've spent in career services, especially those who tracked me down after I left a school. Each of you tested me as I tested you. Without our interactions, this book would not have been possible. You taught me so much and I hope I gave something in return. I came back to career services from recruiting because of you and for you. This book, and my ongoing efforts, are dedicated to everyone of you past, present, and future.

PREFACE

Study Skills as Job Search Skills

At last! A job search publication designed for those who love taking tests—soon-to-be and recent college graduates. I know some will deny, deny, deny. At the writing of this book I've spent over 19 years in higher education (7 as an undergraduate and graduate student and 12 as a career services professional), so I know they do like tests, particularly final exams. I've been a student and I've counseled and taught students. I've worked for student and alumni job seekers in career services capacities at several diverse and well-respected institutions. So, from personal experience I conclude that college students really do enjoy the challenge and exhilaration associated with quizzes and final exams (as well as take-home essays and term papers).

Think about the social dynamics and intrigues of midterm or final periods. "How'd you do?" "Did you study this part of the text?" "Do you think the prof will focus more on lectures or readings?" "Can I borrow your notes?" "Do you want to prep together?" "Is this worth an all-nighter?" These oft-heard questions reveal a bit of anxiety and a great deal of empathetic as well as tactical thinking. Facing the unknown with varying degrees of preparation, students handle these circumstances somewhat differently. Yet, all know how much preparation results in success.

A quick and unscientific survey (I don't have to cite statistical significance or provide hard data) reveals a few of the many approaches individuals and groups use to study for final exams:

- ✔ Reviewing and rewriting notes and outlining readings; condensing as much information as possible into as few pages as possible. Ultimately, creating concise study notes to review, synthesize, analyze, and (depending upon the subject and a twisted desire to rhyme) "memorize."
- ✔ Anticipating possible questions or reviewing old exams (obtained in honorable ways), outlining possible answers, and internalizing concepts behind the questions or simply memorizing answers (or both).
- ✔ Finishing all readings (at the last minute for most); highlighting important materials from texts, periodicals, and notes with color highlighter; creating study lists (not crib notes for unsavory purposes).
- ✔ Reviewing all quizzes taken to date, hoping the professor has a sense of logic (some call it fairness) and inquires regarding critical points or the cumulative sum of information covered to date.
- ✔ Sleeping with texts and notes and hoping that the required knowledge seeps through via osmosis.

Some swear by the "the R.S.V.P. method." No, this doesn't involve confirming attendance at a pretest party designed to relax (or pickle) one's brain. It's a study approach, with the acronym illustrating: **R**eviewing information at hand, including notes, texts, and readings; **S**ynthesizing information deemed relevant, creating outlines, lists, or similar pieces; **V**erifying facts and researching areas with information missing; and **P**reparing to express information in multiple choice, fill-in blanks, short answer or written essay or, occasionally, verbal formats. *No matter the approach taken, effective preparation involves reviewing, rewriting, prioritizing, and internalizing in preparation for specialized written or verbal communications.*

This book is written for those preparing for job search, the most unique "cumulative final" of all. If you realize that the skills required of job search are similar to those required to study, after overcoming initial bouts of anxiety and disorientation over the prospect of finding "the J word" (a job), you will know how well equipped you are to succeed. All students and graduates have skills necessary for effective job search. Reusing the now-familiar (and I hope someday "best-selling") acronym, we identify how easily you can apply this approach to job search:

☆ Review, and document in writing, knowledge of self and knowledge of career fields and job options.

☆ Synthesize knowledge of self and information pertaining to careers and job functions in order to set tentative research goals (worthy of more inquiry) and job search goals (targeted for job search actions).

☆ Verify information regarding research and job search goals, fine-tuning job search goals, identifying and researching in greater detail potential employers, and developing job search strategies.

☆ Prepare to express information effectively via written (resumes, cover letter, fax messages, and follow-up letters) and verbal (telephone calls, informational and employment interviews, and voice mail messages) communications.

Whether you realize it or not, you have all of the skills to be a successful job seeker. You can prioritize, research, summarize, write, and speak toward a specific task. You have done so many, many times effectively in academic settings. All you have to do is apply study skills to a different type of exam, the test of job search.

Assessments (a fancy word for "tests" and "quizzes") in this book are designed so you can progress easily and enjoyably through the process outlined above. They will develop and hone Job Search Study Skills, preparing you to be as successful a job seeker as you are a student (or were, if you're an alum). Every reader should first complete *The Job Search Survival Quiz* (Chapter 1). This device has proven over many years that a humorous checklist can be an informational and motivational force, stimulating appropriate and effective actions. It will also provide a sense of direction, allowing you to determine which assessment you might wish to complete next. You can pick and choose those that relate to circumstance of job search reality or review them all. If, as an example, you are now in the process of developing a resume, *Resume Reality Checklist* (Chapter 4) and *Perfect Resume Review* (Chapter 5) would be of immediate value. If you are preparing for interviews, the *Interview Readiness Indicator* (Chapter 7) would be a timely exercise. In truth, completing all would be of highest value. Preparing for exams requires identification of what you know and what you *don't know* (boy, that's profound). That's exactly what these devices will do. Each quiz is followed by elaboration on relevant topics. This information will be presented as:

♦ *Answer Key and Typical Questions,* with answers to all or selected inquiries and analyses of essential issues.

- ◆ *Study Tips for the Retest,* action-oriented tidbits outlining skills-building and job search steps.
- ◆ *Helpful Resources,* a brief annotated listing of helpful people, places, or things.
- ◆ *Study Skills Summary,* overview of objectives of each chapter (so you can grade how well I did).

Sample resumes, correspondence, phone scripts, and other materials are also included. The *Job Search Secrets Quiz* (Chapter 10), an assessment designed to determine whether material was internalized and to summarize important concepts, is the last quiz. The book ends with an *Appendix: Tips Not Tests,* containing some additional advice for special readers. Now don't get lazy, reading the first and last chapters, thinking that you can fake your way through this self-paced course (see, I do know how students think).

Citing a traditional and thought-provoking homily (sorry, they just seem to pop out of my word processor), "giving credit where credit is due," I must note that students, alumni, and recruiters taught me everything you will read in subsequent pages. You will learn how to study for and pass your job search finals using time-tested techniques (oh, you better get used to alliterations too). We've all head that tests are meant to teach as well as determine what we know, but we don't believe it. These are truly *tests that teach* (that would make a good header for a book review; get the hint?).

Remember that unscientific survey? It also revealed a universal nightmare shared by test takers . . . walking into an exam undressed! Psychoanalysts (or, more appropriately "pseudoanalysts") interpret this vision as representative of a lack of preparation or a sense of security. Without being too Freudian, being "naked" is a fear also shared by job seekers. Many dream the dreaded dream of walking into an interview without clothes. No, not without the *proper* clothes, without *any* clothes . . . buck naked!!! Concepts covered by this text should clad you with the confidence that knowledge of successful job search behaviors will bring. Once read, the insecurity-laiden nightmare of nakedness will disappear.

The book is written in a tone and with content that college grads can relate to and find enjoyable (if you like parenthetical quips mixed in with important advice and information). **Read on, enjoy, learn, and good luck on your job search finals!**

Contents

CHAPTER 1

The Job Search Survival Quiz

The following is a quick and easy assessment of your Job Search Survival Rating. Answer questions by checking the appropriate boxes, tabulate your score as instructed, and match your results with the comments on the following pages.

		Yes	No
(1)	Do you have a distribution-ready copy of your resume within arm's reach?	[ ]	[ ]
(2)	Does at least one version of your resume have an objective statement with a job title and field cited?	[ ]	[ ]
(3)	Have you visited or spoken to your alma mater's career services office in the past six weeks?	[ ]	[ ]
(4)	Have you applied for a posted job within the past week and felt confident you would get an interview?	[ ]	[ ]
(5)	Have you interviewed for a job within the past week without getting nauseous as well as nervous?	[ ]	[ ]
(6)	Have you ever met someone who has a job you would like to have?	[ ]	[ ]

		Yes	No
(7)	Have you ever practiced interviewing with a friend, counselor, or family member?	[ ]	[ ]
(8)	Have you recently followed up a rejection letter, requesting additional consideration?	[ ]	[ ]
(9)	Can you write a thorough description(s) of the job(s) you want on 3x5 index cards?	[ ]	[ ]
(10)	Have you recently solicited the help of a reference librarian for a job search–related task?	[ ]	[ ]
(11)	Can you write the names of three books or magazines pertinent to your field(s) of interest?	[ ]	[ ]
(12)	Has anyone ever looked puzzled and confused when you describe your ideal job?	[ ]	[ ]
(13)	Can you cite the name, address, and phone and fax numbers of at least 25 potential employers?	[ ]	[ ]
(14)	Have your parents promised to support you forever?	[ ]	[ ]
(15)	Have you won the million-dollar lottery at any time in your life?	[ ]	[ ]

For questions 1–13 score 5 points for each "yes" and zero for each "no." Total up your scores for these 13 questions.

A score of 50–65 indicates that you will not only survive, but you will thrive because you have taken important first steps. You are very familiar with helpful resources and can be confident that you will be successful. You are intuitively aware of the nature of job search. *While you may wish to read on, you may want to return this book before you get fingerprints on it or you may wish to give it as a gift to the most needy job seeker you know.*

A score of 40–50 indicates that you may have taken some critical first steps, but don't quite know what to do next. You may need to discuss your goals more carefully with a career services counselor or another job search support person and develop a clearer strategy. You may need to finish your resume or make some decisions on how to identify potential employers and how to follow up initial contacts, but basically you are on the right track. *Read this publication carefully. You'll get a great deal out of it.*

A score below 40 indicates that either you have a unique strategy or that you have yet to take steps in the right direction. *Whatever the case, a call to your alma mater's career services office and a thorough review of this book is definitely called for.*

If you answered "yes" to question 14 or 15, ignore your Job Search Survival Rating, because you obviously don't need a job and if you wanted to find one (just to keep from being too bored), you could depend upon luck, rather than your own efforts. *You may want to purchase and donate numerous copies of this book to your local public library or alma mater's career resource library.*

Seriously, this book has been written to educate as well as motivate. Unless you think you are a very, very lucky person, you should act upon the ideas presented. Every reader should take a critical job search step within a week after completing the book. Don't wait. Don't depend on luck. Utilize skill and intelligence. The assessments in each chapter will make you a more skilled job seeker, more knowledgeable of resources you can use, and more action oriented.

JOB SEARCH SURVIVAL QUIZ ANSWER KEY AND TYPICAL QUESTIONS

Don't be too hard on yourself if you scored below 40. There's always hope, and you (or your parents) might yet win the lottery. You definitely have the skills to be an excellent job seeker. The remaining quizzes will show that. Now, and after each assessment, let's review answers, examine typical inquiries, identify useful hints, and note useful resources.

Do you have a distribution-ready copy of your resume within arm's reach?

Why is a resume so important and do I really have to have it within arm's reach at all times?

A resume is like a job search driver's license. It allows you to respond quickly to postings and effectively seek the help of others. While you really can't carry a resume with you at all times (although you should), it's best to view it as your job search calling card. In fact, I suggest you develop a business card that has your name, address, phone number, school, degree, and graduation date (and maybe, job search goal) noted. This will make it easier to "exchange cards" with someone to whom you should send a resume. Or, you might be creative and make a "mini-resume," an abbreviated resume reduced to a 5x7 inch size, which you can carry with you. With or without an objective, large or small, resumes project the message "I'm looking for a job!" Resumes are more than symbols of job search, they are critical job search tools. You can't complete the process without proper tools. But tools don't finish a project, craftspeople do. The *Resume Reality Checklist* (Chapter 4) and *Perfect Resume Review* (Chapter 5) will address issues related to developing, critiquing, and using your resume effectively.

Does at least one version of your resume have an objective statement with a job title and field cited?

Won't an objective limit me and stop an employer from thinking about other options?

Can't I simply put the name of any job I'm applying for under the objective heading?

Objectives don't limit, they focus. Appropriate goal-directed phrases are like handing reviewers magnifying glasses. Resumes with an objective are focused and seem much "larger" than those without one. Early in the process, it's okay to develop a multipurpose version without an objective. As soon as possible, you should create at least one, perhaps two additional resumes that clearly cite job search goals. Stating a desired position does not eliminate consideration for other options. More accurately, you will uncover these options through effective follow up. Resume communiqués (fancy word for "cover letters") are not one-time-only, hit-or-miss propositions. You can cite an exact job title, and even a firm name, for posted openings or for thoroughly explored opportunities, but don't simply change objectives. Rework your resume's format to highlight skills and experiences that support each new objective. Don't ever be afraid to state goals (in writing or verbally). One of the greatest ironies of job search is that those seeking "anything" often find "nothing." A lack of focus is what truly limits you. Discussions and samples appearing in the *Resume Reality Checklist* and *Perfect Resume Review* will further clarify these issues.

Have you visited or spoken to your alma mater's career services office in the past six weeks?

Why? Isn't it just for business and engineering majors?

*If I go to a small school without any real on-campus
recruiting, isn't it a waste of time?*

*If I'm a graduate living hundreds of miles away how
can it help?*

Career services operations may appear to anxious and, frankly,
uninformed people to be primarily for business and engineering students, because highly visible on-campus recruiting projects this stereotype. Some larger universities do in fact have specialized offices targeted
at particular majors, but most have wide-reaching centralized services
designed to enhance the decision-making and job search potential of all
students and alumni, no matter the major. While smaller schools may not
have large on-campus recruiting programs, they often are better able to
provide individualized attention and stress the importance of alumni
networking. Visit or call your office as soon as possible! Learn about what
they do and do not offer. Even if you live far away from your alma mater,
contact the career services office to learn of services they offer alumni.
Phone counseling and fax resume critiquing are becoming more regular
offerings. Also, don't limit yourself to your school's services. Be curious,
bold, yet polite, and visit the office nearest to you. Reciprocal services
can be available and most counselors seem to melt if you ask for help in
the right ways. *Mr. Recruiter's Tell it All Test* (Chapter 9) and *Tips For
Recent College Grads* (Appendix) offer additional insights.

**Have you applied for a posted job within the past
week and felt confident you would get an
interview?**

*If postings aren't the way most people get jobs, what
good are they?*

*Aren't postings a waste of time, especially those "blind
ads?"*

How can I feel confident?

Postings (including want-ads and on-campus announcements) are
not the way *most* people get jobs, but they are the way that *some* people
are successful. Don't limit your efforts to postings, but don't ignore them.
Responding to postings strengthens job search communication skills.
Writing, calling, and conducting telephone or in-person interviews are
all parts of "reactive" job search. The stronger your skills, the better you

apply them to "proactive" (goal-directed) methods. Blind ads are frustrating, so don't simply send a cover letter and resume, then wait and hope. Follow all responses to blind ads with two additional letters, one sent three days after the initial mailing and the other five to seven days later. Include copies of your resume and original cover letter in each. Your paperwork will be reviewed at least three times and you will be projecting enthusiasm and initiative. Also follow with another note if you have not heard after three weeks. Whatever approach, remember how critical ongoing communication can be. Confidence will come with a sense that you have done your best and that you have followed guidelines outlined in this publication (that's confidence on my part!), and from an awareness that you can (and will) follow up assertively.

Have you interviewed for a job within the past week without getting nauseous as well as nervous?

Are you kidding?

While I never get nervous, I don't get called back, why?

Interviewing is perhaps the most universally feared undertaking, second only to an IRS audit. If you are prepared, it can be an enjoyable way to share your background with an interested (and often interesting) individual. While practice is the best way diminish physiological and psychological symptoms, an attitude adjustment is the best way to eliminate self-perpetuating negative thinking. If you think it's going to be nerve-wrenching and stressful, it will be. Your own thoughts can heighten natural reactions to any situation. The image of walking into an interview naked may heighten anxiety in most, but it can be humorous. Think about the oft-used public speaking desensitizing technique of imagining an audience as naked. If it works, use it. But, don't giggle too much. From this moment on, think of an interview as simply a "conversation with a purpose." Also remember, even those who enjoy talking about themselves may be less effective if they don't stay focused. You interview *for a job*, not *with a company*. The more you direct inquiries (before and during an interview) to understanding the nature of a job and the more you focus responses on qualities possessed to perform job-related tasks, the better. The *Interview Readiness Indicator* (Chapter 7) contains a two-part assessment that covers virtually everything you'll need to be symptom-free, effective, and more important, feeling fully clothed and confident!

Have you ever met someone who has a job you would like to have?

So what if I did, what good will it do?

I don't know much about any jobs, isn't it too late?

As discussed in *Career Vocabulary Inventory and Goal Grid* (Chapter 3), goal orientation is simply a matter of describing job functions. Enhancing your career vocabulary by reading about or, better, by meeting people in certain professions, is essential to success. The more you know about a career field and about particular jobs, the more likely you will find a job within that field. Setting goals and identifying role models won't make a job appear by magic, but these steps will take you far on the path to job search success. Networking (a phrase you've heard over and over) with persons who do what you want to do is ideal. It isn't just using people you know, it's getting to know new people. Simply, it is telling as many people as you can (perhaps everyone) of your research and job search goals. Asking people what they do, how they got started in their field, and what advice they have for someone interested in either "learning more" or "breaking into the field" is effective networking. If you do this long enough and smart enough (you'll get better as you read on and as you practice), you will be successful. It's never too late to study for an exam or finish a term paper. I know you've pulled a few "all nighters" and received admirable grades. Just apply your study skills and research talents to this task, now. It is never too late to learn about careers, set goals, and find a job.

Have you ever practiced interviewing with a friend, counselor, or family member?

What good will practice do if you don't know what an interviewer will ask?

What good will studying for an exam do if you don't know what the professor will ask? What a question! Practicing interviewing is like studying. You don't memorize answers, but familiarize yourself with issues and prepare to face a number of possible questions. The interview test will definitely ask you to note qualifications, cite examples, and project enthusiasm. So, you do know the nature of most questions before you begin studying. Practice will place into short-term memory information that cobwebs or stress would make difficult to retrieve during an interview. Almost all career service facilities offer role-play interviewing. Some even offer videotaping (don't worry about the tilt of your head, where you place your hands, or count the number of pauses). Don't be too critical or analytical about any role-play efforts, no matter the technique. Practice brings to mind, then to mouth and tongue, pertinent information you might need for your oral exam (an interview). The *Interview Readiness Indicator* found in Chapter 7 presents a take-home role-play interview exercise to help you structure a practice session. You really wouldn't go to an interview naked, so don't go unrehearsed and ill-prepared.

Have you recently followed up a rejection letter, requesting additional consideration?

Isn't it "pushy" and inappropriate to follow up a rejection?

Once they determine I'm not a good fit, shouldn't I take "no" for an answer?

If I've said it once, I've said it a thousand times (oh yes, as a parent, I am prone to using stupid paternal, authoritarian phrases), "job search is not an application nor a correspondence process, it is a communication process." If you think job search involves sending resumes and cover letters to employers and waiting, you will end up waiting, and waiting, and, perhaps waiting . . . on tables! You are the only person you can count on in this amazingly unpredictable process. If you continue to communicate appropriately, the process will continue to move in the right direction. Always be polite, but always find a next step to take. I recommend following a pattern of phone, fax, and mail communications over and over. Follow phone calls (even the ones when you can't get past the receptionist) with fax notes, and fax notes with brief letters, and letters with another call. But, don't phone or write simply to be persistent. Have something to say and, most importantly, a goal in mind and a request to make (like a request for information on entry-level options). Ultimately, we hope, this pattern will be positively disrupted with in-person meetings, either employment or informational interviews. When goal directed, persistence does pay off. *The Job Search Correspondence Quotient* (Chapter 6) and *Phone, Fax, and Voice Mail Etiquette Exam* (Chapter 8) highlight how important follow-up communications are.

Can you write a thorough description(s) of the job(s) you want on 3x5 index cards?

Why must I be able to write job descriptions on 3x5 cards?

Won't I be limiting myself if I focus on a
particular job?

I will say again (and again, and again throughout this text), the more focused, the more effective you will be. If you cite a few fields and job functions of interest, others can more easily suggest alternatives. The more "open" you are, the more you receive polite smiles or overgeneralized advice, and very little else. Often, those looking for "anything good, anywhere" find nothing, nowhere. Quite simply, you must be able to describe one or more jobs of interest and, if possible, identify someone who has a job you would like. You will limit yourself only if you cannot cite a job search goal or two (or three) that you find appealing. Even if you just collect appealing job descriptions from books, want-ads, or postings you are researching options well enough to clarify goals. By writing them on index cards you are symbolizing your ability to articulate job search targets. These cards give you and others something to aim at. It is very powerful if you can show descriptions and say: "I'm looking for something similar to this. Do you have any suggestions as to whom I should contact and how I might go about it?" You may find it effective to incorporate desired job descriptions into cover letters and interviews, citing an "ideal position" in the letter or handing an interviewer your "ideal job description." Also, once written, you can enhance your ability to verbalize your goals and your capacity to share qualifications via an interview. You might wish to have the descriptions printed on the back of your business card under the heading *Seeking. . . . The Career Vocabulary Inventory and Goal Grid* (Chapter 3) presents ways to clarify and articulate job search goals.

Have you recently solicited the help of a reference librarian for a job search–related task?

Why a reference librarian? What can this person do?

These professional problem-solvers are amazing at uncovering hard-to-find facts and resources. They can help with goal-setting by suggesting books and magazines that describe career fields and job functions. They can help with employer identification, by suggesting written resources and databases. They can locate national, regional, and local directories that list potential employers and professional associations. And they can help with interview preparation by locating information about potential employers and current events pertaining to specific fields. Think about it. Whenever you bring a fairly obscure inquiry to these individuals their eyes grow bigger, the edges of their mouths turn up in a curious smile, and they begin to work with you to uncover appropriate information. Quite simply, reference librarians are perhaps the most underutilized and extremely valuable job search support persons. Turn them on and they can turn you on! Also a library is an easy-access environment where you feel comfortable completing research and job search tasks. There is no excuse for job search and research inactivity, because public and school libraries are accessible to everyone.

Can you write the names of three books or magazines pertinent to your field(s) of interest?

Why is it so important that I know about books and magazines?

Isn't it enough to know the employers I want to work for and shouldn't I be reading their annual reports?

The more you know about the field you wish to enter, in addition to the employer, not just one or the other, the more likely you will find a job. Interviewers are seeking a sense of focus and commitment from candidates, in addition to specific skills and characteristics. The more you project (in writing, over the phone, and in person) that you are intensely curious about your career field of stated choice, the greater the likelihood you will locate and interview for opportunities. You can't just say "I'm interested." Your actions will speak much louder than your words. By conducting research and, eventually, telling people about how you did your research, you will be enhancing your chances of finding employment. It's amazing, but I often work with students who say they are interested in advertising who have not read David Ogilvy's "Confessions of an Advertising Man," or *Ad Week* or *Ad Age* magazines. Don't locate books and magazines simply to "name drop" or "phrase drop" (questionable interview techniques that evoke images of pigeons and seagulls). Reading books and magazines will make you aware of trends within a field and more knowledgeable of the unique vocabulary of a field and, as a result, make you more likely to project a motivated and informed image. People do like to speak with someone who shares common interests and uses common phrases.

Knowing about employers isn't enough. While reading an annual report can be an effective way to research an organization, it can too often be an ineffective use of your time. Annual reports can inform you about the nature of an organization's business, strategic goals and plans, major influences on past operations, the names of senior management and, of course, the financial status of an organization. But, they often tell you *nothing* about day-to-day job functions. Given the choice of reading an annual report for 15 to 30 minutes, or spending 5 to 10 minutes with three individuals over the phone, addressing questions about the nature of the job you are seeking, always choose the latter. Ideally, you will be able to do both. If you can't, I encourage you to learn as much as you can about a job in question, frame that with knowledge of the field, and spend time in face-to-face or voice-to-ear communications. Also, understand that "goal-setting research" takes place prior to job search activities, and "preinterview research" prior to interviewing. Each requires honesty and an inquisitive and assertive nature.

Has anyone ever looked puzzled and confused when you describe your ideal job?

If I don't really describe a job, how can they be confused?

As will be a recurring theme, goal-directed speech and, ultimately goal-directed behaviors are critical. It's always best to keep in mind the KISS (Keep It Simple Stupid) acronym when projecting goals. I have worked with many, many intelligent students and alums who are amazingly fluent in "circle speak." They can go on and on and not really describe anything. "A corporate oriented . . . marketing kind of . . . strategic . . . management training–type position," is not a clear job search target. It is a perfect example of how circle-speaking job seekers fool themselves into thinking they can express goals. Some people nod their heads and say "that's nice" when confused, because they don't want to appear ignorant or embarrass the speaker. Seek feedback when sharing goals with others. Ask if they know of someone who is working in your field of interest or in a job associated with your goal. These inquiries will reveal whether you have expressed yourself effectively and, ideally, uncover some very important contacts.

Can you cite the name, address, and phone and fax numbers of at least 25 potential employers?

Once I have all of this information do I just send a resume and cover letter, or is there more?

It's important to be able to list potential employers, but it isn't enough. There is more to accomplish before you "send" resumes and letters and much, much more to accomplish after. I have said again and again (I think I've said it a few times in this book already): "job search is neither an application nor a correspondence process." You cannot simply mail resumes and cover letters (no matter how well-written) to potential employers and expect a thorough review of your candidacy followed by a note revealing a thoughtful decision. Names and addresses are easier to come by, using national and regional directories and databases, but this information isn't meant for oversimplified (often ineffective) mass mailings. First conduct a "phone survey" to uncover basic information pertaining to each organization and, whenever possible, to identify a person (or persons) to communicate with. The telephone is *one* underutilized tool, but the fax machine is perhaps the *most* underutilized job search tool. Don't be afraid to fax first and follow with original copies by mail. The *Phone, Fax, and Voice Mail Etiquette Exam* in Chapter 8 will address the best use of all of these "new-fangled" devices. Also, the sample phone scripts, resumes, and job search correspondence that appear in appropriate sections will reveal how you can best "tell your story" and undertake critical follow-up actions.

Have your parents promised to support you forever?

Even if they have, I know you'll get bored after the first few months, so you might as well read the rest of this book and prepare yourself for job search.

Have you won the million-dollar lottery at any time in your life?

You already know what you should do. Purchase many, many copies of this book and donate them to college career services offices and libraries. Yes, even you will get bored after a while, so keep one copy for yourself.

JOB SEARCH SURVIVAL QUIZ STUDY TIPS FOR THE RETEST (ACTION STEPS TO TAKE)

✎   If you have completed a resume, immediately review *The Perfect Resume Review*. After using this device, review your draft with a career services professional, and make any changes you believe will make it more effective. If you don't have a resume, complete it within the next week. Don't put it off. Information in *Resume Reality Checklist* and *The Perfect Resume Review* (Chapters 4 and 5) will get you started. This material will make it easy for you to create a first draft, and ultimately a finished version. You want to have distribution-ready copies at your disposal as soon as possible. Also, don't depend upon a resume-writing service or software. If you must, have a service develop a first draft *with* you (not *for* you), but don't assume that paying any price means that you will receive an effective and individualized resume.

✎ Complete three "informational interviews" (I really don't like that phrase) in order to focus on goals and begin to identify a job search network. It is critical that you be able to articulate your goals. Informational interviewing is easier and less awkward than most think. Chapter 3 (*Career Vocabulary Inventory and Goal Grid*) contains information on this approach. Ask a career services counselor for help if you don't feel comfortable soliciting and completing information-gathering conversations. Don't ever use informational interviewing as a pretense when you actually want an employment interview. If you are sincere in your efforts to learn about another's job, you can find your own with appropriate follow up. Quite honestly, effective informational interviewing is the most important skill you can learn and use. By asking others about their educational and vocational backgrounds you set goals and, ultimately and quite naturally, request employment consideration.

✎ Review want-ads in the past five editions of your Sunday paper (or visit a career services office to review old and current postings). Identify ten that seem "appealing," "intriguing," or "right on target." Don't be concerned about years of experience or academic background stated as requirements. Just identify the ones that look interesting. Now, address these questions: *Do you want to actually apply for any of these positions? What is appealing? What qualifications do you possess that match? Do other firms hire people to perform similar roles? What other publications (or places) post jobs? What do you want to do next?* This exercise can enhance goal setting and it will encourage you to use the very best "reactive job search" skills and to begin to develop creative approaches to "proactive job search." Too often job seekers limit themselves by reading postings and reacting to "openings" (positions cited as available). They ignore goal-directed ways to uncovering hidden jobs.

> ## JOB SEARCH SURVIVAL QUIZ HELPFUL RESOURCES
> ## (PEOPLE, PLACES, AND THINGS)

✔ University and college career services facilities offer much for students, alumni, and, when possible, community members. Contact your school's career services office to become familiar with their offerings. If you are a currently enrolled student, this is easy. Don't procrastinate! Do it now! If you are a graduate, this may be a little more difficult, but you should call now. Find out via a phone conversation what alumni services are available and how you can access them. Also, stop by the nearest two colleges and universities to determine whether you can access services or resources. Don't be afraid to hear "no." Nothing ventured, nothing gained (oh, is that true!). The least you may be allowed to do is review resource materials. Great! If your geographic goal (or home) is in a city different from your school's location, you must contact institutions in that city. Don't be shy.

✔ Books to examine include: *Liberal Arts Jobs*, Peterson's, 1989; *The Complete Job Search Handbook*, Henry Holt, 1988; *Creative Careers*, Wiley Press, 1985; *The Careers In Series*, VGM Horizons; *The Fourth of July Guide to Careers, Internships, and Volunteer Opportunities in the Nonprofit Sector*, Garrett Park Press, 1990; and *The Career Opportunities Series*, Facts on File. Remember our earlier discussion regarding the critical ability to articulate goals. The more you know about a field, the more likely you will enter it. The better able you are to describe a job, the easier it will be to find one. These books will help you examine career fields and job functions and identify potential employers.

✔ Professional associations and chambers of commerce are wonderful, underutilized resources for those exploring options or actively seeking positions within particular career fields. Call the chamber of commerce in your city (cities) of interest and contact an organization associated with your field(s) of interest. If you're having trouble locating an association, ask a reference librarian for help. If you don't ever "look for a job," but simply "look to meet people," you will be successful. Ironically, when we have a job we don't have time to join associations and attend events. When we don't have a job we have the time, but feel awkward. Overcome psychological inertia. Learn about associations related to your field(s) of interest, join when possible, use membership directories to set up informational and employment interviews, attend meetings and, yes, volunteer to work on the newsletter or organize the next function. That will keep you busy and really force you to take effective networking steps.

A skills summary will appear at the end of each chapter. Review the stated objectives to determine whether you have internalized all that you can from the section. If ready, continue to the next. If not, review the chapter again. Remember, your final grade will be based upon individual test scores, so don't hurry onto the next until you have "aced" the one at hand.

JOB SEARCH SURVIVAL
QUIZ STUDY SKILLS SUMMARY

- Identified many of the basic components of successful job search.
- Highlighted often-overlooked steps.
- Previewed concepts covered in subsequent chapters.
- Motivated you to read on and enjoy (I hope)!

CHAPTER 2

Self-Knowledge Screen: The Check Above the Neck

To determine your Self-Knowledge Status, circle answers that *best* completes the highlighted phrases.

1. **Introspection can:**
   (a) Lead to epiphanies of career insight required to set goals
   (b) Cause headaches and stomach cramps if done incorrectly, and should be done only under proper supervision
   (c) Be the covert cause of much frustration and, in truth, delay one's efforts to successfully identify goals and implement job search strategies
   (d) Bring great joy and lower one's blood pressure when associated with the correct mantra
   (e) Both "a" and "c"
2. **In-depth career counseling, including vocational testing, can:**
   (a) Cost a great deal of money, but soothe concerned parents, spouses, or significant others
   (b) Reinforce knowledge already present, yet characterize it in new ways, using easier-to-share terms

(c)   Be a great disappointment for those unwilling to undertake postassessment research

(d)   Reveal steps required for decision-making and, ultimately, job search success

(e)   All of the above

3. **Components most critical to the self-knowledge required of job search success are:**

(a)   Skills, values, interests, and personality traits

(b)   Ambitions and financial aspirations

(c)   Depth of career knowledge

(d)   Logistical, financial, and emotional obstacles

(e)   All of the above

4. **Skills assessment reveals:**

(a)   Potential for success within careers and jobs that use particular skills

(b)   Skills possessed

(c)   Priorities of skills one could use within career fields and job functions

(d)   Both "b" and "c"

(e)   All of the above

5. **Values clarification reveals:**

(a)   A values profile that can impact perceptions of career alternatives, but not predict compatibility or happiness

(b)   Current values, not life-long permanent views of the world

(c)   Values that associate with career fields and job functions

(d)   The financial value of any career field and job function and the earnings potential of particular majors

(e)   Both "a" and "b"

6. **Interest inventories:**

(a)   Conducted by banks to determine what rate they should charge for home and auto loans

(b)   Clarify areas of interest and motivate research of career fields and job functions

(c)   Are the most often misused and misunderstood assessment devices

(d)   Match interests to predict performance in career fields

(e)   Both "b" and "c"

7. **The most underemphasized yet critical component of career exploration and job search is:**
   (a) Assessment of personal characteristics
   (b) Research of potential careers and job functions
   (c) Marketing oneself to employers
   (d) Majoring in appropriate academic area(s)
   (e) Supply, demand, and potential earnings information

8. **The most often confusing and misunderstood component of career decision making is:**
   (a) How to tell mom and dad I don't want to work
   (b) The role of self-assessment
   (c) What is meant by "researching of career fields"
   (d) The intrinsic value of "work" in contrast to the value of "jobs" and "careers"
   (e) The impact of first job on career pathing

9. **"Myers-Briggs" is:**
   (a) An old vaudeville team who made the dance, "the job search shuffle," famous
   (b) An abbreviated phrase used to identify the Myers-Briggs Type Indicator (MBTI), one of the most widely used psychological assessment devices
   (c) A test many use, but few understand
   (d) A mother-daughter team who developed and updated the MBTI
   (e) Answers "b," "c," and "d"

10. **John Holland and the SII are:**
   (a) The designer and construction firm responsible for the tunnels connecting New York City and New Jersey
   (b) A rap group that entertains at many career counseling conventions
   (c) The original theoretician who posited that vocational interests can be described in general ways by six themes, and the test, Strong Interest Inventory, that utilizes this theory to enhance career exploration
   (d) The creator of, and the name of the test, Strong Vocational Interest Inventory, which tells you what careers you should enter
   (e) Both "c," and "d"

Now score your Self-Knowledge Status (SKS). Answers (as mirror images to lessen temptations to cheat) are:

(1) ↄ (2) Ǝ (3) Ǝ (4) ◻ (5) Ǝ (6) Ǝ (7) ꓭ (8) ꓭ (9) Ǝ (10) ↄ

Isn't it strange publishers think you won't look backwards to get answers before doing a multiple-choice quiz? Anyway, for each correct response credit 10 points to your score. Using a typical academic curve:

Scores of 90 and 80 indicate an SKS of "excellent." You have a good understanding of the worth of self-assessment and how it fits into the process of decision making and job search. You are ready to incorporate knowledge of self with knowledge of careers and jobs to set and, ultimately, obtain realistic goals. You've probably had some very good career counseling or have had life experiences that provided the reality checks necessary to instill career focus. Or, you're a career counselor and not a job seeker, so you know all of the tricks (that's not fair).

70 or 60 indicates an SKS of "good." You have had some experience with self-assessment, perhaps testing and counseling, but you haven't quite made the connection between this stage and subsequent ones. You intuitively know self-assessment isn't enough to establish goals, but you are naive or frustrated enough to be unsure of next steps. Or, you're a career counselor who has used the "test 'em and toss 'em" approach; offering exercises, tests, and words, but not guiding clients through identifiable postassessment steps.

Below 60 is, let's say, "not so good." You've either fallen into the terror-filled trap of multiple choice, allowing logic and analytical thought to confuse you, or you are in desperate need of clarification regarding self-assessment and career counseling. All readers should, but low scorers *must* review the annotated answer key. This means job seekers as well as counselors!

Many who take this quiz might disagree with how I judge "right and wrong," so before job seekers or fellow professionals read the answers I want to share insights regarding my background. I was, and remain, proud to call myself a "Career Counselor." After working hard to receive the academic credentials associated with two graduate degrees and being hired into a position with this title, it was imperative that everyone knew what to call me. My education cost too much time, energy and, yes, money to be "hey you, the one who helps people get jobs." Working with students and alums, I followed basic tenets of counseling theory and practice and applied concepts associated with career developmental theories, and I sprinkled in things I learned in career counseling courses. As I read popular self-help books and learned from job seekers and recruiters, I added common sense and behavioral approaches. I also began to allow my natural curiosity regarding career fields and job search techniques to get the best of me. I read, I conducted informational interviews, I listened to job seekers, and I felt more comfortable sharing what I learned in an authoritarian (and, yes, humorous) style.

Having returned to college career services, after recruiting for a management consulting firm and a financial services organization, I now most enjoy calling myself a "Job Search Coach." While career counseling will always be a part of my professional repertoire and an important offering of facilities I manage, career counseling without the end goal of meaningful employment is a luxury few can afford. I am now concerned that some can get caught in quagmire of self-assessment. I am also concerned that the counseling most receive is too assessment-driven, leaving its recipients unsure of appropriate next steps. I have been quoted as saying: "*What Color Is Your Parachute?* is a perfect title, but a far from perfect book, because readers without a parachute might break legs if they jump unprepared into job search from its lofty heights of personal knowledge." This book and its author, Richard Bolles, have contributed much, but I use the quote to underscore some concerns. **Too many people who have completed many wonderful exercises or taken any number of assessment devices can cite Myers-Briggs or Holland codes, note values of particular import, and list significant achievements and skills, *but cannot describe fields of interest or successfully find a job.*** Counselors ask clients to jump from self-assessment into an "ideal career" (an extremely lofty goal) without a parachute or a safety net of career information below. J-O-B-S (a four letter word I am allowed to use in print) are building blocks of C-A-R-E-E-R-S (a seven-letter word that leaves many as horrified as any four-letter word could). Yes, I must confess I use "the J word" and call myself a Job Search Coach frequently. I now proselytize that research is the key to goal setting and job search skills building should be the main objective of all good "career services professionals" (a diplomatic phrase everyone can support).

```
SELF-KNOWLEDGE SCREEN
ANNOTATED ANSWER KEY
```

The following notes correct answers in ***bold italics*** and, unlike most quizzes, identifies why particular responses were best. It's always hard to get a prof to explain why one answer was better than another, but we've done it here. Discussions cover basic concepts associated with self-assessment, career decision making, and job search.

1. **Introspection can:**
   (a) Lead to epiphanies of career insight required to set goals
   (b) Cause headaches and stomach cramps if done incorrectly, and should be done only under proper supervision
   (c) ***Be the covert cause of much frustration and, in truth, delay one's efforts to successfully identify goals and implement job search strategies***
   (d) Bring great joy and lower one's blood pressure when associated with the correct mantra
   (e) Both "a" and "c"

Many would mistakenly identify "a" as the answer, but in truth it is "c." Job seekers would like to contemplate their past and explore inner visions to reveal goals, but this does not happen very easily. Those who counsel (or coach) realize that self-assessment is a critical first step, but few are prepared to address frustrations resulting from clients' unrealistic expectations that it is the first and last step. Goals come from research, the exploration of fields and functions. Exploration takes place in libraries, bookstores, and career resource areas. It occurs by reading and, ideally, by speaking with people knowledgeable of fields and functions. No matter how long or hard you contemplate a desired future, you're limited by career-related experiences of the past. You cannot do your best on an exam if you haven't read all of the required materials. Complete self-assessment as quickly as you can and progress enthusiastically to exploration. That is where you will uncover goals and lessen frustrations.

2. **In-depth career counseling, including vocational testing, can:**
    (a) Cost a great deal of money but soothe concerned parents, spouses, or significant others
    (b) Reinforce knowledge already present, yet characterize it in new ways, using easier-to-share terms
    (c) Be a great disappointment for those unwilling to undertake post-assessment research
    (d) Reveal steps required for decision-making and, ultimately, job search success
    (e) All of the above

Those knowledgeable of career counseling (as counselors or clients) realize "e" is the answer, because all are equally appropriate statements. Those unfamiliar with the field, or quite honestly naive, may have greater expectations for counseling and testing. These individuals, including some well-meaning, yet short-sighted counselors, look for answers within standardized assessments. They might select "b" or "d." Assessments, whether formal or informal, can mark the true beginning of the process we call "job search success," but they can also be disappointing to those who do not enter or complete the explorations phase of the process. No matter the cost (private testing services can charge hundreds of dollars), you must realize that tests will not tell you what you should be or what you would be successful at. At the very least, they provide new and better ways to express things you already knew about yourself. At best, they stimulate research of career options by identifying fields and functions that "match" (statistically and intuitively) test results. No test is predictive of career success or personal happiness, but it can be a wonderful motivator if interpreted properly and used effectively.

3. **Components most critical to the self-knowledge required of job search success are:**
    (a) Skills, values, interests, and personality traits
    (b) Ambitions and financial aspirations
    (c) Depth of career knowledge
    (d) Logistical, financial, and emotional obstacles
    (e) All of the above

Career counselors are fond of echoing that "skills, values, interests, and personality traits are key components to self-assessment," but too few cite the impact other criteria can have. So, if you listened to your counselor closely, or if you had help with this quiz (shame on you), you may have identified "a" as the answer. The correct answer is "e," because all factors cited are equally critical to goal setting and, ultimately, obtaining employment. Self-assessment can be completed with an analysis of skills, values, interests, and personality traits. Utilizing this knowledge to set and articulate realistic goals and build skills required to find targeted jobs involves all factors. Some job seekers set unrealistic goals because they learn a great deal about themselves and then read very little about career options. Suffering a "love at first sight" response, they leap headlong (light-headed) into job search and with upsetting regularity find frustration rather than positive responses. Further research would reveal whether additional studies, specific technical skills, or access to certain individuals or settings would be required to succeed.

A student who wants "an overseas job" but is unable to cite specific jobs, unwilling to contact or visit employers in major metropolitan areas, and unwilling to pay his or her way overseas to find a so-called "ideal job," illustrates this situation. Logistical, financial, and emotional obstacles to completing research and job search activities have too long been ignored. You must learn the skills required to identify and overcome obstacles in order to be successful. By going beyond self-assessment to research and, finally, to job search, you will do just that.

4.   **Skills assessment reveals:**
   (a)   Potential for success within careers and jobs that use particular skills
   (b)   Skills possessed
   (c)   Priorities of skills one could use within career fields and job functions
   (d)   Both "b" and "c"
   (e)   All of the above

Some might mistakenly identify "e" as the correct answer, because many really want tests to predict success. I can't tell you how many times I hear the question "Can you give me the test that will tell me what I should do?" (but I'll guess it has been over 10,000 times). In truth, no test has been developed to predict what you *should* do, although some are designed to motivate your exploring things you *could* do. Skills inventories, card sorts, or exercises are not predictors of potential success. They are simply good mechanisms to identify and prioritize skills you possess (or think you possess). Most devices are not aptitude or achievement tests, but simply self-report questionnaires. Even the best aptitude and achievement tests do not predict your ability to apply your skills to particular fields. It is through research that you identify skills required of entry-level options. After research, you determine whether you wish to undertake all of the experiences involved in ongoing skills enhancement (that's a fancy way of saying "on-the-job training"). Often you must wait for "the test of time" to determine whether you have what is required for long-term success.

5. **Values clarification reveals:**
   (a) A values profile that can impact perceptions of career alternatives, but not predict compatibility or happiness
   (b) Current values, not life-long permanent views of the world
   (c) Values that associate with career fields and job functions
   (d) The financial value of any career field and job function and the earnings potential of particular majors
   (e) *Both "a" and "b"*

The correct answer reveals how important it is not to overindulge on values issues. Yes, I must confess that some call me "a realist," others "a pragmatist," and, more than a few call me "a cynic" when I address "touchy-feely" issues, but I do believe job seekers too often overvalue values. You should consider value systems and how you will respond to intrinsic as well as extrinsic rewards, but it's very hard (if not impossible and dangerous) to associate careers with particular values. In fact, stereotyping might result in individuals not examining appropriate options. A desire to feed one's family and live a life surrounded by material objects and hold a career of prestige should not preclude someone from exploring teaching, but stereotypically individuals who identify these values as important do not research this field. It's best to think of values clarification, and associated exercises, as establishing a list of current feelings. This list can come in very handy when exploring career options and, rarely, when identifying potential employers. It is most valuable when conducting post-offer analysis and when mapping out a long-term career strategy (which really can take place only after 5 + years of postundergraduate employment). As you learn more about yourself and about your reactions to job-related issues, you can take out your list and see where positive, negative, or ambivalent feelings may be coming from.

I don't think someone twenty-one or twenty-two years of age can accurately project yet-to-be clarified values into a lifelong quest for career achievement and happiness. Also, we often forget that values-oriented needs can be met by "avocational" interests (hobbies, volunteerism, and family). Many a businessperson contributes time and money to worthwhile causes, even when value assessments revealed a lower priority when forced to rank roles. So, no device can associate particular values with jobs or careers. Values are within individuals and expressed in various ways. It would be naive at best, and biased at worst, if we were to label certain fields as more "meaningful" than others. Yes, I understand these views may be controversial, or worse, commonsensical, but I have seen too many people seeking career direction become confused and disoriented by issues of values. I encourage these people to do whatever they can to take each and every step as carefully, yet as quickly as possible. Assessment is first followed by "paper-and-pencil" and "people-to-people" research. Research identifies tentative job search goals; then, job search skills-building and, ultimately, fine-tuning, which comes from active job search, yields success. Your next job (particularly your first job) is not your last. Ongoing personal assessment, including values clarification, is required to stay on the right path (no matter how crooked it might seem).

6. **Interest inventories:**
   (a) Conducted by banks to determine what rate they should charge for home and auto loans
   (b) Clarify areas of interest and motivate research of career fields and job functions
   (c) Are the most often misused and misunderstood assessment devices
   (d) Match interests to predict performance in career fields
   (e) *Both "b" and "c"*

The correct answer is "e." Interest inventories can be some of the most intriguing ways to stimulate research, but they can be the most often misused and misunderstood devices. These are the tests most job seekers regularly characterize as the ones "that told me to be a funeral director or army officer." Well, you always said you wanted to work with people. In both of these jobs you do work with people and rarely hear complaints from those you work with. Seriously, like skills inventories these formal tests , informal card sorts, or exercises are not predictors of potential success. They are simply good mechanisms to identify and prioritize interests you possess (or better "express"), for most devices are also self-report questionnaires. Correlating your interests with those in certain career fields and the labeling of your skills profile (whether using one-, two-, or three-letter codes) does not predict that you will be successful or happy in a particular job or field. It is meant to motivate research. Through research you uncover enough information about a field and how you might relate to tasks and people within the field to set tentative goals. Through job search you go through what Darwin might have called "survival of the fittest testing." Those judged "most sincerely interested," "most skills qualified," and "a good fit" receive offers. Once offers are received, review self-knowledge indicators before accepting or declining. With an offer in hand you can conduct more in-depth employer research and make good next (not last) decisions.

7. **The most underemphasized yet critical component of career exploration and job search is:**
   (a) Assessment of personal characteristics
   (b) Research of potential careers and job functions
   (c) Marketing oneself to employers
   (d) Majoring in appropriate academic area(s)
   (e) Supply, demand, and potential earnings information

While each answer has some merit, the best is "b." Assessment is far from the most underemphasized component. If I haven't made it clear yet, I do believe it to be the most overemphasized aspect . It really isn't a part of career exploration, but an important preliminary part of a larger process. Research of fields and functions is truly the most underemphasized component. While every counselor and all job search coaches sing the praises of exploration, too few motivate job seekers to thoroughly complete this stage. Lack of funds to purchase materials, inability to track alumni in particular career fields, and too little one-on-one time with clients are sad-but-true reasons why we sometimes cannot help. Research is ironically perceived as the most time consuming and least exciting part of the process for almost all job seekers. Seniors are busy taking courses, participating in extracurricular activities, and undertaking the socialization (or socializing) required to complete their final year of study. They really don't have enough time to conduct thorough exploration. Financial and psychological pressures to find a job quickly force many to skip this phase and go directly into job search (with little focus and a minimal goal-directed vocabulary). Some try to find out "what's hot" and "what's not," "what can I do with my major," or "what pays the most and is most readily available?" These will forever be the cries of job-seeking Seniors and alumni. In truth, time and life experiences facilitate career exploration well beyond graduation and even after one has served in a first or second job. Like death and taxes, career exploration happens whether you like it or not. Insurance policies and knowledge of tax laws can make both undesirable inevitabilities somewhat rewarding. So, it's always best to plan ahead and expand knowledge. Research is the real key to success. Do it now if you can, or do it later, but please do not be naive enough to think that the research you can conduct now will result in the identification of a "dream job." Environmental and economic factors, including scientific discoveries yet to be made and industries yet to be developed, make exploration an ongoing necessity. If you learn now how to conduct it in the future, you will be well served.

8. **The most often confusing and misunderstood component of career decision making is:**
   (a) How to tell mom and dad I don't want to work
   (b) *The role of self-assessment*
   (c) What is meant by "researching of career fields"
   (d) The intrinsic value of "work" in contrast to the value of "jobs" and "careers"
   (e) The impact of first job on career pathing

You won't be surprised to learn that "b" is the correct answer. While all alternative statements do have merit, and "c" is a very close second, let's agree that the role of self-assessment is misunderstood by many who undertake career decision making. Too many assume self-assessment yields career insights and related decisions. Wrong! Self-knowledge is an important ingredient in the recipe, but research is critical to the final outcome. Those that fixate on self-assessment can easily become confused and frustrated when motivated to conduct the research required of decision making. They don't want to leave what I call the lofty heights of self-knowledge. It has taken a while to climb the mountain. The view is beautiful and they don't want to undertake the practical and potentially risky trek downward. Some counselors allow them to stay up there as long as they like. Some coaches motivate them to continue the decision making journey through the next steps of research, until it ends with stated goals.

9. **"Myers-Briggs" is:**
   (a) An old vaudeville team who made the dance, "the job search shuffle," famous

   (b)   An abbreviated phrase used to identify the Myers-Briggs Type Indicator (MBTI), one of the most widely used psychological assessment devices

   (c)   A test many use, but few understand

   (d)   A mother-daughter team who developed and updated the MBTI

   (e)   *Answers "b," "c," and "d"*

The correct answer is "e." The Myers-Briggs Type Indicator (a.k.a. "Myers-Briggs" or "MBTI") is perhaps the personality instrument most widely used by career services professionals (and others) today. The test, developed by the mother-daughter team of Isabel Briggs Myers and Katherine Briggs, offers a practical application of the eminent psychologist Carl Jung's theory of types. Many college grads studied the theory, but few thought much about it after psych finals were over. But now there is a phenomenon of millions (I didn't count, but it's a safe and documented guess) able to cite four-letter acronyms revealed by this measurement. Many companies, government agencies, counseling facilities, schools, and even a few career services offices (a small personal joke) educate test-takers that only one of 16 possible types best describes each person. Ultimately, a four-letter code (not "four-letter word") identifies a type based on four aspects of personality. The Extroversion versus Introversion "dimension" reveals how we interact with the world and where we direct our energies. Sensing versus Intuition identifies the kind of information we naturally notice and remember. Thinking versus Feeling notes how we make decisions. And, Judging versus Perceiving reveals whether we prefer more structure or more spontaneity. Increasingly, career counselors believe that matching a person's personality type to a career is the best guarantee to satisfaction. I'm not sure how many job search coaches accept this premise, but I am sure that many students and alumni will be offered this device as a self-assessment tool. Yes, it is a good test, but like all assessment devices, it doesn't tell you what to do or what you would be successful at. It tells you about you, not about careers. Knowledge of careers is gained through application of the research and study skills you possess and through the lifelong process of internalizing information (no matter whether you are an "S" or an "I" or any other Myers-Briggs type). Use this intriguing test, but don't depend on it, or expect too much from it.

10. John Holland and the SII are:

   (a)   The designer and construction firm responsible for

the tunnels connecting New York City and New Jersey

(b)   A rap group that entertains at many career counseling conventions

(c)   *The original theoretician who posited that vocational interests can be described in general ways by six themes, and the test, Strong Interest Inventory, that utilizes this theory to enhance career exploration*

(d)   The creator of, and the name of the test, Strong Vocational Interest Inventory, which tells you what careers you should enter

(e)   Both "c," and "d"

I would like to say that "a" or "b" are correct, and you would like to hear that "d" or "e" are correct, but it's really and truly "c." The SII or "Strong Interest Inventory" (known by different names and different initials at different times) has historically been the most widely used career-related assessment. But it remains the most often misunderstood instrument of its kind. A warning is clearly stated in the interpretation information: "Your answers to the test booklet were used to determine your scores: your results are based on what you said you liked or disliked. The results can give you some useful systematic information about yourself, but you should not expect miracles. Please note that this test does not measure your abilities; it can tell you something about the patterns in your interests, and how these compare with those of successful people in many occupations, but the results are based on your interests, not your abilities." Yes, it is the test that matches scores to people in career fields. It is the one we have almost all taken at one time or another. But, it is not "the test that told me to be a Beautician," because no test can tell us what to be! The device is based upon the original work of John Holland, who premised that vocational interests can best be described by six overall occupational "themes." These include: Realistic, Investigative, Artistic, Social, and Enterprising. You get an acronym with this one too, but this time it's three-lettered, revealing the three themes that seem most "dominant." The Strong Interest Inventory (SII) presents information to test-takers in three ways: (1) scores for a "General Occupational Theme," identifying similarity to the six interest patterns; (2) scores for "Basic Interest Scales," identifying similarity to clusters of activities associated with major themes; and, (3) scores noting similarity to the interests of men and women in over 100 occupations via

"Occupational Scales." Interpretive instructions do use phrases like: "They prefer occupations such as design engineer, biologist, social scientist . . ." and " Vocational choices include . . ." when describing themes, but the test is not designed to predict career satisfaction or success. If interpreted well and used properly, as a motivator of research, it can be a useful self-assessment device.

SELF-KNOWLEDGE SCREEN STUDY TIPS FOR THE RETEST (ACTION STEPS TO TAKE)

✎ Identify the career counseling services offered by your school or the nearest college career services office. Explore the nature of assessment activities; whether formalized testing is done and if individual or group counseling is a part of the program. Once you understand the way it's done, and if you judge it to be professional and economical (even if a small fee is involved) do it! Take the actions required to learn about yourself and do so in preparation for thorough exploration of options.

✎ Using the Yellow Pages, referrals by career services professionals, or lists appearing in publications like *What Color Is Your Parachute?* locate three private "vocational counselors," "career counselors," or "testing services." You probably won't find anyone listed under "Job Search Coach." Oh, well! As above, explore the nature of their offerings and costs associated with services. Be careful. Don't commit to anything, yet. You are just exploring how these alternatives might differ from college facilities. You may get a "hard sell," so maintain your willpower and stay in research mode. If after you have done your homework you wish to invest in one of these, okay. At least you can compare and contrast cost-per-services and have a sense of "connection" with a particular counselor or operation. Too often moms and dads pressure college students and recent grads into taking an expensive battery of devices that have little, if any, impact in decision making. If you choose to undertake this approach to self-assessment, and you are committed to complete postassessment research, go for it!

✎ Speak with three career services professionals (no matter what they call themselves) and identify their favorite self-assessment exercise or device. Spend at least five to ten minutes discussing why they value the particular instrument, exercise, or test and ask about strengths as well as weaknesses. Determine if they are "self-help" in nature or whether they require professional interpretation. See if you can uncover any consensus regarding the most appealing activities. Even if you don't, focus on the one test or exercise you felt could be most interesting or helpful and do it. Of course, this can be done as a part of the above-suggested inquiries and should help you determine whether you want to use a college or private counselor or whether you can fly solo with a self-contained device.

✎ Remember, assessment is like using a police artist to create a composite sketch. It may resemble a suspect, but it really isn't a photo. Yet, you can still use it to find the person in question. The process, no matter how thorough or professionally guided, won't create a detailed portrait of you or of potential careers. It will give you something to use when rounding up suspects. Career exploration involves taking the composite with you to locate as many options as possible. After collecting evidence, interrogating people via informational interviews (there's that phrase again), and differentiating fact from fantasy, you decide whether you're ready for the trials of job search. Job search follows self-assessment and research. It doesn't flow naturally, so it requires dedication and hard work. Go for it!

SELF-KNOWLEDGE SCREEN HELPFUL RESOURCES (PEOPLE, PLACES, AND THINGS)

✔ Large bookstores are wonderful places to begin self-assessment efforts. I encourage you to visit two or three and spend several hours examining texts appearing under a variety of different headings. Depending upon the store and its inventory control methods, you thumb through "Self-Help," "References," "Self-Improvement," "Psychology," "Careers," "Job Search," or "Miscellaneous" publications. Don't limit yourself to one category (hey, where did you find this book?). Be curious about the others. Identify two publications that focus on self-assessment. Buy them (or see if a local library has them available to borrow); if you find a publication intriguing and the exercises interesting, do them! In spite of misinterpretations of my infamous quote, I do recommend that you review Richard Bolles' publication, *What Color Is Your Parachute?* Some suggestions are noted below, but so many different books under such a diverse array of categories and titles are available that I like individuals to self-select.

✔ Books to examine include: *What Color Is Your Parachute?* annually by Ten Speed Press; *The Three Boxes of Life*, Ten Speed Press, 1981; *Type Talk*, Delta Book, 1988; and *The 7 Habits of Highly Effective People*, Fireside, 1990. Magazines like *Working Woman, Success,* and *Self* regularly contain quickie self-help quizzes (like the ones in this book). While they may not be scientific, they can be fun and motivational (again, like the ones in this book) and spark your continued efforts. Peterson's *Where to Start Career Planning*, is an annotated and well-indexed listing of hundreds of titles; review of this one publication will reveal many others that would be of value at any stage of decision making and job search. Remember our earlier discussion regarding the tendency to fixate on self assessment. Frankly, the more you know about yourself, isn't necessarily better. While these books will help you examine components of self that relate to career focus, those that identify career fields and job functions and identify potential employers should be reviewed as quickly as possible when assessment is completed. The more you know about day-to-day job responsibilities, potential career paths, and about the lifestyle issues of people who perform in particular job capacities, the better.

✔ I don't want to appear too repetitive, or reinforcing (wow! alliteration and redundancy in the same sentence), so I will merge a few of my most frequent suggestions. A college or university is an amazing place (I don't have to tell you). It offers students, alumni, and (usually) community members diverse services and resources. Counseling facilities, career centers, and libraries are places you should explore. Counseling facilities are not just for those who "really need help." They often offer career counseling for those who "just want to get started." Obviously, career services can offer much, or they would have used a different name (and they often do, so don't get confused). Librarians can help you locate self-help publications that can help you begin your search for self-knowledge. Also, by being very, very curious, and using indexes (computerized and published), you can uncover some hidden gems in publications and magazine articles that are rather obscure, yet valuable.

**SELF-KNOWLEDGE SCREEN
STUDY SKILLS SUMMARY**

✏ Enhanced awareness of basic components of self-knowledge: skills, values, interests, and personality.

✏ Explored role of self-assessment in decision making and job search.

✏ Covered realities of "vocational testing" and suggested how to find right resources.

✏ Addressed impact of psychological issues on goal setting and job search.

✏ Bridged self-assessment to exploration and outreach efforts, while reinforcing critical research phase.

CHAPTER 3

Career Vocabulary Inventory and Goal Grid

When asked "What are your job search or career goals?" frequent responses include:

"A career-oriented position."

"A good job that will use my skills and allow for growth."

"An entry-level management training opportunity."

"A chance to learn and grow . . . to become somebody . . . and maybe attend graduate school."

"I don't know. Whatever I can do with my major. Anything!"

It's not surprising to hear these phrases from those just beginning exploration or job search, but it is shocking to hear them expressed throughout an employment campaign. After probing, some realize it is all right to cite precise goals, and they do. Others cannot improve their responses, no matter how creative the inquisitor. These individuals become frustrated when continually questioned about goals. They repeat the above litany of statements hoping the questions stop. They do stop, and the job seeker is encouraged to complete research.

The ability to express goals (although sometimes "tentative") is critical to job search success. The fear of appearing "ignorant" (the worst thing to call a well-educated soon-to-be or recent college grad) is a reason some speak in generalities. Ironically, those who wish to appear smart by expressing statements like those above are viewed as confused and naive. A strong vocabulary and proper usage are generally interpreted as signs of intelligence. You have the skills required to improve your ability to speak in concise goal-directed phrases. When completing vocabulary building, simple, yet effective, strategies are best characterized by three statements:

"If you can describe a job you can get a job!

It is difficult to concisely and accurately describe goals when you depend on knowledge gained from limited exposure to careers. Many have held summer jobs and internships, and a few have been lucky enough to observe family members performing in various roles. Too few have had career exploration courses or been tested on long lists of career spelling words (until now). I am confident that all job seekers can improve descriptive talents and enhance potential for job search success if they build a broader career vocabulary. You do so by reading books, magazine articles, and job descriptions. We are naturally attracted to want-ads because they are "easy-to-find job descriptions." After reading an ad or announcement, our ability to describe a particular job has immediately been enhanced and we feel confident to take next steps. Use want-ads as vocabulary builders, but do not limit efforts to expand your career vocabulary and, ultimately, finding a job, to this one approach.

"If you've met someone who has a job you would like, you can get a similar job!"

Reading books, reviewing magazine articles, collecting want-ads and postings, and discussing goals with a counselor are easy-to-follow first steps. The most educational and enjoyable, yet challenging, approach involves meeting someone who has held positions of interest. Listening to someone describe past or present jobs is the easiest way to improve your career vocabulary. Yes, it does require asking for help, but you will be surprised how readily others will offer to speak about themselves. If this is all one did for research, and it was done thoroughly, it would be enough to identify goals and facilitate effective job search actions.

"Remember the 3 F's—fields, functions, and firms—in that order!"

For years I have guided research using this wonderful alliteration, yet students and alumni always resist and recite their own three F's—firms, firms, and firms. Rather than first learn about career fields and job functions and later identify firms who consider candidates, they ask: "What firms hire my major?" "What firms are international?" and "Which are the best firms to work for?" So, I try to channel curiosity by starting with firms, working to functions, and, ultimately generalizing about fields. The unspoken fourth F—"focus" is the true goal. The more focused you are the deeper you can explore particular fields and functions, continually enhancing your vocabulary and improving chances that potential employers will hire someone who speaks their language.

CAREER VOCABULARY INVENTORY

This assessment seeks to identify the nature of your overall and goal-directed career vocabulary. For the fields appearing in the three boxes on the following pages, draw lines connecting the fields with correct functional descriptions, with applicable firm names, and with ways one might describe functional options in common language.

In the remaining blank boxes on page 38, list three fields of interest. Describe functions associated with a job in each field; note at least three employers of persons who serve in these functions; and describe the job as if you held it.

FIELDS	FUNCTIONS	FIRMS	COMMON LANGUAGE TRANSLATION
Advertising	*Production and Design Assistant* Works directly with others planning and executing efforts to create and implement cost-effective, strategic, and visually appropriate projects. Guides creation of drafts and finished products based on analyses of markets, finances, and schedules. Uses quantitative and technical skills as frequently as artistic ones. Frequently oversees graphics and production, but regularly interacts with editorial, marketing, sales, and other areas.	Andersen Consulting AMS EDS P&G General Mills Booze•Allen	"I work project by project, balancing many tasks, depending on the stage each project is at. Today I met with a marketing person. She seemed to like the basic concept we developed, but she wanted to see a test run-through and some cost estimates before making any decisions. Programming owes me some revisions first, then we'll see how user-friendly and fast everything is. After, I'll work with her to think of ways to sell the program internally. Without buy-in our work is wasted. When I was in Programming I didn't realize all of the challenges."
Information Systems and Computers	*Account Executive* Works directly with clients planning and executing campaigns. Coordinates efforts of others to create and implement an effective and strategy-driven effort. Guides development of print and broadcast efforts based upon analyses of client products, images, needs, and finances. Uses quantitative skills as frequently as qualitative ones. Orchestrates research, production, copywriting, and other areas, while interacting with marketing and sales professionals.	Wiley Warner Avon Holt, Rinehart and Winston William Morrow Simon and Schuster	"I work project by project, balancing a number of tasks. Today I met with a marketing rep associated with a project. She seemed to like the concept and drafts we developed, but she wanted to see a final copy of the text before making any editorial decisions. Design owes me some paste-ups first, then we'll see if copy and images blend to create what we want. After, I'll think of a way to sell her the total package, both print and multi-media. When I started in the Traffic Department I didn't realize how challenging it would be."
Book Publishing	*Analyst* Works with others planning and executing efforts to implement cost-effective, strategic, and user-oriented projects. Also assesses needs to purchase hardware and software. Guides creation of drafts and finished programs based on analyses of needs, finances, and schedules. Uses quantitative and technical skills more frequently than qualitative ones, but requires strong client relations skills. Regularly interacts with finance, marketing, sales, and other areas.	BBD&O Chiat Day DDB Needham Grey FCB/Leber Katz McCann Erickson	"I work project by project, balancing many tasks, depending on the stage each project is at. Today I met with a marketing person. She seemed to like the basic concept we developed, but she wanted to see a rough copy of text and graphics together before making campaign decisions. Design and editorial owes me some paste-ups first, then we'll see how copy and images blend. After, I'll work with her to think of ways to sell the product. When I started in Sales I didn't realize how challenging it would be."

Now that you've completed the relatively easy part of the exercise, you have more to do. Remember the instructions? In the blank boxes neatly nestled on the next page (I told you I liked alliteration) list three fields of interest. Describe functions associated with a job in each field; note at least three employers of persons who serve in these functions; and describe the job as if you held it. Simply, you're trying to model what appeared in the earlier portion. While you may use the same fields, please don't copy functions, firms, or translations. Enter new information if possible.

FIELDS	FUNCTIONS	FIRMS	COMMON LANGUAGE TRANSLATION

Most find the first portion of this assessment easy, so we won't provide an answer key. Yes, descriptions were by design similar, and some key phrases were omitted for fear of making it too easy, but you should be able to match fields to functions and translations. Some of the firm names might not be familiar, so there may have been some challenge with these connections. In general, most soon-to-be and recent grads already know a great deal about the importance to being able to cite all three F's.

For some the difficulty may have arisen when trying to complete the second portion. This is the simplest, yet most revealing short-answer job search test I can give. If you completed it with ease, you're on your way to job search success. If not, you have a bit more studying to do.

You now realize how crucial your ability to state goals is to job search success. This is a study skill you must learn to use if you are to pass the job search final! No matter how much knowledge you have regarding yourself, if you do not know basics associated with career fields and job functions you cannot effectively identify or communicate with firms you wish to work for. There is no magic way to fill your memory banks with information, although the process is relatively simple. Read books, speak with people, and observe work settings. You cannot read all of the books written on career fields or speak with everyone in the world regarding their career biographies, so you do need a bit of focus before undertaking in-depth research. Remember the three F's? You should, because that's what this exercise is all about. How about the fourth F? *Focus* is required to succeed in all research and job search undertakings. A tiny bit of focus is all that is needed to begin research. If it comes from a self-assessment exercise, great. If it comes from a lengthy list of career vocabulary words, fine. Once you have it, it builds and builds.

If you had difficulty filling in the blank boxes, don't fret, simply continue on to the *Goal Grid* exercise. Be sure to review the study tips and research sections thoroughly. They will contain some guidelines and suggested readings you should find valuable.

GOAL GRID

To identify research options (ideally thought of as "pRe-search Goals" thoroughly explored before active job search begins), or target Job Search Goals, review the listing that follows. It contains the most common (and, hopefully, realistic) entry-level options for recent grads. It was compiled by reviewing easily accessible "careers in" publications, so it didn't take a top secret security clearance to uncover and list about 400 options.

For pRe-search Goals check the box that best reflects your desire to explore particular functional options in the fields noted. Of course, don't check functions that are of little, if any, interest.

For Job Search Goals check the box that best reflects your desire to seek employment in specific functional areas. If fields or functional areas of interest are not identified, please add them to the end of this exercise. Don't be too analytical or judgmental at first. After you have completed the checklist, you will be asked to prioritize.

Fields	Functions	pRe-search Goals		Job Search Goals	
		Strong	*Moderate*	*Strong*	*Moderate*
Accounting	CPA	❏	❏	❏	❏
	Compliance Agency Examiner/Auditor	❏	❏	❏	❏
	Government Agency Budget Analyst	❏	❏	❏	❏
	Internal Auditor Banking	❏	❏	❏	❏
	Internal Auditor Industry	❏	❏	❏	❏
	Tax Consultant	❏	❏	❏	❏
	Tax Preparer	❏	❏	❏	❏
Acting/Drama/ Entertainment	Actor/Actress	❏	❏	❏	❏
	Agent	❏	❏	❏	❏
	Comedian	❏	❏	❏	❏
	Dancer	❏	❏	❏	❏
	Director	❏	❏	❏	❏
	Lighting Technician	❏	❏	❏	❏
	Publicist	❏	❏	❏	❏
	Stage Technician	❏	❏	❏	❏
	Publicist	❏	❏	❏	❏
Advertising	Account Executive	❏	❏	❏	❏
	Advertising Copywriter	❏	❏	❏	❏
	Advertising Salesperson	❏	❏	❏	❏
	Creative Artist and Director	❏	❏	❏	❏
	Media Buyer	❏	❏	❏	❏
	Media Planner	❏	❏	❏	❏
	Photographer	❏	❏	❏	❏
	Production Assistant and Director	❏	❏	❏	❏
	Traffic Coordinator	❏	❏	❏	❏
Aeronautics	Engineer	❏	❏	❏	❏
	Mechanic	❏	❏	❏	❏
	Pilot	❏	❏	❏	❏
	Project Manager	❏	❏	❏	❏
	Quality Assurance Staff	❏	❏	❏	❏
Agriculture	Agriculture Department Worker	❏	❏	❏	❏
	Farmer	❏	❏	❏	❏
	Grain Merchandiser	❏	❏	❏	❏
Airlines	Cargo Staff	❏	❏	❏	❏
	Customer Service Representative	❏	❏	❏	❏

Fields	Functions	pRe-search Goals		Job Search Goals	
		Strong	Moderate	Strong	Moderate
Airlines (Continued)	Pilot	☐	☐	☐	☐
	Purchasing Agent	☐	☐	☐	☐
	Revenue Control Analyst	☐	☐	☐	☐
	Sales Agent	☐	☐	☐	☐
	Sales Representative	☐	☐	☐	☐
	Trainer	☐	☐	☐	☐
Air Traffic Control	Controller	☐	☐	☐	☐
Animal Care	Veterinarian	☐	☐	☐	☐
	Veterinarian's Assistant	☐	☐	☐	☐
	Zoologist	☐	☐	☐	☐
	Zookeeper	☐	☐	☐	☐
Architecture	Architect	☐	☐	☐	☐
	Architectural Drafter	☐	☐	☐	☐
Arts/Arts Administration	Artist	☐	☐	☐	☐
	Assistant Director Museum or Gallery	☐	☐	☐	☐
	Business Manager or Agent	☐	☐	☐	☐
	Curator	☐	☐	☐	☐
	Editor Arts Publication	☐	☐	☐	☐
	Educational Director	☐	☐	☐	☐
	Fund Raiser or Development Staff	☐	☐	☐	☐
	Public or Community Relations Staff	☐	☐	☐	☐
	Restoration Worker	☐	☐	☐	☐
	Registrar	☐	☐	☐	☐
	Research Assistant	☐	☐	☐	☐
Audiology/ Speech Pathology	Audiologist	☐	☐	☐	☐
	Special Ed Teacher or Aide	☐	☐	☐	☐
	Speech Pathologist	☐	☐	☐	☐
Automotive	Engineer	☐	☐	☐	☐
	Finance Manager	☐	☐	☐	☐
	Leasing Agent	☐	☐	☐	☐
	Salesperson	☐	☐	☐	☐
Banking	Auditor	☐	☐	☐	☐
	Bank Examiner	☐	☐	☐	☐
	Branch Manager	☐	☐	☐	☐
	Corporate Finance Analyst	☐	☐	☐	☐
	Credit Analyst	☐	☐	☐	☐
	Financial Analyst	☐	☐	☐	☐
	Lending Analyst	☐	☐	☐	☐
	Loan Officer	☐	☐	☐	☐
	Money Market/Securities Trader	☐	☐	☐	☐
	Operations Manager	☐	☐	☐	☐
	Public Finance Analyst	☐	☐	☐	☐

Fields	Functions	pRe-search Goals		Job Search Goals	
		Strong	*Moderate*	*Strong*	*Moderate*
Banking (Continued)	Retail Banker Research Analyst Trust Officer	❑ ❑ ❑	❑ ❑ ❑	❑ ❑ ❑	❑ ❑ ❑
Building/ Construction	Accountant/Bookkeeper Estimator Expediter Laborer Landscaper Purchasing Agent Supply Salesperson Surveyor	❑ ❑ ❑ ❑ ❑ ❑ ❑ ❑	❑ ❑ ❑ ❑ ❑ ❑ ❑ ❑	❑ ❑ ❑ ❑ ❑ ❑ ❑ ❑	❑ ❑ ❑ ❑ ❑ ❑ ❑ ❑
Catering/Event Planning	Customer Service Rep Manager Planner Salesperson Server	❑ ❑ ❑ ❑ ❑	❑ ❑ ❑ ❑ ❑	❑ ❑ ❑ ❑ ❑	❑ ❑ ❑ ❑ ❑
Census/Survey Work	Analyst Project Supervisor Research Analyst Team Manager	❑ ❑ ❑ ❑	❑ ❑ ❑ ❑	❑ ❑ ❑ ❑	❑ ❑ ❑ ❑
Chemistry	Chemist Lab Technician Quality Control Tester Teacher	❑ ❑ ❑ ❑	❑ ❑ ❑ ❑	❑ ❑ ❑ ❑	❑ ❑ ❑ ❑

College Administration and Support Services	Administrative Assistant
	Admissions Officer and
	  Director
	Adviser
	Alumni Affairs Staff
	Assistant Dean
	Assistant Director
	Assistant to a Dean
	Career Counselor
	Career Information
	  Resource Person
	Career Services Staff
	College Union Staff
	Counselor
	Development Staff
	Disciplinary Adviser
	Finanical Aid Staff
	Foreign Student Adviser
	Fraternity/Sorority Adviser
	Library Staff
	Residence Adviser
	Residence Life/Housing
	  Staff
	Student Activities Staff
	Student Life Staff
	Student Publications
	  Adviser
		❑
		❑
		
		❑
		❑
		❑
		❑
		❑
		❑
		❑
		
		❑
		❑
		❑
		❑
		❑
		❑
		❑
		❑
		❑
		❑
		❑
		
		❑
		❑
		❑
			❑
			❑
			
			❑
			❑
			❑
			❑
			❑
			❑
			❑
			
			❑
			❑
			❑
			❑
			❑
			❑
			❑
			❑
			❑
			❑
			❑
			
			❑
			❑
			❑
				❑
				❑
				
				❑
				❑
				❑
				❑
				❑
				❑
				❑
				
				❑
				❑
				❑
				❑
				❑
				❑
				❑
				❑
				❑
				❑
				❑
				
				❑
				❑
				❑
					❑
					❑
					
					❑
					❑
					❑
					❑
					❑
					❑
					❑
					
					❑
					❑
					❑
					❑
					❑
					❑
					❑
					❑
					❑
					❑
					❑
					
					❑
					❑
					❑

Fields	Functions	pRe-search Goals		Job Search Goals	
		Strong	*Moderate*	*Strong*	*Moderate*
Broadcast Communications	Announcer	☐	☐	☐	☐
	Art Director	☐	☐	☐	☐
	Broadcast Engineer/Technician	☐	☐	☐	☐
	Continuity Writer	☐	☐	☐	☐
	Copywriter	☐	☐	☐	☐
	Disc Jockey/On-Air Personality	☐	☐	☐	☐
	Film Editor	☐	☐	☐	☐
	Graphic Artist	☐	☐	☐	☐
	Layout Artist	☐	☐	☐	☐
	Makeup Artist	☐	☐	☐	☐
	Production/Program Assistant	☐	☐	☐	☐
	Property Handler	☐	☐	☐	☐
	Researcher	☐	☐	☐	☐
	Set Decorator	☐	☐	☐	☐
	Sound Effects Technician	☐	☐	☐	☐
Print Communications	Ad Taker	☐	☐	☐	☐
	Advertising Staff	☐	☐	☐	☐
	Assistant Editor	☐	☐	☐	☐
	Circulation Staff	☐	☐	☐	☐
	Copy Editor	☐	☐	☐	☐
	Copy Reader	☐	☐	☐	☐
	Correspondent	☐	☐	☐	☐
	Editor	☐	☐	☐	☐
	Editorial Assistant	☐	☐	☐	☐
	Freelancer	☐	☐	☐	☐
	Illustrator	☐	☐	☐	☐
	Layout Assistant	☐	☐	☐	☐
	Marketing Staff	☐	☐	☐	☐
	Production Assistant	☐	☐	☐	☐
	Reporter	☐	☐	☐	☐
	Researcher	☐	☐	☐	☐
	Staff Writer	☐	☐	☐	☐
	Technical Writer	☐	☐	☐	☐
Computer/Data Processing	Consultant	☐	☐	☐	☐
	Customer Service Rep	☐	☐	☐	☐
	Data Analyst	☐	☐	☐	☐
	Data Entry Staff	☐	☐	☐	☐
	Data Processor	☐	☐	☐	☐
	Hardware Salesperson	☐	☐	☐	☐
	Information Systems Analyst	☐	☐	☐	☐
	MIS Consultant	☐	☐	☐	☐
	Manfacturing and Production Staff	☐	☐	☐	☐
	Programmer	☐	☐	☐	☐
	Sales Support Staff	☐	☐	☐	☐
	Software Salesperson	☐	☐	☐	☐
	Software Support Staff	☐	☐	☐	☐
	Systems Consultant	☐	☐	☐	☐

Fields	Functions	pRe-search Goals		Job Search Goals	
		Strong	Moderate	Strong	Moderate
Consulting	Administrative Staff	❑	❑	❑	❑
	Consultant	❑	❑	❑	❑
	Operations Staff	❑	❑	❑	❑
	Research Analyst	❑	❑	❑	❑
	Research Associate	❑	❑	❑	❑
	Researcher	❑	❑	❑	❑
Corrections and Parole	Corrections Officer	❑	❑	❑	❑
	Counselor	❑	❑	❑	❑
	Parole Officer	❑	❑	❑	❑
Courier and Freight	Courier	❑	❑	❑	❑
	Customer Service Staff	❑	❑	❑	❑
	Expediter	❑	❑	❑	❑
	Management Staff	❑	❑	❑	❑
	Salesperson	❑	❑	❑	❑
Crafts	Artisan	❑	❑	❑	❑
	Artist	❑	❑	❑	❑
	Salesperson	❑	❑	❑	❑
Design	Decorator	❑	❑	❑	❑
	Interior Designer	❑	❑	❑	❑
Education	Advisor	❑	❑	❑	❑
	Coach	❑	❑	❑	❑
	College Instructor	❑	❑	❑	❑
	Counselor	❑	❑	❑	❑
	Elementary Teacher	❑	❑	❑	❑
	Librarian and Library Aide	❑	❑	❑	❑
	Preschool Teacher	❑	❑	❑	❑
	Program Administrator	❑	❑	❑	❑
	Supply Salesperson	❑	❑	❑	❑
	Secondary Teacher	❑	❑	❑	❑
	Special Ed Teacher	❑	❑	❑	❑
	Substitute Teacher	❑	❑	❑	❑
	Teacher's Aide	❑	❑	❑	❑
	Teaching Assistant	❑	❑	❑	❑
Energy/ Environment	Activist	❑	❑	❑	❑
	Analyst	❑	❑	❑	❑
	Environmental Impact Analyst	❑	❑	❑	❑
	Hazardous Waste Disposer	❑	❑	❑	❑
	Landman	❑	❑	❑	❑
	Lobbyist	❑	❑	❑	❑
Engineering	Aeronautic	❑	❑	❑	❑
	Agricultural	❑	❑	❑	❑
	Architectural	❑	❑	❑	❑
	Ceramic	❑	❑	❑	❑
	Chemical	❑	❑	❑	❑
	Civil	❑	❑	❑	❑
	Computer	❑	❑	❑	❑

Fields	Functions	pRe-search Goals		Job Search Goals	
		Strong	Moderate	Strong	Moderate
Engineering (Continued)	Electrical	☐	☐	☐	☐
	Industrial	☐	☐	☐	☐
	Mechanical	☐	☐	☐	☐
	Nuclear	☐	☐	☐	☐
	Petroleum	☐	☐	☐	☐
	Technician	☐	☐	☐	☐
Film	Copywriter	☐	☐	☐	☐
	Distribution Staff	☐	☐	☐	☐
	Marketing Staff	☐	☐	☐	☐
	Production Staff	☐	☐	☐	☐
	Promotions Staff	☐	☐	☐	☐
	Screenwriter/Editor	☐	☐	☐	☐
	Researcher	☐	☐	☐	☐
	Technician	☐	☐	☐	☐
Finance/ Financial Services	Accountant	☐	☐	☐	☐
	Auditor	☐	☐	☐	☐
	Customer Service Staff	☐	☐	☐	☐
	Bookkeeper	☐	☐	☐	☐
	Broker	☐	☐	☐	☐
	Financial Analyst	☐	☐	☐	☐
	Financial Planner	☐	☐	☐	☐
	Investment Counselor	☐	☐	☐	☐
	Money Manager	☐	☐	☐	☐
	Researcher	☐	☐	☐	☐
	Salesperson	☐	☐	☐	☐
Fitness	Instructor	☐	☐	☐	☐
	Manager	☐	☐	☐	☐
	Marketing and Sales Staff	☐	☐	☐	☐
Foreign Service/ Intelligence	Embassy Staff	☐	☐	☐	☐
	Researcher	☐	☐	☐	☐
	Analyst	☐	☐	☐	☐
Forestry	Forester	☐	☐	☐	☐
	Lumberjack	☐	☐	☐	☐
	Planner	☐	☐	☐	☐
	Ranger	☐	☐	☐	☐
Government	Agency	☐	☐	☐	☐
	City/Local	☐	☐	☐	☐
	Federal	☐	☐	☐	☐
	Special Interest Group	☐	☐	☐	☐
	State	☐	☐	☐	☐
Graphic Arts	Animator	☐	☐	☐	☐
	Art Director	☐	☐	☐	☐
	Book Designer	☐	☐	☐	☐
	Cartoonist	☐	☐	☐	☐
	Designer	☐	☐	☐	☐
	Display Artist	☐	☐	☐	☐
	Fashion Illustrator	☐	☐	☐	☐
	Graphic Designer	☐	☐	☐	☐

Fields	Functions	pRe-search Goals		Job Search Goals	
		Strong	Moderate	Strong	Moderate
Graphic Arts (Continued)	Illustrator	☐	☐	☐	☐
	Layout Artist	☐	☐	☐	☐
	Letterer	☐	☐	☐	☐
	Medical Illustrator	☐	☐	☐	☐
	Package Designer	☐	☐	☐	☐
	Paste-up Artist	☐	☐	☐	☐
	Photographer	☐	☐	☐	☐
	Printer	☐	☐	☐	☐
	Record Jacket Artist	☐	☐	☐	☐
	Storyboard Artist	☐	☐	☐	☐
	Technical Illustrator	☐	☐	☐	☐
	Textile Designer	☐	☐	☐	☐
Health Care	Admissions Staff	☐	☐	☐	☐
	Aide/Assistant	☐	☐	☐	☐
	Billing Staff	☐	☐	☐	☐
	Biomedical/Medical Researcher	☐	☐	☐	☐
	Clincial Laboratory Staff	☐	☐	☐	☐
	Dental Assistant	☐	☐	☐	☐
	Dental Ceramist	☐	☐	☐	☐
	Dental Lab Technician	☐	☐	☐	☐
	Dentist	☐	☐	☐	☐
	Dispensing Optician	☐	☐	☐	☐
	Emergency Medical Technician	☐	☐	☐	☐
	Medical Assistant	☐	☐	☐	☐
	Medical Records Administrator	☐	☐	☐	☐
	Nurse	☐	☐	☐	☐
	Nurse's Aide	☐	☐	☐	☐
	Occupational Therapist	☐	☐	☐	☐
	Occupational Therapy Aide	☐	☐	☐	☐
	Optometrist	☐	☐	☐	☐
	Optometric Aide	☐	☐	☐	☐
	Orthodontic Technician	☐	☐	☐	☐
	Paramedic	☐	☐	☐	☐
	Patient Rep	☐	☐	☐	☐
	Pharmacist	☐	☐	☐	☐
	Pharmacy Assistant	☐	☐	☐	☐
	Physician	☐	☐	☐	☐
	Physician's Assistant	☐	☐	☐	☐
	Physical Therapist	☐	☐	☐	☐
	Physical Therapy Aide	☐	☐	☐	☐
	Radiation Therapist	☐	☐	☐	☐
	Radiology Technician	☐	☐	☐	☐
	Research Assistant/Technician	☐	☐	☐	☐
	Supply Salesperson	☐	☐	☐	☐
	Surgical Technician	☐	☐	☐	☐
	Technologist/Technician	☐	☐	☐	☐
	Volunteer Services Staff	☐	☐	☐	☐
	X-Ray Technician	☐	☐	☐	☐
Hotel/Motel Management	Catering Staff	☐	☐	☐	☐
	Conference Coordinator	☐	☐	☐	☐

Fields	Functions	pRe-search Goals		Job Search Goals	
		Strong	*Moderate*	*Strong*	*Moderate*
Hotel/Motel Management (Continued)	Desk Staff Facilities Manager Management Staff Reservationist Salesperson	❏❏❏❏❏	❏❏❏❏❏	❏❏❏❏❏	❏❏❏❏❏
Human Resources/ Personnel	Compensation Analyst EEO Rep Labor Relations Analyst Personnel Assistant Personnel Generalist Recruiter Trainer	❏❏❏❏❏❏❏	❏❏❏❏❏❏❏	❏❏❏❏❏❏❏	❏❏❏❏❏❏❏
Human and Social Services	Community Organizer Counselor Fieldworker Program Staff or Director Project Assistant Social Worker Social Work Staff	❏❏❏❏❏❏❏	❏❏❏❏❏❏❏	❏❏❏❏❏❏❏	❏❏❏❏❏❏❏
Insurance	Actuary Adjuster Advertising Staff Agent/Broker Claims Representative Computer Programmer Economic Analyst Field Rep Group Sales Rep Investment Analyst Legal Researcher Mortgage Analyst Real Estate Analyst Trainer Underwriter	❏❏❏❏❏❏❏❏❏❏❏❏❏❏❏	❏❏❏❏❏❏❏❏❏❏❏❏❏❏❏	❏❏❏❏❏❏❏❏❏❏❏❏❏❏❏	❏❏❏❏❏❏❏❏❏❏❏❏❏❏❏
Investment Banking	Analyst Arbitrager Associate Operations Staff Trader Salesperson	❏❏❏❏❏❏	❏❏❏❏❏❏	❏❏❏❏❏❏	❏❏❏❏❏❏
Languages	ESL Instructor Interpreter Teacher Translator	❏❏❏❏	❏❏❏❏	❏❏❏❏	❏❏❏❏
Law	Administrator Clerk Law Librarian Legal Assistant Legal Researcher	❏❏❏❏❏	❏❏❏❏❏	❏❏❏❏❏	❏❏❏❏❏

Fields	Functions	pRe-search Goals		Job Search Goals	
		Strong	Moderate	Strong	Moderate
Law (Continued)	Litigation Support Consultant	❑	❑	❑	❑
	Paralegal	❑	❑	❑	❑
Law Enforcement	Agent	❑	❑	❑	❑
	Investigator	❑	❑	❑	❑
	Officer	❑	❑	❑	❑
	Security Guard	❑	❑	❑	❑
Lobbying	Lobbyist	❑	❑	❑	❑
	Organizer	❑	❑	❑	❑
	Researcher	❑	❑	❑	❑
Manufacturing	Engineer	❑	❑	❑	❑
	Operations Manager	❑	❑	❑	❑
	Quality Control Inspector	❑	❑	❑	❑
Marketing	Assistant Brand Manager	❑	❑	❑	❑
	Brand Assistant	❑	❑	❑	❑
	Brand Manager	❑	❑	❑	❑
	Broker	❑	❑	❑	❑
	Consignment Merchant	❑	❑	❑	❑
	Manufacturer's Rep	❑	❑	❑	❑
Market Research	Account Executive	❑	❑	❑	❑
	Analyst	❑	❑	❑	❑
	Interviewer	❑	❑	❑	❑
	Project Manager	❑	❑	❑	❑
	Research Assistant	❑	❑	❑	❑
	Statistician	❑	❑	❑	❑
Merchandising	Contract Administrator	❑	❑	❑	❑
	Industrial Buyer	❑	❑	❑	❑
	Manufacturer's Buyer	❑	❑	❑	❑
	Manufacturer's Rep	❑	❑	❑	❑
	Manufacturer's Salesperson	❑	❑	❑	❑
	Purchasing Agent	❑	❑	❑	❑
	Wholesale Salesperson	❑	❑	❑	❑
Modeling	Artist's Model	❑	❑	❑	❑
	Fashion Model	❑	❑	❑	❑
	Fitting Model	❑	❑	❑	❑
	Photographic Model	❑	❑	❑	❑
	Showroom Model	❑	❑	❑	❑
Music	A&R	❑	❑	❑	❑
	Artist Representation	❑	❑	❑	❑
	Marketing	❑	❑	❑	❑
	Performer	❑	❑	❑	❑
	Promotion	❑	❑	❑	❑
	Record Sales	❑	❑	❑	❑
	Retail Sales and Sales Management	❑	❑	❑	❑

Fields	Functions	pRe-search Goals		Job Search Goals	
		Strong	*Moderate*	*Strong*	*Moderate*
Parks and Recreation	Curator Exercise Instructor Guide Manager Ranger Sales Staff	❑ ❑ ❑ ❑ ❑ ❑	❑ ❑ ❑ ❑ ❑ ❑	❑ ❑ ❑ ❑ ❑ ❑	❑ ❑ ❑ ❑ ❑ ❑
Pharmaceuticals	Brand Manager Laboratory Staff Pharmacist Researcher Salesperson	❑ ❑ ❑ ❑ ❑	❑ ❑ ❑ ❑ ❑	❑ ❑ ❑ ❑ ❑	❑ ❑ ❑ ❑ ❑
Politics	Advanceperson Campaign Worker Fundraiser Press Relations Staff Researcher Volunteer Organizer	❑ ❑ ❑ ❑ ❑ ❑	❑ ❑ ❑ ❑ ❑ ❑	❑ ❑ ❑ ❑ ❑ ❑	❑ ❑ ❑ ❑ ❑ ❑
Printing	Customer Service Rep Press Operations Staff Salesperson	❑ ❑ ❑	❑ ❑ ❑	❑ ❑ ❑	❑ ❑ ❑
Public Relations	Account Executive Assistant Coordinator Director Editor Event Planner	❑ ❑ ❑ ❑ ❑ ❑	❑ ❑ ❑ ❑ ❑ ❑	❑ ❑ ❑ ❑ ❑ ❑	❑ ❑ ❑ ❑ ❑ ❑
Real Estate	Agent Broker Finance Staff Leasing Agent Mortgage Lender Property Manager	❑ ❑ ❑ ❑ ❑ ❑	❑ ❑ ❑ ❑ ❑ ❑	❑ ❑ ❑ ❑ ❑ ❑	❑ ❑ ❑ ❑ ❑ ❑
Recycling	Organizer Center Director	❑ ❑	❑ ❑	❑ ❑	❑ ❑
Restaurant Management	Assistant Manager Manager	❑ ❑	❑ ❑	❑ ❑	❑ ❑
Retailing	Artist Buyer Copywriter Demonstrator Department Manager Executive Trainee Group Manager Merchandiser Photographer Salespeson Window and Display Decorator	❑ ❑ ❑ ❑ ❑ ❑ ❑ ❑ ❑ ❑ ❑	❑ ❑ ❑ ❑ ❑ ❑ ❑ ❑ ❑ ❑ ❑	❑ ❑ ❑ ❑ ❑ ❑ ❑ ❑ ❑ ❑ ❑	❑ ❑ ❑ ❑ ❑ ❑ ❑ ❑ ❑ ❑ ❑

Fields	Functions	pRe-search Goals		Job Search Goals	
		Strong	Moderate	Strong	Moderate
Sales and Sales Management	Area Manager District Manager Manufacturer's Rep Regional Manager Sales Representative Territory Manager	☐ ☐ ☐ ☐ ☐ ☐	☐ ☐ ☐ ☐ ☐ ☐	☐ ☐ ☐ ☐ ☐ ☐	☐ ☐ ☐ ☐ ☐ ☐
Sports	Agent Athlete General Manager Marketing Staff Promotions Staff Ticket Sales Staff	☐ ☐ ☐ ☐ ☐ ☐	☐ ☐ ☐ ☐ ☐ ☐	☐ ☐ ☐ ☐ ☐ ☐	☐ ☐ ☐ ☐ ☐ ☐
Telecommuni-cations	Analyst Customer Service Staff Installer Engineer Operations Staff Salesperson Telecommunication Manager	☐ ☐ ☐ ☐ ☐ ☐ ☐	☐ ☐ ☐ ☐ ☐ ☐ ☐	☐ ☐ ☐ ☐ ☐ ☐ ☐	☐ ☐ ☐ ☐ ☐ ☐ ☐
Translation and Transcription	Translator Transcriber	☐ ☐	☐ ☐	☐ ☐	☐ ☐
Travel and Tourism	Activities Director Agent Guide Promoter Recreation Director Salesperson	☐ ☐ ☐ ☐ ☐ ☐	☐ ☐ ☐ ☐ ☐ ☐	☐ ☐ ☐ ☐ ☐ ☐	☐ ☐ ☐ ☐ ☐ ☐
Union Managememnt	Grievance Handler Organizer	☐ ☐	☐ ☐	☐ ☐	☐ ☐
Urban and Regional Planning	Planner Research Assistant	☐ ☐	☐ ☐	☐ ☐	☐ ☐
Waste Management	Hazardous Materials Staff Risk Manager	☐ ☐	☐ ☐	☐ ☐	☐ ☐

Boy, talk about a long vocabulary list! After completing this rather tedious checklist activity, please take the time to tally totals (Oh no! Not alliteration). Some test takers will have large numbers in boxes below, and others will not. Do not judge goal direction by virtue of breadth of interests, but focus and intensity. When playing with a magnifying glass it takes a very narrow and clearly focused beam of light to ignite a dry leaf, so it is with career exploration and job search. The narrower and more clearly defined your goals, the better. I know! This is counter to what you feel in your gut. You want to "keep my options open." But, you must be prepared to lose the false sense of security associated with that phrase, in order to conduct thorough research and express job search targets. You must build and use research skills if you are to ignite and fuel a blazing job search fire.

Don't be concerned if you identified only a few pRe-search Goals and very few, if any, Job Search Goals. This means you are at the early stages of exploration. The information that follows will help you examine options, improve career vocabulary, and articulate goals more clearly. After additional research you may wish to complete this exercise again to assess your readiness to transform pRe-search options into Job Search Goals. Reviewing the list has already started the process and reading only a few of the texts suggested later will take you quite far. Before you know it, you will be able to return to the *Career Vocabulary Inventory* and fill in those blank boxes. You should do just that. Completing this exercise shows you are really ready for job search.

Those who have entries only in Job Search Goals boxes are focused and ready for job search. You should read the remainder of the chapter to determine whether you might want to undertake a bit more research.

TOTALS	pRe-search Goals		Job Search Goals	
	Strong	Moderate	Strong	Moderate

Now, circle and think about all of your strong pRe-search and Job Search goals and identify your top three of each. Again, if you cannot identify job search goals, do not be concerned. If you cannot identify pRe-search goals, complete the exercise again and be a bit more openminded. Remember, you are not deciding what to do with your life, you are simply trying to gain enough focus to begin some valuable research activities.

Top Three pRe-search Goals	
FIELD	**FUNCTION**

Top Three Job Search Goals	
FIELD	**FUNCTION**

Because of the unique nature of this assessment, there will again be no answer key. Both devices in this section were designed to determine the nature of your career vocabulary and how ready you are to articulate goals.

After completing both, if you are still clarifying pRe-search goals, complete steps outlined in the following study tips section and use resources noted later. Don't worry. You're not behind. This isn't a race, with laurels going to the swiftest competitors. Progress comfortably yet thoroughly through each stage to reap personal rewards.

Those with clear job search goals are ready to take subsequent job search tests. Resume writing will be next, but you will ultimately locate and use directories to identify potential employers, enhance job search correspondence skills, learn about appropriate follow up, become an effective interviewee, and much, much more. All that you will learn, with the specific steps involved, will be covered in the *Job Search Goals and Guidelines* outline later in this chapter. This is a very valuable listing, so copy it and have it available whenever you undertake research or job search efforts.

CAREER VOCABULARY INVENTORY AND GOAL GRID STUDY TIPS FOR THE RETEST (ACTION STEPS TO TAKE)

✎   Using resources noted later, or those suggested by a career services professional or reference librarian, locate and review three publications that provide information on identified pRe-search goals. All college students and grads have the skills required to author great essays and papers. It's ironic when I hear "how do I explore career options?" from talented researchers, writers, and presenters. For many, browsing a career resource collection or general library resources proves an exciting awakening. As few as three books or magazine articles can address questions and guidelines appearing on the following page. Write down the information gathered. You should ultimately have a lengthy crib sheet for each pRe-search goal. Exploration of these notes, incorporating self-knowledge in decision making, will result in setting tentative job search goals.

✎   Tell the next ten people you meet (family members are okay) that you are interested in a particular field or two (do not cite more than two, you'll overload the process). Ask if they know of anyone working in the field(s). In this way you will uncover persons to contact regarding an "information conversation." Yes, an **information conversation!** Stop using the outdated and often misleading phrase "informational interview." Think about it. Do you want to learn about job functions and career options, or do you want "an interview?" This approach has too often been used as a ploy to get a foot in the door, meet a potential employer, and convince someone of your qualification. The old label doesn't really project the informal and inquisitive nature of this exchange. This new phrase better states what you are seeking: some informal time with a knowledgeable person. Sessions when job seekers ask questions are *information conversations.* Those when employers ask questions are *employment interviews.* Now there is only one kind of interview, and all will be much clearer. Isn't it exciting to be a part of the establishment of a new entry into the lexicon of career exploration and job search? Be the first one to use *information conversation,* when requesting help from these ten individuals.

The information conversation is the most effective, and too often the most underutilized research technique. Always be honest when requesting assistance. If you are seeking information only, say so. If you really want job search assistance or employment consideration, don't use an informational conversation as a pretense. You are simply collecting career biographies through discussions with people who work within fields you are researching. Ideally, you will find someone who has (or had) the exact job you would like. Meeting people (particularly alumni of your school) and asking pertinent questions is the most interesting and effective way to narrow goals and identify appropriate next steps. Information conversation guidelines follow. Do it!

✎ If job search goals are clear (and realistic), you are ready to take all subsequent job search steps. You can now develop finely honed job search tools and soon identify a list of potential employers. To review our RSVP approach (did you already forget?) and preview all that is involved, examine the *Job Search Goals and Guidelines* later in the chapter. Also, you are ready to begin resume development as soon as you can. Coincidentally, and conspicuously convenient, the next section guides you through that very process.

✎ In anticipation of your creating a list of potential employers, and to provide closure for those who left this exercise unfinished, return to and thoroughly complete the fill-in-the-blanks portion of the *Career Vocabulary Inventory*. Unless you are able to do so, you are not really ready to take effective next steps. Before you complete the exercise, review the guidelines and locate resources appearing later. After a bit of research, you should have little difficulty.

pRe-search Goals: Questions and Guidelines

What You Need to Know about Fields, Functions, and Firms

This listing notes questions you can ask others or address when reviewing written materials. They can be used during information conversations or as guidelines when completing library research. Whatever the source of your information, the clearer your answers, the better.

Fields and Functions

☞ What job functions and job titles exist within a particular field?
☞ What are the duties and responsibilities of job functions in a field?
☞ What would major projects, or major achievements, be?
☞ You must thoroughly (descriptively) understand job functions before you can determine whether they can be realistic goals that correlate with values, interests, and personality type, and utilize skills and abilities.

☞ In pRe-search identify and (ultimately) analyze as many functional descriptions as possible.

Qualifications Associated with Functions

☞ What capabilities are required to perform responsibilities of job functions in a field of interest?

☞ From a thorough job description you will be able to interpret qualifications required. Old and new want-ads are good for this. You're not yet looking for a job, but you can use want ads as pRe-search tools.

☞ First identify general characteristics and qualities associated with job functions.

☞ Later, you assess continued interest and, perhaps, chances for job search success.

☞ Don't be too quick to eliminate an option because you have yet to gain all cited qualifications.

☞ Be courageous enough to risk rejection, allowing a bit of job search natural selection to occur.

Education, Training, or Experience Required or Desired

☞ What type of education (major, degree, or classes) is stated as "desired" or "required?"

☞ Is licensing, graduate study, or a professional degree required?

☞ Is specialized training (degrees, individual courses or seminars) necessary and readily available?

☞ Where can it be obtained and does it fit into your current academic plans?

☞ Where can you get information about these training or academic experiences?

☞ Is on-the-job experience really necessary to break in?

☞ How can experience be gained (internship, part-time or summer job, volunteer work, full-time job)?

☞ Don't be too quick to judge yourself as unqualified if you don't yet have stated educational "requirements" (specific major or degree) or the desired experience.

☞ If you decide a field or job function is a realistic goal, you can develop a strategy to deal with issues related to education and experience.

First Functions for Entering a Field

☞ How can you enter the field or obtain jobs being explored?

☞ Do you begin through formal training or in entry-level positions, eventually to be promoted to the desired job?

☞ What are these entry-level jobs?

Firms: Organizations and Work Environments

☞ Where do jobs fit in firms with these functions?

☞ What divisions or departments have these jobs and where are they located?

☞ Seek a broader perspective to understand day-to-day job functions and identify future options, not to predict your ability to move "up the ladder."

☞ Would you typically work in an office or on the road?

☞ Would the job typically exist in large cities, small towns, or elsewhere?

☞ Are there typical settings (i.e., schools or stores) associated with fields or functions?

☞ These factors are most important when taking job search action, not when identifying goals. Post-offer analysis gives you additional information and the power to say "no."

Funds and Forecasts (The Hidden F's)

☞ What is the range of starting salaries and potential long-term earnings for jobs or fields of interest?

☞ Where are opportunities now, and where will they be in the future?

☞ Don't let these be critical issues, because if motivated and qualified, and a good job seeker, you will find a job even in an overcrowded field. In time, you will earn financial and other "rewards."

Please write answers to the above when conducting research. Direct application of study skills is called for here. It is difficult to memorize large quantities of information. You do need study notes when preparing for tests. Write it down! Later review of pRe-search notes, incorporating knowledge of self, will clarify job search goals.

The Information Conversation

People-to-People pRe-search

Information conversations involve seeking information only, not job search assistance or consideration. By phone, in person, or by letter, you ask: *"Could I meet with you to learn about your background? I am currently researching options, and your field/job is of particular interest. An information conversation with you could help me formulate my goals."* In truth, it is a pRe-search activity, not really a job search activity. Although it is appropriate to request an information conversation when employment consideration cannot be granted, it should never be used deceptively as a way to meet someone who could hire you. You can react to a *"We're not hiring now!"* response with a request for an information conversation. If granted, you should maintain an inquisitive role, not subtly push your candidacy.

Through brief conversations (although 15-minute sessions have a way of stretching into an hour) collect the career biographies of individuals who work in fields you are researching. Meeting people and asking pertinent questions is the best way to narrow goals and identify effective next steps. Research networks should expand as you conduct information conversations. By asking for additional names each time you have a conversation, you continually multiply your supply of sources. Once goals are clear, you transform your pRe-search network into a job search network.

Basic questions you may wish to ask during an information conversation include:

How did you enter this field?
What are the responsibilities of your job?
What are typical entry-level job titles and functions?
What educational or experience requirements are associated with entry-level opportunities?
What qualities do you believe contribute most to success in this field?
How did you get where you are today?
What are your long-range goals?
What other kinds of organizations hire people to perform the functions you do here?
Do you have any advice for someone interested in this field/job?
Are there any books or magazines I should read?
What advice would you give someone seeking to learn more, and ultimately, enter the field?
Do you know other people (three if possible) I could talk to who have similar jobs?

The more you learn about career biographies, and the more you know about fields and functions, the easier it will be to develop goals and make decisions regarding appropriate next steps. Don't be afraid of using up a "contact" (family friends, for example) to arrange information conversations. You can always follow up an information conversation with a request for job search assistance once you have finalized your goals. Follow-up notes can express your desire to seek an entry-level job, hold an employment interview, or just seek job search assistance. Don't confuse your request for information with other factors.

Be prepared when conducting these somewhat informal sessions. Write your questions down and take notes. Start with people you know or with direct referrals (from friends, family, or through an alumni network) so you can become more comfortable with the process before you contact a stranger. Bring a resume simply to share your background, not for job search purposes. Dress businesslike. Always write thank-you notes and keep these people aware of the outcome of your decision making.

This approach to exploration (better stated as "goal setting by vocabulary building") is difficult for some. Many feel awkward about being nosy and expect that others won't agree to spend the time talking with someone who doesn't have a sense of direction. Honestly, you'll be surprised how willing people are to help and how easy it is to get them to talk about themselves. The easiest ways to start are by speaking with friends or family members or by contacting a college career services office. However you get started, you must do it!

RSVP Revisited: Job Search Goals and Guidelines

What 's Now and What's Next

You should recall the acronym used to identify how to apply study skills to job search actions:

☆ **Review**, and document in writing, knowledge of self and knowledge of career fields and job options.

☆ **Synthesize** knowledge of self and information pertaining to careers and job functions in order to set tentative research goals (worthy of more inquiry) and job search goals (targeted for job search actions).

☆ **Verify** information regarding research and job search goals, fine-tuning job search goals, identifying and researching in greater detail potential employers, and developing job search strategies.

☆ **Prepare** to express information effectively via written (resumes, cover letter, fax messages, and follow up letters) and verbal (telephone calls, informational and employment interviews, and voice mail messages) communications.

If you have identified realistic job search goals you are ready to take effective actions. Reviewing some issues uncovered by the *Job Search Survival Quiz,* and previewing what will be covered in future chapters, to be successful you will:

☞ **Write thorough descriptions of jobs you want on 3x5 index cards.** State geographic and functional goals—what you want to do and where—on paper and, whenever asked. Remember, goal setting involves self-assessment (clarification of skills, values, and interests) and, most importantly, pRe-search of career fields and job functions. Introspection is not enough! You must be able to cite goals, even if they are only exploratory in nature.

☞ **Develop a distribution copy of your resume, with at least one version citing an objective.**
Resumes can be "multipurpose" (without an objective) or "targeted" (with an objective citing goals), but you should develop at least one targeted version. Resumes and all job search correspondence must project goals and qualifications. Cover letters and follow-up notes communicate goals and qualifications and identify desired next steps (i.e., interviews). Writing skills must be fine-tuned and applied to these special projects.

☞ **Identify the names, addresses, and phone and fax numbers of at least 25 potential employers.**
Use directories and other resources to develop a list of employers to contact. Then, don't do a mass mailing. Call first, identify whom to communicate with, begin research on the nature of the firm and learn as much as you can about how the job you want fits into the operations of this organization. Don't research the firm too much and ignore the function.

☞ **Network! Network! Network!**
Share pRe-search and job search goals and resumes (in person or via letters) with friends, family members, faculty, business associates, past employers, and, of course, alumni of your school. Meet someone who has (or had) a job you would like. Ask for exactly what you want, not simply "help." If you want an information conversation, ask for it. If you want the names of firms (and contact person) that hire within functions of interest, ask for them. Identify how your network member can help. Don't simply make a vague request for assistance. Be honest, inquisitive, and appreciative, not pushy or obnoxious.

☞ **Respond to posted opportunities with confidence.**
Use the best resumes, cover letters, and follow-up strategies. Locate and use job postings, such as want-ads, employment agencies, job fairs, and on-campus recruiting programs. Identify whether professional associations have field-specific newsletter and posting mechanisms. Use search firms to uncover hidden postings, but be assertive and don't wait for these services to find you a job. Yes, also use resume data banks, but don't depend on them.

☞ **Conduct a thorough proactive, goal-directed, campaign.**
Inform as many people as possible, as often as possible, about job search goals. Don't wait for postings to appear. Contact persons on your potential employer listing and members of your network on a regular basis. Get involved in professional groups. Do internships, volunteer projects, or take classes while seeking a full-time position.

☞ **Locate and use college or other career services professionals.**
There are a great many career counselors and job search coaches available. Contact your alma mater and local schools, as well as private services. Ask others (including reference librarians) for guidance. You're not alone!

☞ **Follow up all initial contacts and even negative responses.**
Communicate consistently, persistently, yet appropriately with potential employers until an interview (by phone or in person) is given. Use phone, letter, voice mail, or fax communiqués.

☞ **Interview confidently and effectively, with little if any physical or psychological symptoms.**
Communicate your motivations and, most importantly, qualifications to do a job during initial and follow-up interviews.

☞ **Receive, analyze, and accept or decline offers.**
Conduct post-offer analysis and determine whether to say "yes" or "no." While difficult to do (emotionally and financially), rejecting an offer may be the right thing in certain circumstances.

CAREER VOCABULARY INVENTORY AND GOAL GRID
HELPFUL RESOURCES (PEOPLE, PLACES, AND THINGS)

✔ Contact local chapters of professional associations related to fields of interest (research or job search goals). These can be identified via directories available at almost all public or university libraries. Many of the resources cited below also identify these groups. You may at first have to communicate with national headquarters (usually in New York City or Washington D.C.) to do so, but locate the president and membership chair of a local chapter. Contact these individuals and request help arranging information conversations. Start with these two, but you can quickly expand your network to at least five persons who are now serving within functional areas of interest. Membership directories of local chapters are extremely valuable research and job search resources. The more people you meet and speak with who are in a field of interest, the more easily goals will form and the more likely you will enter a field of choice.

✔ Books to examine include: *101 Careers, Wiley,* 1990; *Jobs!* Fireside Books, 1989; *Liberal Arts Jobs,* Peterson's, 1989; *The Harvard Guide to Careers in Mass Media,* Bob Adams, 1989; *Creative Careers,* Wiley Press, 1985; *The Careers In* and *Opportunities In* Series, VGM Horizons; *The Occupational Outlook Handbook,* Bureau of Labor Statistics; and *The Career Opportunities Series,* Facts on File. Some of these resources contain overviews of numerous fields and functions, others just a few. Most can be purchased or ordered from local bookstores. Some are series of books, usually found in large libraries. Frankly, if these are the only books you locate and use to explore career options, you will find more than enough information required to set tentative goals.

While books can be the best resources for basic information, periodicals can provide insight regarding current trends and issues. Use computerized databases or published indexes to locate articles appearing under headings related to your field(s) of interest. You might be surprised how many articles have been written about publishing recently. By locating these pieces you will identify publications that are written for and read by people in the field. Some might contain job search leads. If unfamiliar with computerized search programs or periodical indexes, seek the help of a librarian.

CAREER VOCABULARY INVENTORY AND GOAL GRID
STUDY SKILLS SUMMARY

- ✏ Examined knowledge of basic functions within world of work.
- ✏ Introduced the concept of "The Three F's—Field, Function, and Firm."
- ✏ Highlighted how the fourth F—Focus—can improve potential for job search success and listed variety of functions within fields.
- ✏ Identified level of readiness to articulate goals and steps required to gain additional information and, ultimately, complete job search.
- ✏ Stressed importance of "information conversation" (new phrase for informational interviews that stresses informality and nature of exchange) in exploration and, ultimately, job search stages.

CHAPTER 4

Resume Reality Checklist

As a college career counselor and job search coach, and as a corporate recruiter, I have critiqued or reviewed 11,836 resumes (yes, I counted), given over 2,324 resume-writing workshops, and answered 34,928 questions regarding this aspect of job search. I've heard just about every question and comment on the subject. Check whether you believe the following statements are best characterized as "truths" or "myths," and note comments or questions.

STATEMENT	MYTH	TRUTH	QUESTION/COMMENT
A resume must stand out!		✓	
A resume must be one page!		✓	
A resume must have an objective!			
Nobody reads resumes!	✓		
Functional ones are best for career changers!			

(Continued)

STATEMENT	MYTH	TRUTH	QUESTION/COMMENT
The more resumes distributed, the better!		✓	
A good resume will get an interview!			X
Resumes are more critical than cover letters!			ˑ
Resume-writing services should be used!			X
There's only one way to write a resume!			ˑ

Now, tally up your truths and myths. How many of each did you check?

Identification of 6 or more truths indicates that either you are firm in your beliefs about resume writing or that you are naive enough to believe there is a "right" and "wrong" way to do everything. I don't want to appear cynical (yet), so I won't be too harsh on those who think a majority of the statements are truths (by any general definition). This perspective can be very good, or very bad, depending upon which statements you believe express fact or fiction. Strongly held views can be great motivators or, in some cases, can deter job seekers from taking creative and assertive actions.

Identification of 6 or more myths indicates that either you don't hold any strong views or that you are openminded (or confused) enough for someone (or some book) to give you direction. Again, this could be very good, or very bad, depending upon how much motivation or inertia is created by this state of receptivity. Quite simply, anything that stops you from taking action is *bad* and anything that stimulates activity is *good.*

Identification of 5 truths and 5 myths reveals either a very balanced view or a propensity for indecision and, of most concern, procrastination. Resume writing strikes fear, paralysis, and procrastination in the minds and bodies of too many job seekers. The information that follows should release anyone from the cognitive tug-of-war that causes too many to put off this critical step until another day (or another book).

If the right-hand column is full of questions and you haven't checked any statement as truth or myth, you're either very curious or very cautious. You're probably the student who frequently asks "What exactly is going to be on the exam?" or "Which chapters should I really study?" Don't worry. Simply read the answer key and then check the correct boxes.

RESUME REALITY CHECKLIST ANSWER KEY AND TYPICAL QUESTIONS

A quick glance at the ten statements may lead you to believe that some are myths and others truths. To a "Job Search Coach" (a title we can now use to describe action-oriented and intervention-driven professionals), the now-popular exclamation *"not!"* comes to mind and mouth. For the full dramatic effect of this finely crafted word-picture, imagine a loud chorus of teen-agers all yelling "not!" at the top of their lungs. Now you understand the intensity of my views. **All are overgeneralized myths that too often cause confusion and, worse, delay the process of creating a distribution-ready copy of your resume!** Each has a bit of truth, for that allows myths to self-perpetuate. They grow until someone says the emperors who cloak themselves in the statements truly have no clothes (as the title reveals, I thought a little "nudity" might sell a job search publication). Let's examine what we should now call the "top ten myths" to reveal the "naked truths" behind resume writing (there, I did it again).

A resume must stand out!

What can I do to make my resume stand out?

Should I print it on brightly colored paper?

Should I get creative and print it on a T-shirt?

Your resume should *not* be printed on glow-in-the-dark or unusually colored paper (unless you're an "artist" or seeking employment in a very, very, creative arts-associated field). It should *not* use unconventional graphics (unless you're looking for a desktop publishing or graphics position). It should be on "businesslike" ("boring" for some) bond paper. Appropriate colors include white, off-white, and ivory. Stock can be laid or linen and about 20 pound (not too stiff). If this sounds too technical, just call it "resume paper." It can be purchased at a stationery or bookstore or, most often, from a printer or copy center you use to duplicate copies. Avoid parchment and darker colors. Quite simply, if you can imagine the letterhead of an employer being on the color and quality of paper you are using, you're on track.

Your resume should not be printed on a T-shirt, or delivered in a pizza box. While both approaches have proven successful for job seekers I've worked with, these are exceptions, *not* the rules. You don't have to depend upon "tricks." Some resumes stand out by virtue of experiences documented and formats used. But always keep in mind that actions taken are what make a document dynamic and, thus, more likely to be reviewed. Resumes really don't "stand out." How you use this job search tool makes you, the job seeker, stand out. Resume development and distribution are two parts of a process composed of several behavioral and interactive components. Resumes, cover letters, follow-up letters, phone calls (and messages), faxes, and in-person meetings (with potential employers and others) make up "the total job search." Multidimensional behaviors make the authors of two-dimensional pieces of paper appealing. Your actions in this scenario should speak much louder than the words of your resume!

A resume must be one page!

If it is over a page, won't it be tossed out?

What if I can't condense all that I have done to only one page?

This is the most often cited myth. Most soon-to-be and recent grads should be able to develop one page documents, but not everyone can meet this arbitrary limitation. Some first-time job seekers (those active enough to be named "most likely to do something") will develop two-page versions, while many experienced professionals should create documents that require an additional page. Avoid writing the next version of *War and Peace*, but cite all accomplishments thoroughly and accurately. Yes, it is important to keep resume reviewers in mind when creating this document. But, it is more important to keep your own goals in mind. A resume is not simply a document *they* use. It is a tool that *you* use! Know why you have noted each entry. If after revising initial drafts, the distribution version is more than a page, great! Also, you can create supplemental pages that contain listings of references, descriptions of courses and projects, abstracts of research papers, and writing samples when needed. Then the one-page resume can be supported with additional pertinent materials.

A resume must have an objective!

Won't that limit me?

What if I don't have a sense of focus yet?

Doesn't that mean I should create a new resume for
each job I apply for?

While you should be able to cite an objective, do not postpone resume writing while exploration continues. A multipurpose resume without an objective statement can be used effectively. Resumes without objectives put more "responsibility" on cover letters and follow-up correspondence, and on the interview, but they can be effective. You may ultimately create one resume without an objective and one or two with goal statements, but don't let anything stop you from taking immediate actions. If you must develop your first resume without an objective, fine, but keep exploring options until you can develop one with a clearly cited goal. **Just do it!** (Can that foot-gear company sue me for using that phrase?)

As cited many times in this publication, expressing goals clearly and concisely does not limit you. Focus provides the point of reference required to spark a meaningful reading of your "promotional bro-chure"—your resume. Objectives can be the magnifying glasses needed to make your background seem larger and more dynamic. Resumes are typically reviewed, analyzed, and used to "match" stated goals. Yes, potential employers connect stated goals and perceived qualifications for existing opportunities. But, an objective will not preclude resume reviewers from viewing you as qualified for more than one position. If your greatest fear comes true and you are rejected, you explore why, reexamine options, and retarget follow-up efforts (using a revised resume). Continued communications will expand views regarding your potential to perform in capacities other than those noted in an initial objective. Don't ever be afraid to cite goals verbally and, more importantly, in writing via resume, cover letters, and follow-up correspondence.

With the use of word-processors and personal computers it is possible to change objectives for each position. It is tempting to think that simply changing an objective will result in a focused and more effective document. But that is not the case. If you change an objective you should consider changing other portions of the resume. Major headings, listings of skills, and descriptions of experiences should parallel each objective.

Nobody reads resumes!

Isn't it really a waste of time to send resumes off to
strangers?

Who should I send it to to get it read?

If it isn't read, how can my resume spark interest in my candidacy?

Should I use one of those resume distribution services or resume banks?

People do read resumes; if you count "speed reading." Most resumes are quickly scanned, not thoroughly analyzed. Assuming job search involves a meaningful and in-depth review of your resume can lead to ineffective behaviors. While you must assume that your resume will be read if you take appropriate actions, you must always be prepared to take effective preliminary and follow-up actions. Never send it to a nameless "To Whom it May Concern." Proper preliminary research (a simple phone call) will uncover the person (or persons) who should receive initial correspondence. Pre–job search inquiries and information conversations (in person or by phone) can be very valuable. At one time I echoed "avoid personnel when contacting potential employers." I now believe corresponding with human resource *and* management professionals improves chances of receiving a positive response to requests for employment consideration. Follow-up conversations with initial contacts reveal who is most receptive to continued communications (correspondence, phone, and, hopefully interview).

Yes, we more regularly hear of large organizations and resume referral services ("resume banks") using digitized scanners ("Mr. Machine" to those who think anthropomorphically in order to survive in an ever-dehumanizing society). But, it is not advantageous to base a strategy on a belief that your resume will magically and mechanically arise from a scanned stack. Once computerized screening is complete, living and breathing humans complete supplemental reviews and, eventually, conduct interviews.

Some want us to believe that recruiting will soon be a paperless process, but that is not yet on the horizon. I encourage you to become aware of and use resume banks, but do not assume computer matching will lead to job search success. It didn't take the place of spontaneous match-making and dating did it? Scanning involves associating key words appearing in a resume with predetermined qualification criteria, so you should actively describe past experiences and list capabilities using field-appropriate terminology (suggestions resume critiquers have made for decades). Don't depersonalize the process and give responsibility to *software* when *hard work* is what is really required. In truth, a well-written resume will naturally contain many of the key phrases used by resume scanners as well as screeners to identify viable candidates.

Use as many resume banks as you feel comfortable with. They can't hurt (unless costs hurt a wallet or pocketbook). But, don't depend upon them for positive outcomes. A great many people buy lottery tickets, but few win. Take the chance, but don't spend psychic cash before you've heard from employers. It's relatively easy to complete a data sheet and provide a resume, but don't expect it will result in success. Job search is still a process that requires direct contact with employers and follow up on your part. No matter how sophisticated and computerized the screening process, person-to-person "interface" (that's computerese for "interview") is how employers decide who to hire. Ultimately, people hire people and concern about and investment of time (and money) in mechanical procedures may involve a misuse of energies (and finances).

Well-written resumes, accompanied by well-written cover letters and used by well-motivated individuals, are most definitely read.

Functional ones are best for career changers!

Isn't it best to leave dates off of a resume if I'm trying to make a change and I'm over thirty?

How big a difference does it make if I use this format?

You often hear that career changers should use a functional resume, one that focuses on skills and diminishes the importance of dates. A functional resume can, by virtue of the skills identification required, be effective, but it is not the best format for some career changers. This format should not be used to hide anything, but to focus the attention of reviewers on three or four specialized skills groups. A targeted functional resume, with a clearly stated objective, could be effective. But the secret to career transition is, as we've said all along, the ability to identify and clearly cite goals. Don't expect resume readers to determine qualifications from a general listing of skills. While that is often the hope of those using functional resumes, in actuality this does not happen enough to be an effective or realistic strategy. In truth, reviewers find this format difficult to read. If you use a functional resume (and again, I don't recommend you do) make sure it reveals your knowledge of characteristics required to perform specific tasks within a clearly defined field of interest. Simply, be focused and keep your resume focused.

"Transferable skills," a phrase often cited by career counselors and mimicked by those seeking employment in new areas, is not frequently used by recruiters. All job seekers, especially those changing careers, must be able to cite goals clearly and identify concisely how skills possessed can be used within positions sought. It is the job seeker's responsibility to bridge the past to the desired future via documents of the present (resumes and cover letters). Don't be naive enough to think someone else (particularly a resume reviewer) will do this for you. You transfer your skills and connect them to desired objectives, or you won't be considered a strong candidate.

Leaving dates off of a resume is like waving a red flag in front of a raging bull (do you think the editor will allow this overused metaphor?). Readers typically judge resumes without dates as written by "an older job seeker who doesn't want me to calculate age or someone with something to hide." Don't be afraid to cite when you accumulated academic, employment, extracurricular, volunteer, or personal achievements. If age discrimination is going to take place (and I am sad to say it will), leaving dates off a document will not protect you from this narrowmindedness. Be proud of what you have done and when you did it. Experienced candidates are in demand by many employers, and follow-up actions can broaden a few narrow minds if done effectively, so don't let insecurity motivate resume writing. Also, remember you don't have to cite day, month, and year. You can use phrases like "Spring 1992" or "Intermittently 1985-present" when dating entries.

The more resumes distributed, the better!

Should I conduct a mass mail campaign?

Can I be effective mailing resumes to other states?

This is a myth because it motivates job seekers to invest too much time and energy in "mass mailing" (hundreds of resumes to hundreds of random employers) or "shotgun" (hoping a wide blast will hit something) approaches. You should feel comfortable distributing your resume to as many people as possible, including potential employers, past employers, faculty, friends, and family members. But, don't confuse quantity of resumes distributed with quality of actions taken. The phrase is "ready, aim, fire," *not* "ready, fire, aim?" Yes, the more assertive you are in distributing your resume, the better, but job seekers cannot depend upon "the lottery syndrome." We all hope each lottery ticket purchased at a local convenience store (each round of resumes mailed) will hit the jackpot. Unless you've already won the million dollar lottery, it is your responsibility to take action. You must be focused, citing goals and acting selectively to magnify job search effectiveness. Think of how much heat you can generate by focusing a magnifying glass. Being focused can ignite your job search, with actions fanning the flames.

Long-distance job search is complicated and worthy of a lengthy discussion, but let's take a shot at it. Imagine you are a human resources professional who receives a resume from a qualified candidate in another state. What would you do? Would you contact the person, pay airfare to fly the candidate in for a meeting, or conduct an initial phone interview? Because you probably receive many resumes from "local candidates" with similar capabilities, I doubt you would fly in the long distance candidate or even take the time to call. Therefore, if you truly wish to conduct a long-distance campaign you must be prepared to "defuse" the miles that separate you from an employer. I encourage you to plan several trips to the city/state of interest, mention that you will be visiting soon and express willingness to pay for travel, and suggest the possibility of an initial phone interview in all correspondence. Assertive telephone communications can overcome some of the distance, but they cannot take the place of an in-person visit. You may also wish to present a local address (of a friend, family member, or mail box service) on your resume. You will appear as an immediately available "semilocal candidate" wishing to return home. Simply, if you can drive to the city, it's a realistic target. If not, you need to take some very strategic and well-planned actions.

A good resume will get an interview!

What if mine isn't very good because I haven't worked much?

Should I be a bit deceptive on my resume to get an interview?

At last! After reviewing over half of the ten myths, we evaluate one that reflects how crucial it is for resume writers to perceive themselves ultimately as "resume users." Good resumes, even great resumes, do *not* get interviews. Job seekers using good resumes, good cover letters, and good phone follow-up skills obtain interviews. Those who conduct research required to set and express realistic goals get interviews. Good interview communicators get jobs! Resumes do less than you might expect, or hope. No matter how much we want a magic piece of paper to bring us our dreams, job search will always be the responsibility of job seekers. Good job search tools enhance the efforts of a conscientious job search craftsperson, but alone they don't create a masterpiece.

Rejection is one of the few guarantees in the process, so don't let anxious anticipation stop you from taking action. Your attitude is very important. Your actions can speak much louder than written words. A lack of experience can be overcome by projecting thorough knowledge of fields of interest and by your ability to clearly cite goals.

Never, never be deceptive on your resume. While you may have heard of stories where deception proved successful, these are few and far between and most often the products of some very overactive imagination. You will get an interview and eventually a job as a result of effective behaviors and because you will conduct the ongoing exploration required to identify and present goals.

Resumes are more critical than cover letters!

Employers don't really read long cover letters, do they?

If I don't write very well will it negatively influence my efforts?

While this statement might create much debate among career services professionals, in truth, resumes and cover letters should be perceived as equally important. Otherwise you might erroneously pay too little attention to one or the other, with disastrous results. Each document should be able to stand alone, sparking interest in a candidate. If only one were reviewed (although both sent) either the resume or cover letter should support a candidacy well enough to justify an interview. Together the two documents supplement each other and support your request for an interview more strongly. Some employers read cover letters, and some don't. Those who read well-written and concise documents will be more willing to grant interviews. More importantly, cover letters organize your thoughts, clarify goals, and stress qualifications. In many ways it is best to think of correspondence as interview preparation, not simply as consideration request.

You don't have to write dramatically to develop a good cover letter. Simple directness can go quite far. The truth is that job search requires strong written and verbal skills. Anything you can do to enhance these qualities will improve your chances for success. Don't be bashful. Ask for help from career services professionals, professors, friends, and (if not too stressful) family members.

Resume-writing services should be used!

Should I use one of the services advertised in the classified section of the paper?

What is a good price to pay for these services?

These services *could* be used, but they are not essential. I will never support using others to write your resume. Regularly, each resume looks all too similar to all the others produced by a service. A resume should be a "personalized" presentation of your background. Those who use services often skip the skills identification and review of past experiences that are valuable aspects of the resume writing process. The more you think about yourself and the more you examine past achievements and present them accurately on paper, the better. When someone else does it for you, something important is lost.

Whatever the price (realistic costs range from $25 to $75 depending upon whether duplication is included), if you use a resume writing service, make sure you manage the process, not vice versa. Use them to develop a first draft, but don't hesitate to go back with changes you wish to make (they should be free) and use others to critique the drafts developed by the service. If you invest your money ($25 for "counseling" and $50 for "typesetting and duplication" is fair), you should be able to make changes until you are satisfied. As you will learn a bit later, being able to work on a resume using a word-processor or personal computer is an advantage. If you don't have access to such hardware, a resume writing service may be a viable option. Before you choose one, please do some comparison shopping. Call several, review samples, clarify how much each service is and how many copies you get for what cost and, most importantly, see if they will give you "floppy" with your resume on it. This will give you the ability to make changes in the future if you have access to compatible hardware.

Also, avoid resume-writing software. These programs usually limit the graphic options you have available with basic word-processing software. While they do have user-friendly prompts that may help some procrastinators quickly create a first draft, once the draft is completed changes are often difficult. It is better to use word-processing or desktop publishing software to develop drafts and revise your resume. As you will very soon become aware, via information in the next chapter, creating a resume isn't that difficult.

There's only one way to write a resume!

If any format is a good one, which should I use?

Why isn't anyone responding to my resume?

An old (and overused) axiom says: "there are as many resume formats as resume users." Yet, old counselors (who most often use old and overused phrases) conclude that all resumes can be categorized into three types—chronological, functional, and combined, and that each of these can be multipurpose or targeted. If I remember my college statistics and probability, that means there are in fact only six types of resumes. Career counselors usually motivate clients to be creative when developing resumes. Resume writing guides and publications contain hundreds of examples of different styles. Some identify particular formats as best for particular fields or types of jobs. Some identify particular formats as best for different majors or backgrounds, but it is hard to identify the best way to write all resumes.

A variety of resume styles can be effective for any individual job seeker. In truth, it is often a lack of follow up, not the resume, which leads to so-called "poor results." If you place the responsibility of job search on a two-dimensional object, you are negating your *response-ability* to take action; your ability to respond to job search challenges and take required steps. Give yourself time to be successful, but be very persistent and active. Think about what you are doing (or not doing) after your resume is sent to a potential employer. Identify additional follow-up actions you can take.

You may recall that I did say earlier that all of these statements were myths, laced with a tiny bit of truth. If I am to be totally honest, this myth may have a great deal of truth to it. Now that I've given you a learned professional and objective perspective, I am compelled to reveal a different view that I now hold. *There is a format that can be most effective for all job seekers!* For many, many years I have said over and over "there is no perfect resume" and I have motivated creativity in developing first drafts and final versions. Because I did not want to block any student or alumni from taking action, I repeated this phrase over and over. I teased authors and counselors who regularly used words like "perfect" and "best" and urged clients not to follow "cookie-cutter" approaches. Because I do believe job seekers must take responsibility for their resumes to have full response-ability for job search actions, I never forced anyone to use a predetermined format . . . until now!

The older and wiser I become, the more I believe there is a pretty-darn-close-to-perfect resume format. In the next chapter, we will examine this approach via a critiquing checklist and by means of several samples. Each will illustrate a variation on a basic theme that, I hope, will allow for creativity but provide the quality control and structure needed to develop your perfect resume.

RESUME REALITY CHECKLIST STUDY TIPS FOR THE RETEST (ACTION STEPS TO TAKE)

✎ You may be tired of hearing it (but I never tire of stating) "write or rewrite your resume now!" Don't put off this critical step. If you don't have a resume, complete it within the next week. Do not put it off another day! Information in the next chapter will get you started and sample resumes appearing in this section will make it easy for you to create a first draft and ultimately a finished version. You must have distribution-ready copies ready as soon as possible.

✎ Ask three people you admire for copies of their resumes. You are simply collecting samples that you can compare with those appearing later in this book. If you wish, you can accomplish this task as a part of an information conversation. In addition to asking questions about someone's employment history, you will be able to see achievements on paper. Use these resumes as samples, but don't think that because someone is successful his/her resume is ideal and worthy of copying. In fact, you may be surprised to see how many achievement-oriented and successful people do not have updated resumes available. Remember, don't use information conversations as pretenses for employment interviews. Effective information gathering is the most important skill you can learn and use. After using an information conversation to learn about someone's background and review their resume, you can set goals, enhance your job search skills and, ultimately, request employment consideration.

✎ Look in the want-ads or Yellow Pages to identify three resume services. Obtain information regarding costs, services provided, and availability of sample resumes. Be strong and don't get caught up in the "sales pitch" you may receive. Remember, I do not recommend using these services, but I think it will be valuable to learn about what they offer. Occasionally, they do have some valuable services (particularly word-processing and typesetting) you may wish to use. The more you learn, the better.

RESUME REALITY CHECKLIST HELPFUL RESOURCES (PEOPLE, PLACES, AND THINGS)

✔ Identify whether your school's career services offers resume critiquing. If you are far from your alma mater, contact the nearest college or university career center to determine if resume services are available. Once you've located a critiquing resource, use it! This may involve faxing a copy to your school's office and conducting sessions over the phone. It may, more simply, involve a visit to a local facility. This is usually a cost-effective way to obtain professional constructive criticism and a way to "connect" with a facility that can offer much, much more.

✔ Books to examine include: *Liberal Arts Power*, Peterson's, 1990; *From College to Career*, Ten Speed Press, 1992; *Resumes that Knock 'em Dead*, Bob Adams, 1989; *The 90 Minute Resume*, Peterson's, 1990; and *Damn Good Resume Guide*, Ten Speed Press, 1989. Each will contain discussions of resume-writing techniques and samples of various formats. Whatever you do, don't get confused. Some job seekers suffer from data overload, freezing when they read too many contradictory views. The following chapter is designed to eliminate this possibility. Read it after you've read any other resume writing guide or, simply, don't read others. Resume writing isn't as difficult as some would like you to believe.

✔ If you haven't already used a personal computer for word-processing, visit a campus computer center or a for-fee center like Kinko's. Inform whoever is available that you are a novice, just beginning to work on your resume. Ask for guidance getting started. They will familiarize you with hardware and software (don't let the jargon scare you). If you get personal attention, great. If you are referred to a minicourse or workshop, fine. Whatever, learning how to use computers for resume writing and correspondence is essential to efficient and timely job search efforts. Never delay actions because "mom can't type my letter." Take steps to enhance your computer literacy now! This is the nineties. Also, a little bit of computer knowledge can go a long way with potential employers.

RESUME REALITY CHECKLIST STUDY SKILLS SUMMARY

- ✏ Identified myths and truths associated with resume writing.
- ✏ Clarified issues that might delay drafting of a resume.
- ✏ Introduced the concept of a "perfect" resume.
- ✏ Addressed issues related to resume data banks, resume-writing services, and resume-writing software.

CHAPTER 5

The Perfect Resume Review

Those with "distribution-ready" resumes or who are beginning to revise old versions, may wish to immediately use the *Perfect Resume Review* as a critiquing checklist, but please resist temptation. All readers, especially those who have yet to write a first draft, should become familiar with basic components of and steps involved in developing perfect job search tools.

Also, before assessing the perfection of your efforts you should use the checklist to analyze at least three of the samples appearing on subsequent pages. In this way you will become familiar with the critiquing device and with styles as close to perfect as you can get. Just to play it safe, one of the many samples will appear before the *Perfect Resume Review*. Now, with heightened curiosity, turn to the checklist (page 84) for a quick glance. When done, return to this overview of resume contents and formats.

Samples are meant to help you write the best resume possible, not to upset you. They were selected to illustrate excellent approaches to resume writing, but do not compare yourself to the resume writers. Samples often seem to belong to mythical super–job seekers, but this is not the case. All are slightly modified resumes of real job seekers, most of whom are students and alumni of the University of the Pacific. Because I am so proud of these achievement-oriented individuals and so appreciative of the opportunity I have had to work at this institution, the school's name is on these samples. It's easy to imagine the name of your institution prominently presented. While some information was altered to protect confidentiality and to highlight particular points, these are resumes developed and used by real job seekers.

Samples were selected to present a number of backgrounds and goals; some rather "unique" and "specialized." Don't think "this one doesn't help because I'm not interested in this field and my academic background is very different." Some publications contain samples that are labeled "the engineering resume," "the banking resume," "the marketing resume," "the teaching resume," and so on. I believe this approach does more harm than good. Whatever goals appear on these samples, styles displayed can be applied to your particular area of interest. View each as a format model and analyze how it might be modified for your needs.

To assist you, each document is followed by a discussion of particular approaches and strategies. Also, several of the correspondence samples appearing later are modified versions of letters used by these job seekers. Reading these will reveal how strategies unfolded. When reviewing sample resumes and letters, keep in mind that each job seeker is an individual and that everyone can (and will) find a job. You will be successful with your own background and qualifications. Don't compare your experiences with those of these individuals or judge yourself based upon what appears in samples. Simply use them to stimulate your efforts.

Yes, much has been written and said about resume writing. It's perhaps the favorite topic of verbose career counselors and authors, and well-meaning, yet poorly informed fathers, uncles, and brothers-in-law. **Overviewing in one page what has taken others 632,888 pages (I counted these too), all resumes present some variation of the following headings and content:**

- ✍ **Identifying information**—name, address(es), and phone number(s) prominent and space efficiently displayed.
- ✍ **Objective**—clearly and concisely expressing field and job function.
- ✍ **Education**—noting degree(s), major(s) and minor(s), school(s), graduation date(s) or dates attended, GPA if above 3.0, brief course listing, and (perhaps) special distinctions. For soon-to-be and recent college grads, high school should appear if you are seeking employment "back home." If not, leave it off.
- ✍ **Experience**—citing and actively describing paid, volunteer,

co-op, internship, part-time, or summer experiences. When appropriate, cite accomplishments.

- ✍ **Extracurricular and Community Activities**—citing and describing leadership roles and involvements.
- ✍ **Special Categories**—presenting information under headings including:

    Skills—noting general skills that would be employment related or identifying and describing greatest strengths, documenting capabilities to perform general job functions.

    Qualifications—noting specific skills that would be related to an objective, documenting capabilities to perform specific job functions, or generally identifying and describing greatest strengths.

    Languages—verbal and written proficiencies.

    Papers and Projects—identifying and describing academic or other research, projects, or presentations that project an understanding of field-related knowledge and acquisition of field-related skills.

    Computer Capabilities—noting programming languages, software competencies, and hardware used.

- ✍ **Interests**—if included, citing hobbies and interests. Often omitted for space reasons.
- ✍ **References**—usually cited as "available upon request." On rare occasions, listed on resume, but often on separate reference sheet.

No matter what combination of the above entries appear, distribution copies of all resumes must be free of typographical errors; typed or word-processed using easy-to-read print or fonts; duplicated on light-colored quality bonded paper; and, most importantly, reflect the quality of work you can do for a potential employer.

Resumes are most often categorized as:

- ○ **Chronological**—listing entries in reverse chronological order; the most often used approach.
- ○ **Functional**—presenting basic skills possessed and describing all relevant experiences under skill headings; an approach used frequently by persons seeking to change fields or by students seeking to bridge unrelated backgrounds to a particular goal.
- ○ **Combination**—chronological format with functional component, an excellent way to emphasize and support clear goals. *Without*

revealing too much and diminishing suspense, many consider this a "perfect" approach.

○ **Vita or Curriculum Vita**—lengthy documentation of background, most often used in education-related fields, not by recent college graduates; used (really "misused") as synonyms for resumes.

Resumes are *"targeted,"* with an objective, or *"multipurpose,"* without one. While at first you may not be able to create a targeted resume, ultimately you should be able to do so. Targeted resumes are most effective. *Again, without revealing too much (I am so bad at keeping secrets), many think a targeted combination resume is "perfect. "*

Whatever anyone says or writes, steps required to draft and, finally, duplicate a "perfect" resume are now really very, very simple. Follow the ten steps outlined on the next page to develop a perfect resume efficiently and quickly. How long it takes depends on how much time and concentration you have and on the availability of a computer or word-processor. But time is not at issue here. Good you do immediately; perfection takes a little longer (another strange homily).

TEN STEPS TO RESUME PERFECTION

1. **After reviewing all samples, make a list of headings you wish to use and develop a simple outline of entries you might include.**
    Under each heading note entries you may describe in detail at a later stage. Now you are just trying to identify Items you "could" include, not the ones you "should" include. Make these notations as long as you like. Enjoy!

2. **Develop a draft version by adding detailed descriptions to your outline.**
    Again, don't be concerned about length. A first draft may be longer than one page. If possible, use a personal computer and word-processing software. I prefer Macintosh with Microsoft Word, but whatever works for you is okay. A word-processor with memory storage is also fine for first and subsequent drafts. These systems facilitate making changes and corrections and allow for use of highlighting techniques. Typewriters are really not as effective.

3. **Use the *Perfect Resume Review* to identify areas requiring modifications.**
    Go down the list of questions, noting responses in appropriate columns. Tally your score to determine the quality of your draft. Reflect upon and, more importantly, change areas that received "no" answers.

4. **Rework your first draft.**

   Changes may involve simple spelling corrections, making verb tense consistent, or following a presentation pattern more closely. They may be more complex—rewriting job descriptions, quantifying achievements (i.e., percentage increase in annual sales), or identifying qualifications required to succeed within fields stated as objectives.

5. **Have the revised second draft critiqued by a professional, if possible; then use the *Perfect Resume Review* again.**

   Don't be defensive, but do be receptive to comments. Everyone has an opinion (or two, or three) about resumes. Listen to advice but, ultimately, you determine what should be in the final draft. It is your resume. If you feel awkward about suggested changes, don't include them in the next draft. When fretting over any particular piece of advice, remember, "when in doubt, leave it out." A final review should reveal almost all affirmative responses to inquiries of the Perfect Resume Review.

6. **Complete final editing and proofreading.**

   Use, but don't depend upon, the spell-checker contained in your software. Proofreading involves more than checking spelling. Make sure proper usage rules are followed and that all facts, figures, and, yes, addresses and phone numbers are presented accurately.

7. **Produce a duplication-ready version.**

   Final drafts should, in almost all cases, be created using personal computers and "quality" inkjet or laser printers. If this equipment is not available or if you do not wish to invest in "typesetting," quality electric typewriters or daisy-wheel word-processors will do. Dot matrix printing is not acceptable. Final versions must be crisp, clean, and error-free. Also, if someone develops a resume for you, make sure you have had input. Don't settle for someone else's idea of what is right for you or their idea of perfection.

8. **Identify a quality duplication service.**

   Many copy services provide access to IBM PCs, IBM "Clones," or Macintosh equipment and offer services to produce laser print resumes. You can, for an hourly rate, use a personal computer for drafting and printing resumes and letters. These facilities also "typeset" resumes and sell blank paper and envelopes. Of course, quality duplication is what you are looking for. Use the Yellow Pages and call a few services to compare prices. Visit to examine samples of work and don't settle for something less than "perfect!"

9. **Duplicate resume(s).**

   Resumes can be "printed" or "word-processed" with a new copy developed each time you need one or they can be "duplicated," creating multiple copies from one "master." Whatever the case, finished versions must be on quality bond paper, projecting professionalism. Conservative colors (white, ivory, and gray) of traditional laid or linen bond (not parchment) paper are recommended. You may wish to purchase blank pages and envelops that match the resume for your job search correspondence. Photocopied duplicates must be clean and residue-free.

10. **Repeat steps 5–9 whenever necessary.**

    Resumes are not chiseled in stone, so feel comfortable making changes or additions. Active job search will teach you much about how to attain goals and, if done properly, will enhance your knowledge of desired jobs. The process itself often demands that you revise resumes about three to six weeks after you begin. There is no better way to revitalize a job search and no better reason to follow up with potential employers than a revised resume. Thank goodness for word-processors and computers. It's easier than ever to reach perfection!

I.M. QUALIFIED

3444 Pacific Avenue • Apartment 111 • Stockton, California 95204 • (209) 999-9999

OBJECTIVE

Pharmaceutical or Health Care Product Sales.

QUALIFICATIONS AND CAPABILITIES

- Experienced working with physicians, health care professionals and patients. *Confident of abilities to successfully sell and service these customer groups.*
- Sales oriented and experience in retail sales. *Confident of abilities to assess customer needs, understand products, educate customers regarding applications, and effectively to close sale.*
- Capable of applying health care experience and knowledge of business practices to develop and implement marketing strategies. *Understand special nature of pharmaceutical sales and sensitivities which must be applied to sales efforts.*
- Patient, persistent, and task-oriented. *Can interact successfully with patients as well as with physicians, nurses and allied health workers working in pressure-filled and time-restricted settings.*
- Outgoing, persuasive, willing to take risks, respond positively to challenges and capable of turning rejection into motivation. *Focused on a successful career in pharmaceutical sales.*

EDUCATION

UNIVERSITY OF THE PACIFIC, Stockton, CA.
Bachelor of Science in Business Administration, anticipated May 1993
Curriculum included courses in all areas of business, including marketing, strategic planning, finance, accounting, and human resources.

HEALTH CARE RELATED EXPERIENCE

1992-Present   UNIVERSITY OF THE PACIFIC SCHOOL OF BUSINESS, Stockton, CA.
Research Assistant: Assisted professor with health care industry market research. Developed questionnaire and scripting for user evaluation study for Health Care Evaluation Inc. Arranged brochure for the 11th annual Conference of the American Association for Advances in Health Care Research. Also, assisted in a customer satisfaction survey for St. Joseph's Hospital.

Summer and   IMQ RADIOLOGY, Bakersfield, CA.
Winter 1985-1992   *Office Assistant:* Filed financial, reports, checks, insurance forms and x-rays. Assisted in billing procedures using Medocs software for data entry. Also, answered phones, directed patients and developed x-rays.

GENERAL BUSINESS EXPERIENCE

1992-Present   UNIVERSITY OF THE PACIFIC SCHOOL OF BUSINESS, Stockton, CA.
Teachers Assistant: Helped develop an authors guide to submission requirements for marketing publications by Southwestern Publishing. Surveyed Girl Scouts from Terra del Orro Council to determine most popular activities. Also, corrected papers for marketing classes.

Winter 1992   SOCAL GAS, Bakersfield, CA.
Office Assistant: Reorganized filing system and updated books.

Spring 1991   KAPPA ALPHA THETA, Stockton, CA.
through Spring 1992   *Vice President Finance*

1986-1993   Held various sales and restaurant positions during summers and part-time jobs to support self during school.

I.M. QUALIFIED

Comments and Analysis

✍ Name appears bold and in larger font size. Address presented on one line to save space. Objective is clear and concise, supported by a Qualifications and Capabilities section.

✍ Qualifications and Capabilities project knowledge of targeted field and function. Each bulleted statement shows that skills assessment and research was undertaken. It is an essential component of a "perfect" resume.

✍ Italicized "can do" statements reveal realistic awareness of traits required to succeed in desired job.

✍ Format is easy to scan, with presentation patterns easily identifiable. Caps and italics used to highlight employers and titles as well as school and degree.

✍ Goal-related employment and projects appear under headings Heath Care and General Business.

At last, an example of resume perfection! It is focused. It highlights qualifications realistically and it presents related experience in an easy-to-scan format. The Qualifications and Capabilities section presents goal-specific qualities and attributes, not an overgeneralized listing of basic skills. The targeted presentation of related experiences contains active descriptions.

I.M. Qualified is a soon-to-be graduate who thoroughly explored options. As a result of experiences working in a doctor's office and an academic project, she determined to seek a pharmaceutical or health care sales position. The most important part of this document is the Qualifications and Capabilities section. After several information conversations she identified skills she wanted to include and nicely correlated them to what would be required to be successful. She didn't list "sales ability," but connected qualifications to italicized capabilities, informing reviewers that she really knew what it took to succeed in pharmaceutical sales. Documents reflecting this much commitment to and knowledge of a career field and job functions regularly yield employment interviews.

Don't let this apparent focus fool you too much, I.M. did identify two other options, so she created another targeted and one multipurpose document. It's a perfect resume when you think it is the only one used by the job seeker, even if this isn't the case.

I.M. used contacts associated with her job at a radiologist's office and her health care market research project to locate persons willing to hold information conversations. Eventually, these individuals provided job search advice and leads. Directories listing pharmaceutical firms were easy to find, but the names of local salespersons or regional managers weren't. It took a little effort, and some awkward phone calls to corporate headquarters, but the information was obtained. She was assertive enough to also "cold call" several local pharmacies to uncover names and phone numbers of area reps. Boy, did that impress recruiters during interviews. I.M. implemented a dual-pronged strategy, contacting centralized human resource professionals at corporate headquarters and regional managers close to school and home. Ultimately, a recruiter who no longer visited campus provided the most useful referrals.

Although this is a resume used by a business student, the style could be used by someone with any academic background. In fact, a sample appearing later shows how it was "transformed" by someone with a different major, yet a bit more experience.

This is not "a pharmaceutical sales resume," but a format to use for any goal. Samples that follow will prove that claim.

Before you review all samples, and before you judge the quality of your resume draft, examine the *Perfect Resume Review* checklist and use it to assess three of the samples. By doing so you will be better prepared to use the device on your own resume.

THE PERFECT RESUME REVIEW

Use this critiquing checklist to determine how close to perfect resume drafts and final versions are. Also use it to determine the quality of sample resumes. After each review tally "yes" checks for all 45 questions.

FIRST GLANCE AND OVERALL APPEARANCE	Yes	No
Is it easy to read, with headings highlighted?	❏	❏
Can you look at, instead of look for information?	❏	❏
Is the placement of headings and content consistent?	❏	❏
Can you scan down the page and identify a pattern?	❏	❏
Is CAPITALIZATION, **bold type**, *italics*, or placement used to highlight important information?	❏	❏
Can you scan down the page quickly and identify important information?	❏	❏
Does it look professional and businesslike, free of typographical errors and misspelled words?	❏	❏
Does it present a "job well done" image?	❏	❏
Do the name, address(es) and phone number(s) stand out?	❏	❏
If more than one address and phone number appears, is it apparent why?	❏	❏
Are most important topics first?	❏	❏
If more than one page, are most important entries on the first and does a name appear on the second?	❏	❏

OBJECTIVE STATEMENT

If included, does it reveal knowledge of a desired field by using appropriate phrasing? ❏ ❏

Does it cite job titles, job functions or skills, or a combination of these? ❏ ❏

SKILLS SUMMARY OR QUALIFICATION SUMMARY

If an objective appears, are skills or qualifications presented in terminology appropriate to the stated goal? ❏ ❏

Do skill categories or qualification statements project knowledge of traits desired within fields of interest? ❏ ❏

If no objective appears, are skills categories or qualification statements easily identified as desirable? ❏ ❏

Are they tightly worded, avoiding overgeneralized "enjoy working with people" phrases? ❏ ❏

If an objective appears, do qualification statements directly connect to the stated goal? ❏ ❏

Do they demonstrate knowledge of a targeted field, stressing field-specific characteristics? ❏ ❏

EDUCATION

Does it present school(s), degree(s), area(s) of concentration, courses, honors? ❏ ❏

Are only appropriate experiences presented (high school is not necessary in most cases)? ❏ ❏

If an objective appears, are related academic experiences highlighted? ❏ ❏

Do they appear earlier or later in the document, and is it apparent why? ❏ ❏

Are grades or grade point averages presented (typically for recent grads), if complimentary (over 3.0)? ❏ ❏

Does an overall grade point average or subject-specific averages appear? ❏ ❏

EXPERIENCE AND SPECIAL HEADINGS

Are entries described using active phrases, with accomplishments noted and facts and figures used? ❏ ❏

If entries are simply cited, with no descriptions, are they obviously of less importance? ❏ ❏

Are experiences grouped according to headings related to a stated objective? ❏ ❏

Do headings like Marketing-Related Experience, Teaching Experience, Sales Experience appear? ❏ ❏

Are job titles as well as organizations highlighted? ❏ ❏

Could they easily be found by someone scanning the resume? ❏ ❏

Are experiences presented in reverse chronological order, with dates appearing? ❏ ❏

If not, is there an obvious logic behind the presentation? ❏ ❏

Do all heading titles catch the eye and reveal the true nature of entries that follow? ❏ ❏

Do headings like Languages, Papers and Projects, and Related Experience highlight important data? ❏ ❏

EXTRACURRICULAR AND COMMUNITY ACTIVITIES

If listed, are leadership positions noted, responsibilities described, and accomplishments noted? ❏ ❏

Do all descriptions seem relevant? ❏ ❏

Are activities presented clearly, avoiding acronyms, with little-known groups and awards described? ❏ ❏

Are they all chronologically relevant or obviously meaningful (i.e., not too far in the past or afield)? ❏ ❏

INTERESTS, PERSONAL DATA, AND REFERENCES

If interests are included, is the presentation brief and does it appear late in the resume? ❏ ❏

If personal data is presented, is information positive and supportive of the candidate's efforts? ❏ ❏

If references are listed, are name, title, organization, and phone for each presented concisely and easy to read? ❏ ❏

If a statement concerning availability upon request appears, is the statement brief and appearing last? ❏ ❏

Is availability of supplemental materials (i.e., sample of works or portfolio) noted? ❏ ❏

Over 35 "yes" checks indicates a "darn close to perfect" resume. Depending upon questions with "no" responses, the resume might require fine-tuning or major revisions. Paying particular attention to questions receiving "no" checks, make changes and use the checklist again (and again) until a draft is "perfect" and duplication and distribution ready. Quite honestly, only you can judge what is truly perfect and, as revealed in the steps outlined earlier, resume perfection is a goal you will continue to reach for in subsequent revisions.

JUSTIN TIMETOHIRE
55 Babbling Brook Road • Carmichael, CA 95608 • (916) 944-1111

Objective
Lobbying or Non-Profit position that builds on existing skills and professional experience.

Qualifications
- Internship with lobbyist whose clients include Blue Cross of California, City of San Diego, and Charter Medical Corporation.
- Observed efforts required to assess needs of clients, determine strategies, and prepare testimony for committee meetings.
- Contributed to process required to track status of pending legislation, read and analyze bills to determine impact on client organizations, correspond with legislators regarding issues, and write reports documenting results of lobbying efforts.
- Conducted research and assisted with writing of report citing funding grants received by City of San Diego for fiscal year 1991-92.
- Consulted with homeless shelter to determine feasibility of transitional housing and employment services.
- First hand knowledge of challenges associated with interacting with state and local agencies, officials, and office holders.

Lobbying and Non-Profit Experience
L & L and Associates Governmental Advocacy, Sacramento, CA
Office Assistant/Intern, Summer 1992
- Kept updated and detailed records of all bills of importance to firm.
- Researched and prepared a report on all funding grants received by the City of San Diego.
- Filed documents with the Fair Political Practices Commission.
- Tracked bills using legislative data base.

Stockton Shelter for the Homeless, Stockton, CA
Student Consultant, Spring 1992
- Helped formulate a model for transitional housing in the City of Stockton.
- Interviewed director of shelter in Sacramento and reported on program effectiveness and implementation logistics to determine whether a similar program would be possible in Stockton.
- Attended and evaluated community meetings held to discuss proposed shelter expansion.

Other Experience
UOP Office of Student Life, Stockton, CA
Student Advisor, 1990-92
- As Orientation Coordinator, helped plan and implement Orientation for over 1,100 students.
- Supervised staff of 25 student advisors.

Smith, Smith, Smith & Schwartz Law Office, Sacramento, CA
Receptionist, Summers 1991

Weinstocks, Sacramento, CA
Sales Associate, Part-time 1987-90

Macy's California, Sacramento, CA
Sales Associate, Part-time 1986-87

Education and Honors
University of the Pacific, Stockton, CA
Bachelor of Arts, International Affairs and Commerce, May 1993.
- Dean's Honor Roll, Spring and Fall 1991
- Overall Grade Point Average: 3.4

Albert-Ludwigs University, Freiburg, Germany
Completed European Studies Program, Fall 1992

JUSTIN TIMETOHIRE

Comments and Analysis

✍ Name appears bold and in larger font size. Address presented efficiently on one line. Objective is clear and concise, presented in bold and supported by a Qualifications section.

✍ Qualifications lists accomplishments and experiences that support targeted objective. Each bulleted statement shows knowledge of skills required to serve within lobbying or non-profit roles.

✍ Bullet format, using three-dimensional boxes, used for all citations, making it easy to scan experience descriptions as well as achievements.

✍ Format is easy to review, with presentation patterns easily identifiable. Reader can look at, not look for, information. Bolding and italics used to highlight organizations and titles, as well as schools and degrees or programs.

✍ Lobbying and Non-Profit Experience heading appearing immediately after Qualifications highlighted most directly related employment and projects.

Another example of resume perfection; yet it shows a variation in visual presentation. It doesn't really matter whether headings appear on the side or whether they are centered, or whether caps and bolding or just size and bolding are used as highlighting techniques. What matters is the focus presented and the listing of realistic qualifications for the target fields.

Justin Timetohire is another soon-to-be graduate who was smart enough to have sought related internships and projects while in school. Through these and through a few courses, he became focused on to the stated objective. While the objective does in fact present two work settings, not particular job titles, it still projects focus. The rest of the document nicely supports the initial goal statement. Students who don't complete internships as undergraduates can (as you will see in a bit) do so the summer after graduation.

As with almost all perfect resumes, the most important part of the document is the Qualifications section. Related achievements are proudly and clearly presented in the most prominent position.

Justin leveraged relationships with previous employers as well as he could. Quickly he realized consideration would not be granted as easily as he had hoped. Fields he wished to enter did not offer many entry-level options and availability of any position was based on tenuous funding and on "political" issues (obviously). Justin knew he was in for a lengthy campaign so he explored taking related summer courses; inquired regarding summer internships with organizations he contacted; and examined year-long intern programs associated with executive and legislative branches of several states.

Applications for formal programs were completed, with decisions expected late-summer. Job search communications continued throughout spring. As of graduation, Justin had no offers, so the summer internships strategy was implemented. After a flurry of calls to almost all contacts, he received a summer position. After he updated his resume to include the new entry he had a reason for recontacting everyone and rekindling interest. Justin awaits word from state programs and continues to communicate with others regarding entry-level positions. He even had time to take a summer seminar in grant writing (great idea!).

Although this is the resume used by an International Affairs and Commerce student for a very clearly defined purpose, the style could be used by job seekers with any academic background.

One of Justin's letters appears as a sample in the correspondence section.

ANNA ESTRELLA

4040 Pacific Avenue • Stockton, California 95211 • (209) 444-1313 or 944-4499
67 Chabeau Drive • Castro Valley, California 94552 • (510) 577-7777

OBJECTIVE

Intern or Student General Music or Choral Teaching Position.

QUALIFICATIONS

- Experienced as volunteer and paid music teacher.
- Have taught Classroom Music in elementary and directed Choir in high schools settings.
- Strong academic background in general music, choral music and in music education.
- Coursework and field observations provided strong foundation for teaching.

EDUCATION

UNIVERSITY OF THE PACIFIC, Stockton, California.
Bachelor of Music, Choral Concentration, expected May 1993.
Preliminary Single Subject Credential, expected May 1993.
Overall GPA: 3.22/4.0 Music GPA: 3.6/4.0

Coursework includes: Voice and Choral Music, Music for Teenagers and Secondary School, Music for the Child and Elementary School, Conducting, Educational Psychology, and Skills Teaching.

MUSIC AND CHORAL TEACHING EXPERIENCE

ANNUNCIATION SCHOOL, Stockton, California.
Part-time General Music Teacher, Kindergarten - 6th Grade, Fall 1992.
- Prepared and presented lesson plans introducing students to basic music theory, various music styles, history of music and other related topics.
- Lead students in singing and music appreciation activities and assisted with Children's Choir.
- Provided feedback to students and parents regarding progress.

CLEVELAND ELEMENTARY SCHOOL, Stockton, California.
Practicum Teacher, 1st and 4th Grades, Spring 1992.
- Prepared and presented lesson plans introducing students to basic music theory, various music styles, history of music and other related topics.
- Lead students in singing and music appreciation activities.
- Assisted with Children's Choir and helped prepare students for special UOP Conservatory event.
- Provided feedback to students and parents regarding progress.
- Strengthened teaching skills through feedback of Master Teacher and Practicum Supervisor.

LINCOLN HIGH SCHOOL, Stockton, California.
Practicum Teacher Assistant, Fall 1991
- Directed and assisted with Concert Choir and Women's Choir.
- Conducted warm-up and sight-reading exercises and helped individual students in both groups.
- Directed Winter Concert performance piece for Women's Choir.
- Strengthened teaching skills through feedback of Master Teacher and Practicum Supervisor.

ACTIVITIES AND HONORS

- Alpha Chi Omega Women's Fraternity, 1989-93.
- UOP Panhellenic President, 1992-93.
- Served on numerous UOP committees dealing with Responsible Options to Alcohol and Drugs (ROAD), student life, and other campus issues, 1989-93.
- Music Educators National Conference, 1990-93.
- American Choral Directors Association, 1990-93.
- Order of Omega Greek Honor Society, 1992-93.
- Mortar Board Honor Society, 1992-93.

ANNA ESTRELLA

Comments and Analysis

✐ Name appears bold and in larger font size. Two addresses presented efficiently on two lines. Objective is definitely clear and concise and supported by Qualifications.

✐ Using creative pencil graphics, Qualifications note accomplishments and experiences that support targeted objective.

✐ Bullet format used throughout, making it easy to scan experience as well as activities and honors.

✐ Format patterns easily identifiable. Reader can easily find information. Caps and italics used nicely to highlight organizations and titles, as well as schools and degrees or programs.

Another example of resume perfection. Anna's goal is very clear, and procedures for seeking teaching positions are rather formalized, but good job search tools will make her efforts more effective and easier. Resume screening is still used to determine who receives interviews for teaching positions.

Anna is one of those special individuals whose background stands out, and the format used makes it stand out even more. Reviewers can see that she is a strong candidate who has achieved in the classroom as a student and someone who will also achieve in the classroom as a teacher.

She is very targeted, as is her job search document, but she cannot be passive and wait for opportunities to come to her. A copy of the letter of inquiry she used for initial contact appears later.

Clem Corson

888 Presidents Drive • University of the Pacific • Stockton, CA 95211 • (209) 947-9900

OBJECTIVE   Sports management internship with established agency.

QUALIFICATIONS AND CAPABILITIES

- ❑ Researched operations of major agencies including, MGI, PROSET, ADSPORT INTERNATIONAL, and CORPRO SPORTS, and approaches used for contract negotiation and promotional representation.
- ❑ Aware of need to be appropriately aggressive, identify clients' goals, and develop and implement strategies to meet clients' financial and image objectives.
- ❑ Capable of completing detailed research, documenting findings, drafting correspondence and basic contractual agreements, and completing follow up fax and phone communication.
- ❑ Can use business skills to research contract options and financial ramifications.

EXPERIENCE   RUFF AND COMPANY, Sacramento, CA.
Real Estate Development Project Manager, Summer 1992.
- Performed project bid analysis.
- Managed off-site improvements and coordinated on-site progress meetings.
- Managed project through public approval process.

CORY AND HAREY REAL ESTATE, Palo Alto, CA.
Real Estate Intern, Summer 1990.
- Conducted land acquisition research
- Mapped municipalities' zoning and general plan designations.
- Assisted in multi-project management.

SIERRA RIDGE CONSTRUCTION, Sacramento, CA.
Assistant to General Contractor, Summer 1991.
- Performed general construction jobs at all phases of construction.

KPAC RADIO, Stockton, CA.
On Air Personality, 1991-92.
- Produced and hosted sports talk show and comedy radio programs.
- Hosted program with highest ratings.

TELENET PHONE SYSTEMS, Menlo Park, CA.
Account Executive, Summer 1990.
- Solicited new accounts and marketed various sales programs.
- Conducted multi-sales presentation meetings.

COLLEGIATE ACHIEVEMENTS

ARCHANIA TEETER-TOTTER MARATHON
Chairperson, Summer 1992.
- Raised over $6,000 for AIDS research and education.
- Sold numerous corporate sponsorships for most successful student fundraiser in UOP's history. Sponsors include: I Dig Volleyball, Coors Light Beer, Primadonna Casino, PG&E, Honda Motor Company, KJOY Radio, Sherwood Broadcasting.
- Arranged for political leaders to endorse event and speak at opening ceremonies.
- Directed corporate sponsored volleyball tournament.
- Gained state-wide television, radio, and newspaper coverage.

NATIONAL ASSOCIATION OF HOME BUILDERS
President Student Chapter, 1991-92.
- Arranged for prominent real estate figures to speak to membership.
- Coordinated numerous development site field trips for membership.

ARCHANIA FRATERNITY
Vice President, 1992.
Rush Chairman, 1992.

Clem Corson

Page Two

UNIVERSITY OF THE PACIFIC BASKETBALL
Division I Team Member, 1989 - 91.
GREEK MAN OF THE YEAR
Nominee, 1992.
INTER-FRATERNITY COUNCIL, 1991-92.
Secretary, 1991-92.
CALIFORNIA REAL ESTATE SALES LICENSE, 1992.

EDUCATION   UNIVERSITY OF THE PACIFIC, Stockton, CA
Bachelor of Arts - English, anticipated December, 1993.
Emphasis in Broadcasting Communications.
Course work includes Business and Real Estate Law.

CLEM CORSON

Comments and Analysis

✍ Name is bolded and in larger font. Address on one line with borders presents letterhead appearance. Objective is very brief and concise.

✍ Qualifications and Capabilities section is most critical. Bulleted statements project very focused and thorough examination of field of interest and awareness of what would be required to perform roles of intern.

✍ Bullet format, with three-dimensional boxes used in Q&C section and traditional bullets used for other citations, allows for quick scanning of experience descriptions and identification of achievements.

✍ Presentation patterns are easily identifiable on both pages. Yes! A two-page format can be perfect, if the first page carries the second. This "do-it-all" individual could not (for logistical and psychological reasons) edit to a briefer version. While most soon-to-be and recent grads *should* be able to craft a one-page document, some *could* create wonderful two-page versions. Also, too many try to edit in their minds prior to developing a first draft. Don't edit before you write. Do so after. Some of the space-saving approaches illustrated in these samples may show you how to "shrink" yours down to size. Caps and italics highlight organizations and titles, as well as school and degree.

This two-page document is another perfect resume. Clem Corson is a Senior seeking an internship in a tough-to-crack field. The entire Qualification and Capabilities section clearly shows the first bulleted statement is true. All other statements reveal a realistic awareness of what would be involved in an internship. Clem did his homework! He researched a field and seeks the appropriate next step (even for those who have graduated), an internship. Samples of correspondence appearing later reveal much more about Clem's job search.

IDA AMANDA CHANCE

P.O. Box 2041 • Stockton, CA 95288 • (209) 986-6464

Objective and Qualification Summary

Catering and event planning position that builds on and utilizes:

O Apprenticeship with Bay Area caterer whose clients include professional athletes, entertainers, as well as major corporations and philanthropic organizations.
O Experience negotiating with florists and other vendors, as well as with hotels and other venues.
O Ability to assess client needs, develop initial plans and estimates, present options to clients, finalize plans, and implement all arrangement. Knowledgeable of set-up styles used for different events.
O Knowledge of floral design and decorating needs, having creating themes and motifs.
O Capability of maintaining effective communications, by letter, phone, fax or in person, with vendors, clients, and event staff. Have used computers to generate correspondence and organize data.
O Awareness of various audio/visual needs for specific events.
O Capacity to work with different budgets, schedules, themes, and sizes, and meet client needs.
O Ability to deal effectively with on-site last-minute challenges.

Catering and Event Planning Experience

Some Food Catering, Danville, California
Apprentice Planner [Part-time 1991-present]
O Design theme and develop menu based upon assessment of clients' wishes.
O Order, prepare, cook, and display hors d' oeuvres, main dishes, and desserts.
O Contact and communicate with vendors for food and decoration needs.
O Adapt private and public facilities to meet logistical and thematic needs.
O Monitor on-site preparation and implementation.

Other Experience

Lincoln Unified School District, Stockton, California
Art History Curriculum Development Intern [Spring 1991]
O Developed and presented art history lessons to junior high school faculty and students.

University of the Pacific, Stockton, California
Art History Teacher's Assistant [Fall 1990-Spring 1991]
O Lectured weekly, graded work, and provided private tutoring.

Assemblyman William Baker, Walnut Creek, California
Campaign Coordinator [Summer 1990]
O Recruited, trained and oversaw volunteers.
O Coordinated precinct material distribution, organized phone banks, polled and registered voters.

Cal-Homes, Dublin, California
Sales and Marketing Aide [Summers 1989 and 1990]
O Collected literature from competitive home building groups to update marketing materials.
O Answered customer inquiries and concerns.
O Proof-read and processed all sales contracts, purchase orders and custom feature requests.
O Distributed and monitored promotional materials at all sales sites.

Education and Honors

University of the Pacific, Stockton, California
Bachelor of Arts, Art History, May 1991.
Overall GPA 3.5/4.0   Major GPA 3.7/4.0
O Semester Abroad, Siena, Italy, Fall 1989
O National Dean's List and UOP Dean's List
O Naomi Cannon Award for outstanding achievement in Art Department
O Outstanding Young Women of America 1991 recognizing community service
O Greek Scholar Award

IDA AMANDA CHANCE

Comments and Analysis

✍ Name is bold, in larger creative font. Address on one line with a double-line border, creating letterhead appearance, which is also used for correspondence.

✍ Combined Objective and Qualification Summary clearly presents target and supports it with proven capabilities to perform related tasks.

✍ Bullet format, with three-dimensional circles, is a bit creative but still businesslike. Used for Objective and Qualification section and all other citations, allows for quick scanning of experience descriptions as well as academic achievements.

✍ Bolding and italics highlight presentation patterns. Catering and Event Planning Experience follows Objective and Qualification Summary's key points and cites most significant employment.

Ida knew what she wanted and her resume and actions showed it. She was leveraging her job search, as illustrated by the resume, on an apprenticeship. Ida knew her options: find another apprenticeship, an entry-level sales position with hotels, conference centers, catering facilities, or an event planning job within a corporate public relations department or public relations firm. It is rare that planning responsibilities are offered entry-level candidates. Most frequently, first roles are associated with booking (selling) engagements or implementing someone else's plans. The field wasn't an easy one to enter at a professional level, but Ida had a perfect resume and a positive and confident attitude.

GINA JOBYET

3333 Twin Tree Avenue • Stockton, CA 95211 • (209) 444-9449

OBJECTIVE Pharmaceutical sales position.

QUALIFICATIONS AND CAPABILITIES

➢ Sales professional, experienced in consumer product and retail sales. *Confident of abilities to assess customer needs, understand products, educate customers regarding applications, and effectively close sale.*

➢ Capable of applying marketing experience and knowledge of sales practices to develop and implement marketing strategies. *Understand special nature of pharmaceutical sales and sensitivities which must be applied to sales efforts.*

➢ Patient, persistent, and task-oriented. *Can interact successfully with physicians, nurses and allied health workers.*

➢ Outgoing, persuasive, willing to take risks, respond positively to challenges and capable of turning rejection into motivation. *Focused on successful career in pharmaceutical sales.*

CONSUMER PRODUCT SALES EXPERIENCE

NIKE SHOES AND SPORTSWEAR
Sales Representative, 1989-1992
Represented Nike in Sacramento to Porterville and East Bay areas.

➢ Ranked 2nd in Region - 1992 Quarter bookings up 112% from 1991.
➢ Increased Sport Casual line from $860,000 to $920,000.
➢ Met and exceeded increasing quota for 10 consecutive months.
➢ Increased top accounts significantly from 1990-92 with World of Shoes, Dublin, increasing from $227,000 to $350,000 and J's World of Shoes, Stockton, increasing from $190,000 to $300,000.
➢ Increased 60% of assigned accounts, with highest increases including Smith's Shoes (722%), Sports Stuff Sporting Goods (184%), and Shoes 4 U (196%)

Technical Field Representative, 1989-90
Responsible for promotions, special events, CIF, and clinic presentations.

➢ Recognized by VP for excellent customer service, product knowledge and dedication.

TED E. BEAR, INC.
Sales Representative, 1988-89
Marketed gift and holiday items and greeting cards in Lodi to Fresno and Mountain Regions.

➢ Pioneered 18 new accounts.
➢ Achieved recognition on Stars list for sales in excess of $8,000 to $10,000 per week.

RETAIL SALES AND MANAGEMENT EXPERIENCE

P'ZAZZ CLOTHING
Buyer, Assistant Manager, Sales Associate, Part-time 1988-present

UNLIMITED DRESS
Sales Manager, 1986-88
Recruited, trained and developed staff; oversaw merchandising, inventory control, and payroll.

➢ Store ranked 4th in California Region with sales increase of 183% in 1987.

OTHER EXPERIENCE

UNIVERSITY OF THE PACIFIC ATHLETIC DEPARTMENT
Coordinator, 1989-present
Supervise and choreograph dance squad, assist with special events and fundraising.

EDUCATION

UNIVERSITY OF THE PACIFIC, Stockton, CA
Bachelor of Communications, 1986

REFERENCES AVAILABLE UPON REQUEST

GINA JOBYET

Comments and Analysis

✐ Example of a perfect resume used by alumna with over seven years of experience.

✐ Illustrates how viewing a sample can impact a resume writer. Doesn't the Qualifications and Capabilities section look familiar? The temptation to copy resume samples if they match your goals is great, but resist copying exact phrases. If you wish, model a format like this one, using active verbs and highlighting accomplishments quantitatively and qualitatively, but don't copy.

✐ Qualification Summary clearly presents target and supports it with proven capabilities, in italics, to perform related tasks.

✐ Three-dimensional arrows used to bullet information are creative yet appropriate.

✐ Distinct categories for sales highlights significant background and presents goal-driven and numerically documented achievements.

✐ Overall format is easy to scan with major categories identified at first glance.

Gina wanted to transition from consumer product and "merchandising-oriented" sales to pharmaceutical sales. As an experienced salesperson she had the assertiveness and tenacity required to reach her goal.

Gina was a great salesperson, but could she (as stated in the Q&C section) interact with a new clientele? Pharmaceutical sales is not just selling a product and using traditional marketing and promotions techniques. It requires understanding of very special and, often sophisticated, product. Frequently a science background is "required" (think of that as "desired," it rhymes and keeps you motivated).

As Gina's efforts continued, as she met more persons in the field and had information conversations as well as employment interviews, she toned down her sales persona and projected her sincere interest in and curiosity about health care issues and pharmaceuticals.

After a prolonged search (see copies of correspondence and note dates appearing), Gina Jobyet sold herself long enough, hard enough, and well enough to reach her goal.

HIRAM E. NOW

31 Lincoln Street #9 • San Francisco, California 94777 • (415) 323-9888

SUMMARY OF SKILLS
- Advanced writing and research skills.
- Particular strengths involve organization, creative thought and planning.
- Computer competent; proficient with Microsoft Word on Macintosh.
- Strong work ethic and good interpersonal skills.

EXPERIENCE

University of Zimbabwe, Harare, Zimbabwe.
Tutor of English. February - March 1993
- Produced, filmed and edited video regarding life and culture in Zimbabwe, Africa.
- Assisted in teaching English to children.

Carousel Stationery, Davis, California.
Office Supplies Salesperson. September 1991- February 1992
- Assisted customers with technical questions and special orders.
- Dealt with catalog and bulk sales.

San Joaquin County Arts Council, Stockton, California.
Internship, Administrative Assistant. February - May 1992
- Compiled 24 page guidebook for annual tour of artists' studios.
- Planned and implemented California State Summer School for the Arts awards ceremony.
- Assisted with planning of "Black Tie & Blue Jeans" fund raising event and art auction benefiting the County Arts Council.
- Handled general office tasks which included document filing, writing press releases, typing and receptionist duties.

University of the Pacific, Stockton, California.
Producer. 1991-92
- Filmed and produced half hour long video presentations, "Dad's Day" for visiting fathers and "Tiger Times", promoting Greek life on campus.
- Filmed and produced hour long video documenting four years on campus and sold to graduating students.
- Designed and constructed the sets for "A Tribute to Andrew Lloyd Weber".

Kelly Temporary Services, Sacramento, California.
Office Assistant. May - August 1991
- Created new position for Sacramento Cable involving cable box retrieval.
- Reorganized dispatch system for more efficient service to customers.
- Improved customer relations.

EDUCATION

University of the Pacific, Stockton, California.
Bachelor of Arts, May 1992.
Major in Liberal Studies, emphasis History.
Minor in English.
Minor in Studio Art.

College Semester Abroad, Siena, Italy
Overseas studies of Italian language, life, and culture, Spring of 1992.

REFERENCES AVAILABLE UPON REQUEST

HIRAM E. NOW

31 Lincoln Street #9 • San Francisco, California 94777 • (415) 323-9888

OBJECTIVE

Event planning position.

SUMMARY OF SKILLS

- Particular strengths involve organization, creative thought and planning.
- Confident of abilities to assess needs of clients, translate needs into alternative plans, and, ultimately, implement selected options.
- Capable of preparing cost estimates and negotiating costs and services with vendors.
- Advanced writing and research skills applicable to developing effective correspondence, writing proposals, and creating promotional materials.
- Strong work ethic and good interpersonal skills will be demonstrated by willingness to work hours required to plan and implement details and personal efforts to address last minute issues.
- Computer Competent. Proficient with Microsoft Word on Macintosh.

PROJECT MANAGEMENT AND ADMINISTRATIVE EXPERIENCE

University of Zimbabwe, Harare, Zimbabwe.
Tutor of English. February - March 1993
- Produced, filmed and edited video regarding life and culture in Zimbabwe, Africa.
- Assisted in teaching English to children.

Carousel Stationery, Davis, California.
Office Supplies Salesperson. September 1991- February 1992
- Assisted customers with technical questions and special orders.
- Dealt with catalog and bulk sales.

San Joaquin County Arts Council, Stockton, California.
Internship, Administrative Assistant. February - May 1992
- Compiled 24 page guidebook for annual tour of artists' studios.
- Planned and implemented California State Summer School for the Arts awards ceremony.
- Assisted with planning of "Black Tie & Blue Jeans" fund raising event and art auction benefiting the County Arts Council.
- Handled general office tasks which included document filing, writing press releases, typing and receptionist duties.

University of the Pacific, Stockton, California.
Producer. 1991-92
- Filmed and produced half hour long video presentations, "Dad's Day" for visiting fathers and "Tiger Times", promoting Greek life on campus.
- Filmed and produced hour long video documenting four years on campus and sold to graduating students.
- Designed and constructed the sets for "A Tribute to Andrew Lloyd Weber".

Kelly Temporary Services, Sacramento, California.
Office Assistant. May - August 1991
- Created new position for Sacramento Cable involving cable box retrieval.
- Reorganized dispatch system for more efficient service to customers.
- Improved customer relations.

EDUCATION

University of the Pacific, Stockton, California.
Bachelor of Arts, May 1992.
Major in Liberal Studies, emphasis History.
Minor in English.
Minor in Studio Art.

College Semester Abroad, Siena, Italy
Overseas studies of Italian language, life, and culture, Spring of 1992.

REFERENCES AVAILABLE UPON REQUEST

HIRAM E. NOW

Comments and Analysis

✍ The first is an example of a perfect "multipurpose" (no-objective) resume.

✍ Very simple and well-presented format.

✍ Summary of Skills cites four basic abilities, applicable to a variety of employment settings. Cannot be as strong without an objective serving as focal point, but still presents significant skills.

✍ Bullets identify important information. Those under Experience highlight capabilities and achievements.

✍ Format is easy to scan.

Hiram had just returned home after an amazing postgraduation year in Zimbabwe. He wasn't very focused, yet he wanted to begin job search and be ready to respond to postings. The best he could do was create a perfect multipurpose resume. Hiram realized goal-direction would enhance job search potential and an objective would strengthen his resume, but he just wasn't ready to finish research and commit to a written goal. He contacted his alma mater's career services office and he identified and used several community career services. Hiram was quite surprised to find more than one useful center that charged reasonable rates and had great resource libraries and posting mechanisms.

While Hiram E. Now wanted things to happen quickly (as his name implies), he soon realized how critical it was to project focus. After four weeks he felt comfortable creating a second version of his resume. This second one illustrates how you can subtly, yet simply, change a multipurpose document into a targeted one.

✍ Objective presented boldly in a few words.

✍ Summary of Skills now supports goal statement, with particular abilities highlighted as associated with event planning.

✍ Experience heading is now Project Management and Administrative Experience to support stated goal.

The new resume wasn't dramatically different from the old, but it was definitely stronger. Hiram's search continued with a sense of focus as well as freedom, with a targeted resume for event planning positions and a multipurpose one for all others. Correspondence samples illustrate some of his efforts.

IVANA B. ASTAR

333 President's Drive ☆ University of the Pacific ☆ Stockton, CA 95211 ☆ (209) 459-5548
7 Rodeo Canyon Road ☆ Arroyo Grande, CA 94420 ☆ (805) 456-6677

QUALIFICATIONS AND ACHIEVEMENTS

☆ Undergraduate studies, extracurricular activities, and employment experiences developed strong communication skills and project-driven work ethic.

☆ Able to motivate self and others to achieve as a team member.

☆ Sales and customer service experience enhanced abilities to communicate effectively with clients and customers, dealing with concerns, or marketing products or services.

☆ Confident of abilities to develop written materials and correspondence and of abilities to develop and make presentations.

☆ For communication course, worked in small group to develop a "Stress Management Workshop." Researched topic, determined priorities and activities for two hour period, delivered "mini-lectures" on special issues, selected and conducted exercises, and compiled written materials distributed to participants.

EDUCATION

UNIVERSITY OF THE PACIFIC, Stockton, CA
Bachelor of Arts, anticipated May 1993
Major: Communication
Emphasis: Interpersonal and Organizational Communication

RETAIL AND CUSTOMER SERVICE EXPERIENCE

1991-present

MACY'S WEST, Stockton, CA
Sales Associate, Full-time Summer 1991, Part-time Fall 1991-present

☆ Assessed customers' needs and sold apparel and accessories in Children's department.

☆ Addressed questions, dealt with returns and concerns, maintaining high level of customer service.

☆ Also brought merchandise from storage areas to sales floor and maintained displays to enhance customer appeal.

Summer
1992-present

QUAIL LAKES ATHLETIC CLUB, Stockton, CA
Receptionist, Part-time

☆ Checked in members, answered phone, booked appointments and completed new member registration procedures.

☆ Also, sold pro-shop items and served as snack bar host.

OTHER EXPERIENCE

Summers
1990 and 1989

CROW CANYON COUNTRY CLUB, Danville, CA
Lifeguard, Full-time

☆ Checked members in, taught swim lessons, and guarded pool area.

ACTIVITIES

UOP VARSITY WOMEN'S SWIMMING, 1989-1992.

KAPPA ALPHA THETA SORORITY, 1992-present.

PUBLIC RELATIONS STUDENT SOCIETY OF AMERICA, 1992.

REFERENCES

Available upon request.

IVANA B. ASTAR

Comments and Analysis

✍ Another "multipurpose" and perfect resume.

✍ Format is easy to scan with effective use of three-dimensional stars as bullets. This is a bit flashy, but Ivana wasn't communicating with conservative employers.

✍ Retail and Customer Service Experience heading projects focus in absence of objective statement.

✍ Bullets used effectively, allowing for quick review.

Ivana wanted a resume to use for on-campus recruiting. She had not yet completed self-assessment and research required to cite goals, but she didn't want this convenient job search process to pass her by. The resume was used primarily for retail firms and sales-oriented organizations, so creative graphics were appropriate. It proved easy to use during interviews, because she kept citing and expanding on the five key qualifications and on achievements and activities.

Ivana B. Astar is a student who has some very basic strengths, but isn't quite a star yet. This resume is like those of many soon-to-be grads. The typical retail, athletic club, and country club experience, supported by academic and extracurricular experiences, may seem familiar (look at your resume). The format may be the perfect way to present yourself.

Her stardom will come with focused and furious job search actions. After research is completed on public relations, advertising, retailing, hotel and resort management, and consumer product sales, Ivana will implement an effective strategy. Targeted resumes will be developed with supporting Q&A sections. Ivana is typical, yet unique. She will complete pRe-search and job search efforts successfully because she realizes that actions, not just a resume, will show others how she reaches for the stars.

Tom T. Eiger

88 Padre Paseos • Santa Barbara, Ca. 93333 • (805) 968-3636

Education   UNIVERSITY OF THE PACIFIC, Stockton, Ca.
Bachelor of Science in English, May 1993
In addition to liberal arts curriculum, completed courses in accounting, marketing, and strategic planning.

SEMESTER AT SEA, Pittsburgh, Pa.
Completed courses during semester long voyage throughout Far East, Africa, and South America. Visited Japan, People's Republic of China, Taiwan, Malaysia, India, Kenya, South Africa, Brazil, and Venezuela. Fall 1992.

CATE SCHOOL, Carpenteria, Ca.
Graduated, June 1989.

Marketing Related Courses and Projects

Promotion and Advertising
Advertising Theory
Strategic Management
International Marketing

Completed simulation game which modeled airline industry. Learned impact that pricing, gasoline costs, maintenance, and sales have on profits. Also explored issues related to leasing versus purchasing equipment, factors influencing stock price, and strategic positioning versus competitors.

Developed concept for new product, a yardage book for golfers, and worked through all phases required of turning idea into reality. Wrote business plan, surveyed potential consumers through questionnaire and focus groups, completed pro forma statements, and developed prototype product. Product selected by class as most likely to succeed in the market.

Activities   UNIVERSITY OF THE PACIFIC BASEBALL TEAM, 1989-1990

ALPHA KAPPA PHI FRATERNITY 1989-1993
Pledge Trainer, 1992
Chaplain (House Speaker), 1991-92

Employment   RED LOBSTER, Stockton, Ca.
Waiter, Summer 1993

COTTAGE HOSPITAL, Santa Barbara, Ca.
Patient Assistant, Summer 1992

EL CAPITAN RANCH PARK, Santa Barbara, Ca.
Ranger, Summer 1991

Additional part-time and Summer employment income used for education.

References   Available upon request.

TOM T. EIGER

Comments and Analysis

✍ How did this one sneak in?

✍ A very good format effectively used by many college job seekers, but not really a "perfect" one. It doesn't have an objective or summary of qualification.

✍ Different font for name and address highlights by contrast.

✍ Marketing Related Courses and Projects heading and contents are important. Identifies semitargeted courses and, most importantly, skills building and applicable projects. Good way for liberal arts student to cite business-related courses and projects.

✍ Resume highlights academic background and achievements, because "employment" (labeled as such) did not build sophisticated skills.

While this isn't a perfect resume, it shows how to get close with a different format. It also shows how someone looking for a job "back home" can subtly slant a resume. Tom presents only his home address. He identifies his private secondary school (not often done for soon-to-be grads), because he wants the name recognition. He also presents courses and projects as "marketing related," even if he isn't exactly sure what he wants. Too many students leave projects off their resumes. I encourage you to present as many of these skills-developing achievements as you can. Headings can appear as Papers and Projects or as Related Courses and Projects.

Tom T. Eiger is evolving strategy and increased focus will be what makes him stand out among his peers. Tom isn't focused, although he promises his career counselor that he will continue research and become more goal directed while he promises his parents that he will keep his options open. What a dilemma (a too often typical dualism—Well-meaning parents may also gain something from this book). This resume is marketing oriented, yet it allows for action during exploration. Again, all actions will be directed at home, so he is very targeted regarding geographic preferences. All that remains is functional focus.

I.M. UNIQUE

777 Bonn Drive ❑ Stockton, CA 95244 ❑ (209) 454-9732

SUMMARY OF QUALIFICATIONS

❑ Textiles development experience.
❑ Design and private label manufacturing experience.
❑ Six years buying line experience.
❑ Knowledgeable of production, design, sales, and marketing operations.
❑ Direct store line management experience with expertise in marketing designer clothing
❑ Excellent managerial, organizational, communication and problem-solving skills.
❑ Extensive knowledge of Macintosh computers and applications such as Microsoft Word, Works and Excel, Claris McDraw II, Aldus Pagemaker, Graphsoft MiniCad Plus, Autodesk AutoCAD, Generic CADD, Specular Infini-D, Adobe Illustrator and Photoshop.

PRODUCTION AND PRODUCT DEVELOPMENT EXPERIENCE

DESIGN INTERNATIONAL / D. ECOLLECTION, San Francisco, CA
Textiles Developer / Buyer (July 1992 to Present)
❑ Researched textile development from fiber to finished fabric.
❑ Worked with yarn and greige textile mills in establishing criteria and specifications.
❑ Collaborated with finishing plants to develop low environmental impact methods for preparing and finishing textiles .
❑ Worked directly with textile converters in developing new environmentally friendly textiles.
❑ Established quality and performance standards for new textiles.
❑ Performed and coordinated textiles testing for developmental textiles.
❑ Maintained all textiles related archives.
❑ Purchased and coordinated importing textiles from overseas vendors.
❑ Negotiated price and delivery.
❑ Conducted costing analyses.
❑ Monitored vendor relations and resolved conflicts.

FASHION FUSIONE, Stockton, CA
Project Coordinator (June, 1988 to August 1991)
❑ Researched design and color trends.
❑ Proposed and developed line offerings.
❑ Coordinated sample production.
❑ Sourced and secured fabric for sample and production runs.
❑ Established and maintained costing guidelines
❑ Constructed flat patterns by use of computer aided design (CAD) technology.
❑ Sourced production sites based on quality, price, and reliability, and supervised quality control.
❑ Coordinated and sourced trims, labels, and hang tags.
❑ Formulated complete merchandising program.

MERCHANDISING EXPERIENCE

FASHION FUSIONE, Stockton, CA
Manager/Buyer (June, 1986 to August, 1991)
❑ Envisioned and realized concept of state-of-the-art designer clothing boutique.
❑ Handled initial research and negotiations in securing appropriate location.
❑ Designed, planned and supervised interior and exterior layout, fixtures and construction.
❑ Created complete store image including logo, packaging and stationery.
❑ Secured exclusivity with European designers (Montana, Byblos, Moschino, and Girbaud).
❑ Created, designed, produced and marketed private label line to supplement major designers.
❑ Performed management functions including budgeting, accounting and staffing.
❑ Coordinated all promotional and marketing activities.

EDUCATION

UNIVERSITY OF CALIFORNIA DAVIS, Davis, CA
Course work towards BA, *Textiles and Clothing,* 1992 - present.

UNIVERSITY OF THE PACIFIC, Stockton, CA
BA, *International Relations,* 1988.

I.M UNIQUE

Comments and Analysis

✍ Extremely targeted resume without objective, used by alum with strong post-grad experience.

✍ Summary of Qualifications presents focused background and projects sense of direction.

✍ Three-dimensional boxes used as bullets highlight pertinent and goal-directed information. Being "boxed in" is desired result.

✍ Specialized experience headings categorize background in two distinct, yet related areas.

This is a perfect resume for someone with experience seeking to remain in (or reenter) a particular field. Even without an objective, it presents a focused and qualified person with extensive Production and Product Development as well as Merchandising skills and achievements. Once you've read the accompanying cover letter appearing later, not much else remains to be said on paper; I.M. Unique will do all of the talking through employment interviews and networking conversations. I.M. will be prepared to show (via resume, cover letter, and follow-up correspondence) as well as tell about qualifications (in face-to-face meetings).

JOB SEARCH COACH

1234 Employment Drive
Stockton, CA 95311

Home: (209) 487-3309
Office: (209) 946-2361

SUMMARY OF QUALIFICATIONS

- Directed comprehensive facility offering career development and employment services to diverse students and alumni.
- Managed undergraduate and MBA college relations and recruiting efforts of major financial services organization.
- Managed Associate (MBA) recruiting for strategic management consulting firm.
- Experienced with operations of numerous graduate and undergraduate career planning and placement facilities.
- In various capacities improved recruiting procedures, policies, and literature and enhanced recruiters on-campus relationships.
- As recruitment and career services professional facilitated screening, selection, and decision-making phases of job search.
- Have interviewed and hired professional, support, and student personnel and performed broad human resource functions.
- Experienced with developing and implementing seminars and workshops and writing career-related materials and publications.

CAREER SERVICES AND PLACEMENT EXPERIENCE

University of the Pacific Career Services, Stockton, CA.
Director, 1990-present.
Overall administrative and counseling responsibilities for comprehensive career services facility. Programming, budgeting, staffing, and out-reach. Individual and group career counseling, resume writing, job search strategy, and interview skills assistance. Administrative oversight of On-Campus Recruiting and Alumni Career Advisory Network programs. Supervision and training of full-time counseling and administrative staff, graduate assistants, and student workers. Compilation and distribution of recruiting, offer, and salary data. Solicitation of external corporate and foundation funding.
- Expanded services and hours and reorganized staff to address school liaison and function-specific areas of responsibility.
- Improved promotional efforts to increase student usage as well as faculty and employer awareness of services.
- Developed recruiting registration procedures which indexed students by stated goals and enhanced employer involvement.
- Authored promotional and educational materials as well as statistical reports regarding services and status of graduates.
- Contributed to development of new outreach, programs and services, including Career Focus Program, Educator Recruiting Day, Alumni Career Forum, Faculty Forum and Award, Career Services Newsletter, column in student newspaper, and resume collections for minority students, student athletes, and other special populations.

Dartmouth College Career and Employment Services, Hanover, N.H.
Associate Director, 1982-1987.
Administrative and counseling responsibilities for full-time and leave-term job search activities. Programming, budgeting, staffing, and out-reach. Individual and group career counseling and job-search skills development. Administration of Recruiting Program, involving over 100 organizations and 400 students, and of ongoing job development efforts. Supervision and training of full-time staff and student workers. Compilation and distribution of on-campus recruiting, offer, and salary statistics.
- Increased number of recruiting organizations by approximately 10% annually.
- Developed and implemented computer assisted recruiting sign-up procedures.
- Initiated and directed San Francisco and Chicago Career Days off-campus consortium recruiting events.
- Reorganized and computerized entry-level job posting, recruiter information, and salary reporting systems.
- Developed programs and materials on job search topics and conducted videotaped roleplay interviews.
- Involved in searches for counseling, support, and student personnel and designing renovated facilities.

Haverford College Career Planning Office, Haverford, PA.
Career Counselor, Part-time 1981-82.
Individual career counseling and workshops dealing with career goals, resume writing, interview skills, and job search.
- Developed and presented "Majors and Careers: What Can I Do With A Major In?," workshop, and "Interview Skills," weekly workshop involving video feedback of roleplay interviews.

Rosemont College Counseling Center, Rosemont, PA.
Career Counselor, Part-time 1981-82.
- Developed and presented "Majors and Careers: Making Decisions," workshop and counseled individuals on career issues.
- Led weekly sessions dealing with career-related issues with women who were non-traditional students.

Bryn Mawr College Career Planning Office, Bryn Mawr, PA.
Workshop Leader, 1981.
- Developed and presented "Arming for the Interview," handouts and workshop, including videotaped roleplay interviews.

Southern Methodist University Career Center, Dallas, TX.
Assistant Director, 1980-81.
Involvement in programming, budgeting, spending, staffing, and public relations.
- Assisted in planning move to new location and designing new facility.
- Aided in searches for Career Center counseling and support staff, and for Counseling and Testing Center counseling staff.
- Disseminated career and salary information to academic and business communities and to media.

JOB SEARCH COACH PAGE TWO

Southern Methodist University Career Center, Dallas, TX.
MBA Placement Coordinator, 1979-81.
Overall coordination of career planning, job search, on-campus recruiting, and job development activities for MBA candidates and graduates. Compilation and distribution of Resume Book and Salary Survey. Coordination of Career Seminar Series.
• Expanded Career Seminar Series, improved Resume Book format and design, and improved Salary Survey to provide additional statistical data as well as a post-graduation update.
• Increased on-campus recruiting each year and coordinated job development efforts.

Southern Methodist University Career Center, Dallas, TX.
Career Counselor, 1978-81.
Initiation of new programs, procedures, and out-reach efforts. Individual and group counseling and job search skills development. Participation in on-campus recruiting and job development. Compilation and dissemination of career and salary data to students, staff, faculty, and employers. Involvement with all majors and levels, including alumni. Co-teaching career planning course.
• Developed registration system.
• Wrote and updated resume writing, interview skills, job search strategy, and career research materials.
• Annually updated "Career Planning and Placement Handbook" and "Exit Survey and Annual Report."

RECRUITMENT EXPERIENCE

Merrill Lynch Consumer Markets, Princeton, N.J.
Manager of College Relations and Recruiting, 1989 - 1990.
Overall management of on-campus recruiting for Consumer Markets Development and MBA Programs. Developing overall and school specific strategies. Creating recruiting literature and developing on campus presentations. Nurturing relationships with career services professionals, faculty, and students to enhance knowledge of organization and opportunities. Overseeing call-back and decision making processes. Creating and monitoring budget. Supervising Recruiting Coordinator. Working with Steering Committee as well as program management professionals.
• Revised literature and established an information-based approach to school relationships.
• Proposed new vehicles for enhancing college relations, including Summer Intern and Associate Financial Consultant Programs.
• Developed New Jersey Career Services Day, hosting 30 career services professionals for an information exchange session.

Strategic Planning Associates, Washington, D.C.
Director of Recruiting, 1987-1989.
Overall management of on-campus and experienced Associate (MBA) recruiting. Determining targets for U.S. and Europe hires (full-time and summer) and developing school specific targets and strategies. Developing relationships with career services professionals, faculty, and students to enhance selection and conversion efforts. Monitoring accept and decline status and disseminating information to firm and school personnel. Creating and monitoring budget. Supervising Recruiting Coordinator and Recruiting Secretary.
• Enhanced relationships with 6 Core Schools and initiated relationships with 7 Peripheral Schools.
• Brought Ad Hoc (experienced) recruiting into mainstream of overall process.
• Performed critical analysis of recruiting programs and presented findings to Chairman.

SELECTED PUBLICATIONS

Liberal Arts Jobs, Peterson's Guides, Spring 1986, Fall 1989.
Liberal Arts Power! How to Sell It On Your Resume, Peterson's Guides, Spring 1985, Fall 1989.
Arming Yourself For A Part-time Or Summer Job, Olympus Publishing, Spring 1982.
" The Secrets of Job Search Success, " Careers and the College Grad, 1993
"Job Search Trends for the New Decade," Careers and the College Grad 1991
"Significant Other Support: You Can Help a Job-Seeking Partner, Careers and the MBA, 1990
"Beyond The Analyst Experience: To B or Not to B (B School)," Careers and the College Grad, 1989.
"The 'Flyback' Syndrome" in Management Column, *Delta Sky Magazine*, January 1987.
"Resume Books: Boons or Boondoggles?," Journal of College Placement, Winter 1982.
"Flyback Fever" in Careers and the MBA 1982, Harvard Business School, 1982.
"Arming MBAs For The Job Search," Journal of College Placement, Summer 1981.
"You Can Help Students Seek Part-time Employment," Journal of College Placement, Summer 1980.

EDUCATION

University of Pennsylvania, Philadelphia, PA.
Doctoral Coursework in Psychological Services, 1981-82
Master of Science in Psychological Services, emphasis in Counseling Psychology, August 1978.
Bachelors of Arts in Psychology and Sociology, Cum Laude, May 1975.

Stanford University, Stanford, CA.
Master of Arts in Education, Secondary Teacher Education Program, June 1977.

REFERENCES AVAILABLE UPON REQUEST

JOB SEARCH COACH

Comments and Analysis

✍ Another very targeted perfect resume without an objective, used by experienced professional.

✍ Summary of Qualifications presents focused background and projects sense of direction.

✍ Specialized experience headings categorize background into two distinct, yet related areas. General descriptions of positions appear first, followed by bulleted achievements.

✍ Bullets first highlight general qualifications and later, under Experience headings, specific goal-directed accomplishments.

✍ Two-page format appropriate, easy to follow, presenting most important information on first page.

You've often heard "put your money where your mouth is." Well, this is a case of putting your resume where your words are. If you haven't guessed it, this is a modified version of the author's resume (with name and identifying information changed to protect the innocent or guilty). It is not presented here to show my background (although I am very proud of what I have achieved), but to illustrate a perfect format used by a person with a great deal of experience seeking to remain in a particular field. The use of bullets to highlight basic qualifications and, later, to note achievements after general descriptions is the perfect approach for "very experienced" (euphemism for "old") and targeted job seekers. While the print is reduced and smaller than you should use, this two page model is packed with pertinent information. The next version (I'm always updating and improving) will have a separate Publications attachment page, expand on achievements at UOP, and use a larger font size. The publications addendum will have this book prominently noted and I hope, have some positive comments from readers attached.

If you wish to forward comments, concerns, or constructive criticisms (the alliteration thing is still with me), or if you wish your resume considered for future editions, send letters to University of the Pacific Career Services, Stockton, California 95211. Also, the office number appearing on the resume is correct, so give me a call if you have a question or comment. Career services colleagues should know that I am willing, ready, and, most importantly, inexpensive (free in most cases) if you would like to arrange a campus seminar addressing topics appearing in this book. Please call to discuss this possibility. I would enjoy working with you and your students and alumni.

I. Wanda Interview

4666 Tall Oaks Dr. • Rocklin, CA 95787 • (916) 644-4662

SUMMARY OF QUALIFICATIONS

- Completed undergraduate degree with honors and 3.5 Grade Point Average.
- Able to research topics related to international politics and business.
- Can think analytically to determine impact of decisions and actions.
- Good writing and editing skills. Can develop lengthy reports or concise synopses.
- Skilled in Microsoft Word and Word Perfect. Familiar with IBM and Macintosh.
- Competent in written and conversational German. Have studied and traveled in Austria and throughout Europe.
- Coursework in Contemporary World Issues, International Security, History of Eastern Europe, Soviet History, Environmental Problems and Perspectives, Comparative Politics, Cross-Cultural Training, and German language classes.

EDUCATION

UNIVERSITY OF THE PACIFIC, Stockton, CA
Bachelor of Arts in International and Regional Studies, Cum Laude, May 1993.
Overall GPA: 3.5/4.0
Dean's Honor Roll six semesters

INSTITUTE OF EUROPEAN STUDIES, Vienna, Austria.
Studied German and Eastern European issues, Spring 1991

INSTITUTE OF EUROPEAN STUDIES, London, England.
Studied law and history, Summer 1991

ACTIVITIES AND HONORS

TEXAS A&M STUDENT CONFERENCE ON NATIONAL AFFAIRS, 1993.
Selected to represent UOP School of International Studies at conference on "The United States: Facing the Challenges of a New World."

WORLD AFFAIRS COUNCIL OF NORTHERN CALIFORNIA, 1993.

DELTA DELTA DELTA SORORITY, 1990-1992.
Raised funds for cancer research and scholarships.

OPEN ASSEMBLY FOR THE SCHOOL OF INTERNATIONAL STUDIES, 1990-93.
Recruited speakers for conference on international affairs.

PHI KAPPA PHI ACADEMIC HONOR SOCIETY, 1993.

DELTA PHI ALPHA GERMAN HONOR SOCIETY, 1993.

PATRON OF THE PACIFIC SCHOLAR, 1989-1993.

EXPERIENCE

UOP SCHOOL OF INTERNATIONAL STUDIES, Stockton, CA
Office Clerk and Word Processor, 1991-1992.

UOP FINANCIAL AID OFFICE, Stockton, CA
File Clerk, 1988-1991.

MANPOWER TEMPORARY AGENCY, Roseville, CA
Receptionist and Word Processor, Summer 1990.

CHRISTOPHER C. CRANE & ASSOCIATES, North Highlands, CA
Word Processor, 1987-1989.

I. WANDA INTERVIEW

Comments and Analysis

✍ Another perfect "multipurpose" resume.
✍ Format is easy to scan with effective use of bullets.
✍ Summary of Qualifications identifies academic achievements and general skills.

I. Wanda Interview wanted a resume for on-campus recruiting and, more importantly, for requesting information conversations. While a resume isn't necessary when requesting information-gathering sessions, it can facilitate the process. Be careful not to project an "I really want an employment interview, but I'll settle for an information conversation" attitude. Clear telephone messages and cover letters help.

I. Wanda was quick to present "international" when quizzed about goals, but she could not go beyond that intriguing and beguiling phrase. She had not yet completed research required to cite goals clearly. After a bit of reading, I. Wanda realized that a postgraduate internship in Washington, D.C., a lengthy trip to her geopolitical dream location, a postgraduation study-abroad program, or teaching English abroad would be feasible options. This resume was first to be used to obtain additional information and, whenever necessary, to effectively respond to posted openings or formal programs. It could be revised once goal setting was complete.

I. Wanda's resume clearly identifies an academic achiever and an active individual. The Summary of Qualification, Education, and Activities and Honors sections clearly project this image. The multipurpose format doesn't deter from initial efforts, but she realizes a second version, with an objective and supporting Summary of Qualifications section will soon be needed.

Sammie Day Attraina

Present: UOP McCaffrey Center Apartments #666 • Stockton, CA 95221 • (209) 946-9987
Permanent: 26 Adobe Drive • Las Cruces, NM 88001 • (505) 523-8963

Objective

Athletic trainer position in a clinical setting.

Qualifications and Capabilities

- Can create and administer rehabilitation protocols utilizing state of the art modalities.
- Have supervised and instructed undergraduate student trainers, developed policies and procedures for student trainer programs, and administered budgets, purchasing, and personnel matters for clinic operation.
- Master thesis examined epidemiological factors involved in soft tissue injuries sustained by rodeo athletes.

Athletic Training Experience

August 1990-
present
UNIVERSITY OF THE PACIFIC, Stockton, CA
Graduate Assistant Athletic Trainer, Served as head softball and field hockey trainer and assistant football and basketball trainer. Under direction of Susie Smith, M.Ed., A.T.,C. and Charles Christian, M.S., A.T., C.

August 1990-
present
PACIFIC SPORTS MEDICINE CENTER, Stockton, CA
Athletic Trainer, Assisted in physical therapy rehabilitation protocols. Under supervision of Mary Miles P.T., A.T.,C.

September 1990-
November 1990
WOODDALE HIGH SCHOOL, Wooddale, CA
Athletic Trainer, Responsible for injury prevention of varsity football team. Under direction of Head Coach Michael Marks.

August 1985-
May 1990
NEW MEXICO STATE UNIVERSITY, Las Cruces, NM
Student Athletic Trainer, Actively involved with prevention, rehabilitation and education of injuries sustained by football, volleyball, and track and field athletes. Under supervision of Richard Mendem M.S., A.T.,C.

1989-90 **Volunteer Trainer,** New Mexico State University Rodeo Team, Las Cruces, NM

1989 **Volunteer Trainer,** World Finals Rodeo, El Paso, TX

1991 **Volunteer Trainer,** Grand National Finals Rodeo, San Francisco, CA

Education

UNIVERSITY OF THE PACIFIC, Stockton, CA
Master of Arts, Sports Sciences, May 1992
Emphasis: Athletic Training

NEW MEXICO STATE UNIVERSITY, Las Cruces, NM
Bachelor of Science, Athletic Training Education, May 1990
Emphasis: Sports Medicine

Affiliations and Certifications

- Certified Member of the National Athletic Trainer Association
- Certified Member of the American Red Cross
- Certified Member of the American Heart Association
- Member of Rocky Mountain Athletic Trainers Association

Sammie Day Attraina

Present: UOP McCaffrey Center Apartments #666 • Stockton, CA 95221 • (209) 946-9987
Permanent: 26 Adobe Drive • Las Cruces, NM 88001 • (505) 523-8963

References

Susie Smith, M.Ed., A.T.,C.
University of the Pacific
Stockton, CA 95221
(209) 944-2237.

Charles Christian, M.S., A.T.,C.
University of the Pacific
Stockton, CA 95221
(209) 944-2223.

Mary Miles , P.T., A.T.,C.
Star Clinic
75 West March Lane
Stockton, CA 95237
(209) 962-3437.

Richard Mendem, M.S., A.T.,C.
New Mexico State University
Box 30331, Department 3225
Las Cruces, NM 88013-0001
(505) 666-7726.

SAMMIE DAY ATTRAINA

Comments and Analysis

✍ A specialized targeted resume, but a format applicable to a number of fields and functional alternatives.

✍ Two addresses presented efficiently on two lines, used for dual-location search. Creative heading is attractive, yet professional.

✍ Objective and Qualifications and Capabilities sections clearly present a sense of focus and achievements.

✍ Related experience prominently labeled, with bolded headings clearly visible.

✍ Addendum Reference page illustrates form all can use.

Sammie Day Attraina knows what she wants. She is trained for what she wants (no pun intended) and she has documented all she has done very, very well. This resume shows how a very targeted and well-credentialed professional can create a perfect job search document. She will someday be a trainer. All that remains is a constant regime of hard work and exercising of job search skills.

The attachment page, presenting references, is most appropriate for clinical or academic professions, but all can use this format for a reference page. References are not as critical as you might think. If you want individuals noted to contribute effectively to your efforts, keep them informed and clearly ask when you need help. Request a call to a particular potential employer or ask for help with interview preparation. The more active references are and the more they support job search behaviors, the better. A list of names, addresses, and phone numbers doesn't really do very much, but active people can.

Hiram "Hi" Tech

1236 W. Stadium Dr. Apt. #6 • Stockton, CA 95206 • (209) 988-4690

Objective   Electronics research and development.

Qualifications and Achievements

- Practical and academic experiences developing products for industry and consumers enhanced creativity, problem solving , and troubleshooting skills.
- Classes in programming and circuit design have provided tools for development and refined understanding of professional design process.
- Currently designing laser display system with raster scan configuration using low-inertia galvanometer and acoustooptic laser beam modulator.
- UNIX shell written with emphasis on recursive data base management, multiprocess communications, in-process memory management, and window/menu environment with resources based on curses.
- Microprocessor design with 8088, 6803 with multiprocessor configuration using wakeup feature™ and direct memory access circuitry.
- Eprom burner designed for Macintosh for use in development of microprocessor based systems.
- Twelve years of computer programming using UNIX, VMS, C, Pascal, FORTRAN, 68000, 8088, and 6800 assembly language. Limited exposure to FORTH. Limited exposure to Macintosh Toolbox™.
- Courses included microprocessor design, state machine design, electronic circuits, systems, automatic control systems, and project design.

Engineering Experience

January -
May 1992   SIEMENS MEDICAL RESEARCH, Erlangen, Germany
Co-op Programmer: Wrote software-diagnostic subroutines used in debugging a magnetic resonance imager. Tested software with the imager.

June 1989 -
January 1990   HAMMETT & EDISON, INC., Burlingame, CA
Junior Co-op Engineer: Assisted in design of commercial radio, television, and microwave links for broadcasters. Wrote UNIX shell with user friendly environment for in-house use.

Summer 1989   DIALOG INFORMATION SERVICES, Inc., Palo Alto, CA
Programming Assistant Intern: Served as head of beta testing, assisted in programming and documenting program manual for ImageCatcher™ for Mac.

Education   UNIVERSITY OF THE PACIFIC, Stockton, CA
Bachelor of Science in Electrical Engineering, May 1993

FOOTHILL COLLEGE, Los Altos Hills, CA
General education courses, Fall 1986 - Spring 1989

UNIVERSITY OF LONDON UNION, London, England
Attended Foothill semester abroad program, Winter 1988

Interests   Built and fly remote controlled helicopter. Traveled to Hawaii, Alaska, Europe, and former Soviet Union. Enjoy photography, hiking, and fishing.

HIRAM "HI" TECH

Comments and Analysis

✍ Another perfect specialized targeted resume with a format applicable to numerous technical fields and functions.

✍ Use of quotations show how nick-name or Anglicized version of hard-to-pronounce name can be noted.

✍ Qualifications and Achievements section present all significant information using bullets.

✍ Engineering Experience heading shows only related background. Other employment omitted.

Hi's resume is very simple to follow and presents a perfect way to present a technical background. He did consider including an Engineering Courses and Projects section, but determined the Q&A section noted all pertinent information and presented him as an experienced candidate, not simply a student. Addendum pages, presenting abstracts of projects are included when appropriate. While I do not believe there are special formats for special fields, this one can be effectively used by technical and engineering job seekers.

LANCELOT (LARRY) LADD

Manor Hall #230 • University of the Pacific • Stockton, CA 95221 • (209) 964-3387
22 SW 35th • Portland, OR 97376 • (503) 723-6800

EDUCATION
UNIVERSITY OF THE PACIFIC, Stockton, CA
Bachelor of Arts, International Affairs and Commerce, May 1993

ECOLE SUPERIEURE DES AFFAIRES DE GRENOBLE, Grenoble, France, 1991-92
Major: Maîtrise de Gestion (Management degree in Marketing)

CERTIFICAT PRATIQUE DE FRANCAIS ECONOMIQUE ET COMMERCIALE, May 1991
(Parisian chamber of commerce document certifying qualifications to do business in France)

International Business Related Courses: Administration and Human Behavior, Marketing,
French Business and Culture, Sales Marketing, Marketing Analysis, International Finance

INTERNATIONAL AND GENERAL BUSINESS EXPERIENCE
ALLIANCE UNIVERSITAIRE DE GRENOBLE, Grenoble, France
Marketing Intern, (April-June 1992)
• Completed survey and analysis to determine members' perceptions and develop strategy to increase
  membership and provide more effective programs and services
• Interviewed members of business community regarding perceptions of Alliance and used results to develop
  extensive questionnaire
• Distributed 400 questionnaires, tabulated results and analyzed responses, and presented to the Board
  with recommendations for future actions

INTERNATIONAL ASSOCIATION OF ECONOMICS AND MANAGEMENT STUDENTS (AIESEC), Stockton, CA
Exchange Officer, (September 1992-May 1993)
• Processed applications and contracts, developed budgets pertaining to International Traineeship
  Exchange Program
• Planned and presided over Exchange Committee meetings
• Participated in meetings with other officers to discuss future projects of AIESEC-Pacific
• Attended conferences on leadership and communication skills

BLUE CROSS & BLUE SHIELD, Portland, OR
Assistant to the Director of Space Planning and Design, (July-September 1991)
• Managed inventory of all equipment in the four buildings in Portland area

WORLD TRADE CENTER, Portland, OR
Marketing Intern, (June-August 1990)
• Developed list of prospective members of Trade Center
• Planned and coordinated Open House events

OTHER EXPERIENCE
UOP FINANCE CENTER, Stockton, CA
Documentation Clerk, (1989-91)

UOP FINANCE CENTER, Stockton, CA
Accounts Receivable Clerk, (1991-93)

LANGUAGE AND COMPUTER SKILLS
FRENCH: speak, write, and read fluently
LAOTIAN: speak fluently
GERMAN: reading knowledge

COMPUTER: Operate Macintosh IIsi, IBM personal computer and other IBM compatibles,
           WINDOWS 3.1, Microsoft Word, EXCEL, Word 5.1, PCSM, Paintbrush

COLLEGE ACTIVITIES
AIESEC-PACIFIC
1992-93 President
1990-92 Vice-President of International Traineeship Exchange Program
1989-90 General Member of AIESEC-Oregon

OPEN ASSEMBLY OF SCHOOL OF INTERNATIONAL STUDIES

PI DELTA PHI, UOP FRENCH CLUB
1992-93 President

LANCELOT (LARRY) LADD

Manor Hall #230 • University of the Pacific • Stockton, CA 95221 • Etats-Units • Tel: 19.01.20.99.64.33.87
21 ans (née le 3 3 70)
Célibataire
Nationalité américaine

FORMATION

1989-93	UNIVERSITY OF THE PACIFIC, Stockton, CA *Bachelor of Arts, International Affairs and Commerce*
1991-1992	ECOLE SUPERIEURE DES AFFAIRES DE GRENOBLE, Grenoble, France 2ème année de Maîtrise de Sciences de Gestion, Option Marketing
1990-91	CERTIFICAT PRATIQUE DE FRANCAIS ECONOMIQUE ET COMMERCIALE DE LA CHAMBRE DE COMMERCE ET D'INDUSTRIE DE PARIS

STAGES

1992
(Avril-Juin)
ALLIANCE UNIVERSITAIRE DE GRENOBLE, Grenoble, France
- Rédaction d'une étude de marché sur les membres actuels et potentiels
- Gestion d'entretiens semi-directifs avec une dizaine de membres du Conseil Administratif
- Rédaction d'un questionnaire détaillé basé sur les réponses reçues pendant les entretiens
- Presentation des recherches au Conseil d'Administration

1991
(Juin-Août)
WORLD TRADE CENTER, Portland, OR
- Rédaction d'une liste des membres potentiels pour l'association
- Responsable de la préparation des réunions des nouveaux membres

EXPERIENCE PROFESSIONNELLE

1991
(Juin-Sept)
BLUE CROSS & BLUE SHIELD OF OREGON (assurances medicales), Portland, OR
Assistante du Responsable du Décor
- Gestion inventaire d'équipement des 4 bureaux à Portland
- Responsable de parc de stationnement

1991
(Jan-Mai)
UNIVERSITY OF THE PACIFIC, Stockton, CA , Service des Finances
- Mise en place des services de documentation: Service de prêts pour étudiants

1991
(Sept-present)
UNIVERSITY OF THE PACIFIC, Stockton, CA , Service des Finances
- Accounts receivable clerk: Responsable des comptes journaliers

LANGUES

Français:	courant
Anglais:	courant
Allemand:	bonnes notions

INFORMATIQUE: BASIC, Excel, Microsoft Word, Word 5.1, WINDOWS 3.1, PCSM, Macintosh
IIsi, Paintbrush

DIVERS

Sports et Loisirs: Tennis, Volley-ball, Natation

Activités: AIESEC (*Association International des Etudiants en Science Economiques et Commerciales*)
- 1990-91 Vice-Présidente des Stages en AIESEC-University of the Pacific
- 1991-92 Membre général à AIESEC-Ecole Supérieure des Affaires
- 1992-93 Vice-Présidente des Stages en AIESEC-University of the Pacific

Open Assembly of School of International Business (OASIS)
organisation des étudiants en relations internationales pour la promotion et l'appreciation de sujet culturels internationals

Pi Delta Phi, UOP
association honoraire: culture et langue française
- 1992-93 Présidente

Voyages: Allemagne, Angleterre, Canada, Etats-Unis, France, Italie, Mexique, et Suisse

---

LANCELOT (LARRY) LADD

Comments and Analysis

✍ Another not-quite-perfect "multipurpose" resume.

✍ Simple, yet effective format. Desired nickname is noted in parentheses.

✍ Bullets highlight information under International and General Business Experience category, noting capabilities as well as achievements.

✍ Easy to scan and presents a very strong academic and achievement-oriented background.

Larry wasn't very focused, yet he wanted job search to begin as soon as possible. As with many recent grads, Larry wanted something "international" and created an appropriate resume. Larry realized that exploration and focus would enhance job search potential and an objective would strengthen his resume, but his busy schedule didn't allow for research needed to identify particular goals within an international arena. This resume served all immediate purposes well.

Larry enthusiastically and regularly used his career services office while examining international or overseas options. He visited the local French consulate, communicated with the French American Chamber of Commerce, and subscribed to a French language and a Parisian newspaper. He responded to several postings. Job search went on well beyond graduation. It included effective follow up with on-campus recruiters and other organizations. A summer job kept Larry close to school and to the resources he found in the nearest major city. Finally, following the advice of a professor, Larry contacted an alumna who was also a recruiter. These interactions are documented in correspondence samples appearing later. Well, deeds combined with words seemed to pay off and Larry received an offer and accepted it. While he used the French version of his resume when responding to appropriate postings, it wasn't the version used to land the job.

✍ Tres Bon! Oui?

✍ Shows knowledge of particular format used in targeted country.

✍ Illustrates bilingual ability even when contacting domestic firms.

The French resume is an adapted translation of the English, using country-appropriate format. Even in a language I don't understand, it is easy to recognize academic and employment achievements as well as particular skills. What do you think? Larry's new job doesn't require use of French now, but who knows what the future will bring. He will keep both versions updated and ready to go.

Now that you've reviewed numerous variations on a "perfect" theme and examined insightful analyses, I will share just a few more samples. Below is a modified copy of a letter I received from a very enthusiastic and motivated student who worked with me for several months before leaving sunny California for points east. Taking Horace Geeley's advice in reverse, this westerner sought a publishing-related opportunity in the New York metropolitan area. As I knew he would, after a few months he found a job and forwarded me the following:

Burt,

New York is fabulous!!! It's everything I hoped it would be—so far. It took two months of pounding the pavement, but it finally happened. I got a job with a Fortune 500 Company, working on Country Home Magazine.

I am the assistant to the National Director of Advertising and I'm now playing in the big league. I'm very excited about my new job. I've got great benefits, a good salary, fun people to work with, a very easy commute, and a boss who wants to teach me all sorts of valuable information. Another great plus; I have a cubicle that faces a window!!!

I worked with agencies and every one of them wanted me to change my resume. I thought you might like to see what the current trend for resumes is in New York.

I should go now—lots of fun things for me to do!

Thanks and keep in touch,
Eddie

This note raises several issues. Search firms do have "preferred" (not "perfect") formats. While I don't believe there is a "hot resume for New York" or a "Chicago-acceptable style," or an "Engineering and Technical resume," I do encourage all job seekers to view resumes as works-in-progress, never as finished products. If after you develop your resume you desire to change it for the better, do so!

The "before and after" presentation that follows shows how to revise a resume to meet requests of search professionals. When asked by a search firm to revise your resume, do it. You can use your "personalized" version for other efforts, but don't argue with someone who is providing you a special service. Some search firms, depending upon field-specific focus, subtly encourage candidates to begin in administrative positions. The revised version is certainly more administrative oriented than the original. No matter. Your first job is not your last, but it is often the most difficult to land. Any help you can get should be appreciated.

EDDIE TORNOW
345 Rose Blossom Lane • Novato, California 94945 • (415) 893-9876
245 Purchase Street • Apartment 2-B • Rye, New York 10588 • (914) 423-8654

OBJECTIVE
Publishing position using knowledge of and experience in editing, promotion and production.

PUBLISHING EXPERIENCE
EPOCH YEARBOOK, UOP, Stockton, CA
Editor in Chief, 1991-1992. Supervised staff of 35. Selected, hired, and supervised assistant editors, publisher, and photographer. Researched, wrote, and edited stories using Macintosh Microsoft Word and Microsoft Works. Designed layouts using PageMaker. Distributed books, supervised book and advertisement sales.

PACIFIC PULSE ORIENTATION NEWSPAPER, UOP, Stockton, CA
Staff Writer, 1992. Researched and wrote stories, conducted interviews, edited copy.

CALLIOPE LITERARY MAGAZINE, UOP, Stockton, CA
Copy Editor/Reader, 1991-1992. Read, edited, selected material to be published in university literary magazine. Publicized magazine.

SALES AND PROMOTIONAL EXPERIENCE
FINE ART COLLECTIONS, Corte Madera, CA
Assistant to Vice President and Dealer/Owner, 1988-1991. Handled requests from dealers, salespeople, publishers, and gallery directors nationwide. Received, logged, and titled artwork. Assisted with payroll. Worked with IBM.

TRANSAMERICA FINANCIAL SERVICES, San Rafael, CA
Customer Service Representative, 1988-1990. Sold $.5 million in second mortgages in eight months. Serviced accounts, underwrote and solicited mortgages. Interviewed and trained employees.

EDUCATION
UNIVERSITY OF THE PACIFIC
Bachelor of Arts, 1992
GPA: 3.03
Major: *Communication*
Emphasis: *Organizational Communication and Public Relations*

PUBLISHING AND PROMOTIONS PROJECTS AND SKILLS
- Assisted with planning and implementing "UOP Night at the Ports," a faculty and student evening of fun with Stockton's minor league baseball team
- Wrote 20 page Career Planning booklet containing exercises, information, and graphics
- Revised Epoch Training Manual updating and adding new information
- Designed Media Kits, researched media lists, developed themes for special events
- Completed extensive library research training
- Developed and utilized strong editing and proofreading abilities

ACTIVITIES
Public Relations Student Society of America
Student Representative to Communication Department
Resident Hall Community Council — Treasurer
Interview Committee for Prospective Deans
Numerous planning committees
Extensive domestic travel

EDDIE TORNOW
245 Purchase Street • Apartment 2-B • Rye, New York 10588 • (914) 423-8654

EXPERIENCE

9/90 to 6/92   **UNIVERSITY OF THE PACIFIC**
Various Departments

Heavy phones, typing, dictation, filing, facsimile, proofreading
Arranged meetings, luncheons, travel, special events, promotions
Wrote and proofread correspondence
Assisted with publicity and promotions for special events and student services
Greeted and assisted Regents/Donors/Guests
Researched, wrote, edited stories for yearbook and newspaper
Interacted with top University officials
Assisted students with requests and questions

6/88 to 8/90   **TRANSAMERICA FINANCIAL SERVICES**
Administrative Assistant/Customer Service Representative

Heavy correspondence
Heavy client contact
Updated customer accounts
Maintained accounts payable/receivable
Typed, filed, heavy phones, facsimile
Underwrote and solicited loans
Purchased and maintained office supplies
Interacted with appraisers, title offices and other lenders
Contact with upper management
Interviewed and trained new employees

88 to 90   **FINE ART COLLECTIONS**
Administrative Assistant to Vice President

Assisted requests from dealers, sales associates, publishes, clients
Heavy phones, typing, filing, facsimile
Received, titled and logged artwork
Assisted with payroll
Assisted with special events

EDUCATION

UNIVERSITY OF THE PACIFIC
Bachelor of Arts, Communication, 1992
GPA: 3.03

SKILLS

Microsoft Word, Microsoft Works, PageMaker, WordPerfect
Editing, writing, research, media kits, media lists, news releases, promotions, special events

---

THE PERFECT RESUME REVIEW STUDY TIPS FOR THE RETEST (ACTION STEPS TO TAKE)

✎ Well, I am tired of saying it, so just do it! Follow the *Ten Steps to Resume Perfection* and use the *Perfect Resume Review* to create a distribution-ready version (or versions) of a perfect resume.

THE PERFECT RESUME REVIEW HELPFUL RESOURCES (PEOPLE, PLACES, AND THINGS)

✔ Enough said! In addition to books noted in the previous chapter, you may want to examine: *The 90-Minute Resume*, Peterson's 1992; *Just Resumes: 200 Powerful and Proven Successful Resumes to Get That Job*, Wiley, 1991; and *Perfect Resume Strategies*, Doubleday, 1992. Avoid data overload and the propensity for paralysis when you've read too many contradictory views. Honestly, and modestly, this chapter provides enough information and motivation to accomplish this critical job search task.

THE PERFECT RESUME REVIEW STUDY SKILLS SUMMARY

✏ Overviewed basic components of effective resumes.
✏ Identified steps required to quickly complete a resume.
✏ Presented simple and easy-to-use critiquing checklist.
✏ Illustrated sample resumes and analyzed formats and approaches.

CHAPTER 6

The Job Search Correspondence Quotient

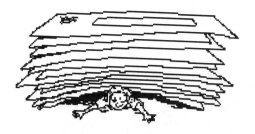

Contrary to what many think, job search is *not* an application; nor is it a correspondence process. It is a communication process requiring ongoing, upbeat, and appropriate goal-directed interaction. While critical communications take place face-to-face (employment interviews and information conversations), preliminary and follow-up efforts are most often in written form. All job search correspondence must reflect quality writing skills and appropriate attitudes.

In almost all job-search circumstances resumes are accompanied by cover letters or follow-up notes. Don't simply "circulate" your resume to everyone without proper follow-up correspondence. If you have a surprise encounter with someone who can offer job search advice or consideration, follow your meeting with a note identifying and requesting next steps. Simply giving someone your resume doesn't really initiate effective job search.

Resumes and cover letters should each be able to "stand alone" and spark a reviewer's interest, but as a united job-search presentation they are much more powerful. A "perfect" targeted resume may not require as much support for an accompanying letter as a multipurpose document. No matter the format, your resume must have the very best example of your writing style attached.

Basically, job search correspondence takes four forms:

✍ *Letter of Application*—used when applying for a particular opportunity that has been posted in a newspaper or through another announcement mechanism.

✍ *Letter of Inquiry*—used to express interest in a particular functional area and to inquire whether an employer has "opportunities" (present or future openings) in that area.

✍ *Letter of Introduction*—used to set the scene for on-campus interviews or confirm arrangements; also used to request information conversations; written by job seekers or references.

✍ *Follow up Letters*—thank-you and follow-up notes (or faxes); *essential to job-search success.*

The following devices highlight components of quality job search correspondence and give you ways to assess the quality of your efforts. Before identifying the Job Search Correspondence Quotient of your draft letters, use each test to judge three of the samples. Samples illustrate a wide variety of scenarios, but there is no way to cover (no pun intended) all circumstances. Those provided should provide motivation to act. Some are letters used by job seekers whose resumes appeared earlier. When reviewing these, note how the resume supports the cover letter and vice versa. Also, after each quotient quiz, a few basic do's and don'ts will be presented.

Use samples as inspirations for your efforts. Although reviewing samples may tempt you, don't copy. Correspondence comes as much from your heart as your head and hands. Clearly, individuality and sincerity are factors that characterize great letters. Others are enthusiasm, and, most critically, goal-directedness. Be yourself! Also, *never* have anyone else write letters for you. Others can get you started, critique your drafts and help you develop stronger skills, but you should author all correspondence. There is nothing more disappointing than a "canned" cover letter. As a recruiter who has read many, I urge you to put a lid on this approach. Create and use your own style, but make sure it is businesslike and simple. Each sample letter is followed by brief comments, with some providing insight to actual job search strategies and circumstances.

Review cover letter drafts and samples. Enter appropriate scores in one box associated with each of the four critiquing criteria. Total all scores to determine the Job Search Correspondence Quotient (JSCQ) for a particular document. Make photocopies so you can use this device as often as needed.

Cover Letter Quotient

Critiquing Criteria	Excellent *Most* *definitely!!!* (5 points)	Good *Yes, I* *think so.* (4 points)	Fair *Maybe it* *did, but …* (2 points)	Poor *Huh, I don't* *know!?!?* (1 point)
Stated purpose clearly and early, addressed to appropriate individual(s).				
Cited title(s) or function(s) sought and used name of firm. Referred to enclosed resume.				
Projected knowledge of field, function, and firm, connecting past achievements, skills, and experiences to future job.				
Clearly cited desire for employment interview or information conversation (by telephone or in person) and next steps writer will take.				
TOTALS				

Job
Search
Correspondence
Quotient!

▼

A **Cover Letter JSCQ of 20–15 is best characterized by the statement:** *"Give that person an interview? I should give that person my job!"* It will be very well received by almost all reviewers. If it does not result in an employment interview it most certainly will initiate a relationship which, if nurtured by further communications, will ultimately yield employment consideration. Don't let a letter like this go to waste. Follow up immediately, persistently, patiently, and politely.

A **Cover Letter JSCQ of 14–10 is best characterized by the statement:** *"Not bad. I'll check to see if we have any immediate needs, but not until after lunch."* It will be well received by some, but it won't be put in a "special stack." Improvement should be made. They will most often be associated with second or third assessment criteria. Even if actual job titles are not presented, an excellent letter reflects knowledge of functional areas of interest and clearly cites skills possessed to perform within these roles. Some good letters can be summarized as "I want to work for your firm. Here's a summary of my academic and extracurricular background and a general discussion (usually too general) of my skills. Read my resume, determine if I'm qualified for anything in your firm, and contact me if I am." That's clearly not the best first communication. Initial documents should, if requesting employment consideration rather than information, project goals. If you cannot do this, review earlier chapters or transform the letter into a request for an information conversation.

A **Cover Letter JSCQ of 10 or less is best characterized by the statement:** *"This one gets a rejection letter, but save it for the staff meeting. We might need something to laugh about."* It will be well received by very few. These documents are summarized as: "Anybody, read my resume, determine if I'm qualified for anything in your firm, and contact me if I am." That's definitely not the way to go about it! Again, job search is rarely successful when you give responsibility to others. If your draft letter received a score of 10 or below, review the samples to better understand what should be included and revise your document until its JSCQ is over 15.

Do keep track of all correspondence and document all calls and other communications. An organized communicator is an effective job seeker. While some may use sophisticated databases and mail-merge systems, simple file folders containing photocopies will suffice. You can make notes on the folder or on the copy.

Do get a name or just leave off the salutation. "To Whom It May Concern" or "Dear Sir/Madam" does more harm than good.

Do identify specific jobs or functional areas of interest in all communiqüés, especially initial letters of inquiry or application.

Do make sure to state what you would like to happen next, most likely "a phone or in-person interview."

Don't tell the reader a lot about his or her organization, like "your firm is one of the leaders in the field and among the best in the world." Tell about your goals and your abilities to serve within desired capacities. Impress the reader with your knowledge of self and clarity of goals, not with facts from an annual report or newspaper article. Remember, if you can describe a job, you can get that job. Cover letters describe qualified candidates for particular jobs.

Review thank-you note drafts and samples. Enter appropriate scores in one box associated with each of the four critiquing

criteria. Total all scores to determine the Job Search Correspondence Quotient (JSCQ) for a particular document. Make photocopies so you can use this device as often as needed.

Thank-You Note Quotient

Critiquing Criteria	Excellent Most definitely!!! (5 points)	Good Yes, I think so. (4 points)	Fair Maybe it did, but ... (2 points)	Poor Huh, I don't know!?!? (1 point)
Cited date of interview or conversation (phone or in person) and expressed gratitude to appropriate individual(s).				
Noted title(s) or function(s) being considered for and reinforced one key point (qualification for job) raised in meeting.				
Stated "I want the job" or "I want to continue the process (employment consideration or information exchange) and take next steps." Enclosed resume as "reminder."				
Clarified status (as candidate or information gatherer) and identified next steps writer will take. Suggested "creative" options (i.e., lunch, internship, part-time or trial employment).				
TOTALS				

Job
Search
Correspondence
Quotient!

↓

[   ]

After using this device and revising drafts, *all* thank-you notes will receive a JSCQ of 20–15 !

A Thank-You Note JSCQ of 20-15 is characterized by the statements: *"I thought we had the right candidate, now I'm sure!" "This one is very persistent and communicates effectively. Let's keep the candidacy active." "We've got at least one finalist." "The note proves he can do the job, let's make a decision soon."* And, at the very least, *"Put the note in the file. There are a few things to think about before we decide."* It may not have a major impact on decision making, but it will be well received by those involved in the process. It can set the scene for ongoing follow up, even if you receive a rejection or nothing-available notice.

Do write and mail (or fax) notes after all communications, not just in-person interviews.

Do state desires clearly. Use phrases like "I want the offer," "I would very much like to meet for a formal employment interview at a mutually convenient time and date," or "I most certainly would like to continue the interview process and, as you noted, interview with others on the staff."

Do, whenever possible, send individual notes to all you met during a multi-interview callback. They don't have to be "individualized and unique," but they shouldn't be identical. It is fine to send one note to a centralized coordinator if you ask him or her to convey your appreciation to others, but it isn't as effective.

Don't ask for feedback regarding interview performance after being rejected, but do ask for continued consideration. It is tempting to find out "why," but it's rare to find employers willing to do so, either for fear of legal issues or because it is awkward to analyze the situation with the person who was "dinged." It is more effective to follow up a rejection with a thank-you note. No matter how strange this seems, it can pay off. It may have been a close decision, and if an internal candidate was selected his or her job will be available. State that your interest remains strong and that you wish continued consideration. Request additional employment interviews or information conversations. Ask to be considered for part-time or project work.

Don't delay. Speed is critical. If the note can impact decision making it will do so immediately after an interview or phone communication. Consider fax or express mail (or hand delivery).

Review follow-up note drafts and samples. Enter appropriate scores in one box associated with each of the four critiquing criteria. Total all scores to determine the Job Search Correspondence Quotient (JSCQ) for a particular document. Make photocopies so you can use this device as often as needed.

FOLLOW-UP NOTE QUOTIENT

Critiquing Criteria	Excellent *Most definitely!!!* (5 points)	Good *Yes, I think so.* (4 points)	Fair *Maybe it did, but ...* (2 points)	Poor *Huh, I don't know!?!?* (1 point)
Cited date of previous correspondence, interview, or conversation and briefly summarized outcomes.				
Noted status (as candidate or information gatherer) and identified desired next steps (employment interview, information conversation, referral to another person).				
Noted title(s) or function(s) desired and reinforces qualification statements in earlier correspondence (quotes or refers to enclosed copy). Enclosed resume as "reminder."				
Identified next steps writer will take. Suggested "creative" options (i.e., lunch, shadow day, internship, part-time or trial employment).				
TOTALS				

Job
Search
Correspondence
Quotient!
▼

After using this device and revising drafts, *all* follow-up notes will receive a JSCQ of 20-15 !

A Follow-up Note JSCQ of 20-15 is characterized by the state-

ments: *"This person is very persistent and communicates effectively. I guess I'll give him a few minutes."* *"What a polite pest, but nicely done. The least I can do is set up an informal meeting with one of our recent hires."* and *"Put this new note in the file. It must be getting thick by now. I really wish we had something."* Follow up neutral as well as negative communications politely, yet patiently. If you stop communicating the process stops!

Do keep records of all communications so you can refer to them in correspondence and track how frequently you contact potential employers.

Do transition from requests for employment interviews to requests for advice and information conversations. Ultimately, the more people you talk to in fields of interest, the more likely you will find your job.

Do identify specific jobs or functional areas in all communiqués, especially initial letters of inquiry or applications.

Do state in every follow up what you would like to happen next; an employment interview, an information conversation, or a sense of the decision-making timetable.

Don't write every week, but **do** keep communications flowing. A pattern of "letter, call, fax" every three to six weeks after initial communications is a good one to follow. Initial correspondence is followed up immediately, but subsequent unsolicited contacts shouldn't be as quick.

Remember, before identifying JSCQs of your own letters, use each test to judge appropriate samples.

Hiram "Hi" Tech

1236 W. Stadium Dr. Apt. #6 • Stockton, CA 95206 • (209) 988-4690

February 26, 1993

SOFTWARE ENGINEER POSITION
470 Potrero Avenue
Sunnyvale, CA 94086

I am writing in response to your notice in the February 23, *San Jose Mercury News.* I would like to be considered for the Software Engineer position requiring a background in microcontroller development.

I trust the enclosed resume, specifically the Qualifications and Achievements section, highlights for you the capabilities I offer. Briefly, I have successfully worked in research and development capacities in classroom and co-op environments. Currently I am working on a laser display to be used in the entertainment industry. This display system features a 6803 microprocessor with direct memory access to the video ram which I mapped between $100 and $4F20. In addition, I have also designed a serial multiprocessor configuration using the 6803. Other experience includes microprocessor design with the Intel 8088. My programming experience includes 68000 assembly language, C and Unix. Also, my experiences within organizations like Seimens, Hammett & Edison, and Dialog Information Services have taught me the importance of quickly fitting into a team and working to my fullest capacity.

I would be very pleased if I could elaborate on my projects, work experiences, and educational achievements via a personal meeting. It is through an initial conversation that you can get to know me and learn more about my background. Of course, I will then have the opportunity to learn about the nature of this position and the firm involved.

Again, I do want to meet with you, or one of your colleagues, to support my candidacy for this position. Thank you for your consideration.

Sincerely,

Hiram "Hi" Tech

HIRAM "HI" TECH

Correspondence Comments

- ✏ Letter of Application in response to "blind" ad in newspaper.
- ✏ Directed reader's attention to Qualifications and Achievements section, the heart of the resume.
- ✏ Because no name is indicated in posting, no salutation appears.

Hiram "Hi" Tech

1236 W. Stadium Dr. Apt. #6 • Stockton, CA 95206 • (209) 988-4690

March 3, 1993

SOFTWARE ENGINEER POSITION
470 Potrero Avenue
Sunnyvale, CA 94086

I recently responded to your notice in the February 23, *San Jose Mercury News* for the Software Engineer position requiring a background in microcontroller development. I hope you had the opportunity to review my cover letter and resume (copy enclosed), and determined that I have the qualities you are seeking in a candidate. If this is the case, I should be hearing from you soon regarding an interview.

If no decision has been made, please allow me to reinforce my interest in meeting with you or one of your colleagues regarding this position.

Thank you again for your consideration.

Sincerely,

Hiram "Hi" Tech

HIRAM "HI" TECH

Correspondence Comments

- ✏ Immediate follow up after initial response to "blind" ad in newspaper.
- ✏ Reinforces interest and ensures additional review of candidacy, including copy of original correspondence.
- ✏ Allows for reading after initial "flood" of letters were reviewed, enhancing chances for more thoughtful analysis of candidacy.

Hiram "Hi" Tech

1236 W. Stadium Dr. Apt. #6 • Stockton, CA 95206 • (209) 988-4690

March 10, 1993

SOFTWARE ENGINEER POSITION
470 Potrero Avenue
Sunnyvale, CA 94086

Responding to "blind ads" is always difficult when you want to follow up appropriately. The more I think about the Software Engineer position as described in the February 23, *San Jose Mercury News,* the more eager I am to hear regarding your judgment of my qualifications. Enclosed is a copy of my original correspondence to remind you of my background.

I will now be patient regarding this position, yet I remain eager to hear from you and, I hope, meet with you.

Thank you again for your consideration.

Sincerely,

Hiram "Hi" Tech

HIRAM "HI" TECH

Correspondence Comments

- ✑ Additional follow up after initial response to "blind" ad in newspaper.
- ✑ Reinforces interest and ensures additional review of candidacy, including copy of original correspondence.

Hiram "Hi" Tech

1236 W. Stadium Dr. Apt. #6 • Stockton, CA 95206 • (209) 988-4690

April 7, 1993

SOFTWARE ENGINEER POSITION
470 Potrero Avenue
Sunnyvale, CA 94086

I contacted you regarding a Software Engineer position posted in the February 23, *San Jose Mercury News* over 4 weeks ago. I assume that you have already identified qualified candidates, but I would like to restate my interest in meeting to discuss similar opportunities. As I have done before, enclosed is a copy of original correspondence.

I do hope that you find my background worthy of an informal conversation to discuss potential future openings.

Thank you again for your continued consideration.

Sincerely,

Hiram "Hi" Tech

HIRAM "HI" TECH

Correspondence Comments

✏ Long-term follow-up one month after initial response to "blind" ad in newspaper.

✏ Seeks to rekindle interest in candidacy, if still viable, or begin exploration of other options.

✏ One way to uncover hidden potential employers and seek information conversation.

✏ Rarely done, so potential for success varies, but well worth the effort.

JUSTIN TIMETOHIRE

55 Babbling Brook Road • Carmichael, CA 95608 • (916) 944-1111

August 17, 1993

Mary Sue Smith
Director
Colorado Conservation Political Action Committee
P.O. Box 2345
Boulder, CO 56743

Dear Ms. Smith,

It was nice of you to speak with me the other day. Jim Johnson of L&L Associates said that you would be helpful, and he was definitely right. As per our conversation, I would like to meet you to explore ways I can help you with Colorado Conservation Political Action Committee's lobbying operations. As detailed on my resume, I have had very applicable experiences with L&L in Sacramento and I have developed appropriate skills in a number of other settings.

You probably hear from many people of their desires to enter lobbying because of their interests in serving the public and impacting the political process. While I am strongly motivated to do so, I know it's not all fun and games and "helping others." I do understand the realities of the field, yet still think of it as a passion rather than a job. Experiences with L&L, Stockton Shelter for the Homeless, as well as my undergraduate studies have nurtured within me a "can do" attitude and, more importantly, "done well" skills. I have tracked and researched legislation, learned and followed procedures and policies of regulatory agencies, and honed the skills required to communicate with office holders and agency administrators. It would be wonderful if I could become a full-time or part-time member of your staff.

Let's meet to discuss your reactions to this possibility. I will call soon to confirm appropriate next steps. If you wish, contact me in care of the address and phone above.

Sincerely,

Justin Timetohire

JUSTIN TIMETOHIRE

Correspondence Comments

- Letter of inquiry written as follow up of initial phone conversation.
- Reminds reader of initial referral.
- Justin should ask Mr. Johnson to follow with a recommendation letter targeted to Ms. Smith.
- Focuses on experience, not simply wishes, and stresses realistic knowledge of field.
- Clearly states desired next step; a meeting, and what Justin will do next; make a call.

CONNIE GOHOME

875 24th Street
Sacramento, CA 95888
(916) 465-6666

8 Maple Avenue
Shady Grove, MN 55669
(612) 486-8765

August 22, 1993

Dr. Sue Perry Intendent
Superintendent
Maple Glen School District
2234 Main Street
Maple Glen, MN 55556

Dr. Intendent:

I will soon be relocating to Minnesota to rejoin my family, and I am interested in pursuing a position with Maple Glen School District. The last two-and-a-half years I have taught second, seventh, and eighth grades. As my resume indicates, I would welcome consideration for general elementary positions or for opportunities which would use my ESL and bilingual teaching abilities. Teaching is my chosen profession and I now wish to apply all that I have learned where I have friends and family, where I was taught by wonderful men and women just a few years ago. I have contacted the Minnesota Department of Education to verify requirements necessary to teach in Minnesota and I have taken steps to complete them.

My academic background, a degree in Liberal Studies, along with a California Preliminary Multiple Subject Teaching Credential, with a Bilingual Cross-cultural Emphasis in Spanish; and my employment history are noted on the enclosed resume. But a resume and cover letter can tell you only so much. I would very much like to discuss my qualifications with you by phone and, if appropriate, arrange for an in person interview when I return to Minnesota.

I will be contacting you soon to confirm receipt of this letter and to discuss the next steps I should take. Prior to my contacting you, please forward any application or relevant information. Please, do not allow the distance from California to Minnesota to negatively influence my candidacy. I do so much want to work for your district. Thank you for your time, and I look forward to speaking with you.

Sincerely,

Connie Gohome

CONNIE GOHOME

Correspondence Comments

- ✏ Letter of inquiry written as first step after using directory to locate appropriate districts.
- ✏ Reinforces desire to return home, but doesn't stress this as the only reason.
- ✏ Refers to resume, encourages phone interview as next step, and requests application materials.
- ✏ Identifies, yet diminishes long distance issue.
- ✏ Creative pencil border appropriate for education or related position.

Clem Corson

888 Presidents Drive • University of the Pacific • Stockton, CA 95211 • (209) 947-9900

October 27, 1992

Ms. Jordan Elizabeth
MGI
2346 East 75th Street, Suite 12
New York, NY 93499
FAX: (212) 765-4334

Dear Ms. Elizabeth:

First, thanks for being so helpful to someone making a "cold call" to MGI. I hope I didn't appear too pushy, but sometimes my enthusiasm gets the best of me. I do so much want to work for your firm as a Summer Intern.

As you suggested, here is a draft copy of my resume and of the letter I would like to send Mr. Weston. Your comments would be very much appreciated. Please call me in care of the number above or, if possible, fax me at (209) 944-8876.

You were most generous offering to help with my efforts to obtain an internship in sports representation. After one phone call I feel as if I've met a role model and I would welcome the opportunity to continue our telephone and correspondence relationship. Of course, I do hope we have the chance to meet someday.

I will call to confirm receipt of these materials and to discuss your thoughts.

Again, and again, thank you.

Sincerely,

Clem Corson

P.S.   I faxed this note as well as a copy of my resume so you would receive them quickly. Of course,
originals will follow by mail soon.

CLEM CORSON

Correspondence Comments

- ✉ Fax note, expressing gratitude for advice and offer of assistance.
- ✉ As discussed in initial phone conversation, draft resume and cover note enclosed.
- ✉ Simple and to the point.

Clem Corson

888 Presidents Drive • University of the Pacific • Stockton, CA 95211 • (209) 947-9900

November 15, 1992

Mr. Mark Weston
President
MGI
One Sports Management Plaza, Suite 234
Cleveland, OH 44111

Dear Mr. Weston:

I would like the opportunity to work as an intern for MGI in London, New York, Boston, or Cleveland during the Summer or Fall of 1993. You may receive many similar requests, but what makes me different is my accomplishments, drive, enthusiasm, and the strength of my commitment to the field. I hope all of these criteria are reflected in the enclosed resume. I am proud of what I have achieved as a student, as a campus leader, as a fund raiser, and as a young person who has already been successful in the competitive field of real estate. I hope I will soon be just as proud of what I will accomplish at MGI.

During the past few months, I have been doing extensive research on MGI and on your competitors in the areas of client representation and event management. Yes, it is my sincerest goal to someday enter the field and become a successful agent. I originally took an interest in becoming an agent when I began assisting a few current and past University of the Pacific football players. I offered to help screen potential representatives for these pro prospects and I have been doing so for over eight weeks. I have learned so much in two months, yet now realize how much more I have to learn. My efforts with these soon-to-be pros (copies of materials regarding these players is enclosed) and, just as important, conversations with people like Jordan Elizabeth, an MGI agent in New York, have served to reinforce my career objective.

I understand that MGI recently put on the Jimmy Connors versus Martina Navratilova tennis match. You created the event, represented the athletes, secured the television rights and offered pay-for-view via Trans World International (an MGI subsidiary); you marketed sponsorships and corporate affiliations, and even had your clients broadcast the event. These are exactly the types of activities I would like to become involved with. It seems that only MGI does things on this scale.

As cited above, I would welcome consideration for an internship with MGI. I know if you gave me a chance, I could be an asset to the firm. I will call your office soon to confirm receipt of this letter and, hopefully, to discuss appropriate steps. I do understand that you might refer this request to a member of your staff, so I will inquire with your assistant regarding who I should communicate with.

Thank you so much for your time and consideration.

Sincerely,

Clem Corson

Enclosures

CLEM CORSON

Correspondence Comments

- ✉ Letter of inquiry clearly (immediately) noting sincere and strong interest in an internship.
- ✉ Personalized story is well told, reflecting knowledge of self, but knowledge of field is also projected.
- ✉ Mailed after feedback received by initial contact.
- ✉ Copies of final draft also sent Jordan Elizabeth with request for continued advice and help.

Clem Corson

888 Presidents Drive • University of the Pacific • Stockton, CA 95211 • (209) 947-9900

January 29, 1993

Mr. John McMohan
MGI
One Sports Management Plaza, Suite 234
Cleveland, OH 44111

Dear John:

I would like the opportunity to formally thank you for your support of my candidacy for an intern position and accept the offer made recently by phone. Obviously, I am very excited about this opportunity and I am enthusiastically looking forward to working at MGI. At present, my plans are to travel to Cleveland and begin work on Monday, June 21st. I hope this date is okay. If not, please let me know.

I will call your office soon to confirm receipt of this letter, to discuss whether my plans meet your approval, and to clarify any additional information you require. Also, I may need some advice regarding temporary housing.

Again, I am looking forward to being a member of the MGI team.

Sincerely,

Clem Corson

CLEM CORSON

Correspondence Comments

- ☎ Acceptance letter.
- ☎ Brief, accurate, and clear, restating phone conversation.
- ☎ If compensation was involved, could restate offer amount and title, confirming information presented in verbal or written offer.

ANNA ESTRELLA

4040 Pacific Avenue • Stockton, California 95211 • (209) 444-1313 or 944-4499
67 Chabeau Drive • Castro Valley, California 94552 • (510) 577-7777

March 27, 1993

Mr. Richard Reviewer
Director of Personnel
Stockton Unified School District
9776 3rd Street
Stockton, CA 96544

Mr. Reviewer:

The intent of this letter and accompanying resume is to make known to you my goal and desire to become an elementary school teacher in the Stockton Unified School District. I have spent the past several years preparing myself to enter the field of elementary education. Upon completion of my student teaching this May, I will receive my Preliminary Multiple Subjects Credential.

I trust my consistent demonstration of academic success, both as a student and as a student teacher, and my proven devotion to the welfare of children, make me a strong candidate for employment with SUSD. The enclosed resume and my recommendations, available through University of the Pacific, are indicative of not only the person I am but also the type of teacher I will become.

I have demonstrated reliability and hard work in all aspects of my life, and teaching will be no exception. My determination to influence young children and make an impact on my community can only be accomplished if I am given the opportunity. I do wish to become an elementary school teacher in the Stockton Unified School District.

I respectfully request an interview at your convenience. It is through a conversation that I can share my motivations and goals, not simply my accomplishments. I will call to confirm receipt of these materials and to discuss next steps.

Sincerely,

Anna Estrella

Enclosure

ANNA ESTRELLA

Correspondence Comments

✆ Traditional, yet effective letter of inquiry.
✆ A bit formal, yet effective.

HIRAM E. NOW

31 Lincoln Street #9 • San Francisco, California 94777 • (415) 323-9888

November 16, 1993

Mr. Public Relations Person
Public Relations Firm
San Francisco, CA 99951

Dear Mr. Person:

It's taken me a while, but I now have a sense of career focus. With your help, I can increase the clarity with which I view and understand event planning as a potential career. I would be so grateful if you, or one of your staff, could give me 10 to 15 minutes of your time for an information conversation.

Simply, I want to ask questions like:

- How did you break into the field and what are other entry-level jobs?
- How do you start the process of planning an event and maintain positive relations with clients throughout the process?
- Have you recently hired someone to perform entry-level tasks and, if yes, what are these tasks?

As you can see, I am trying to identify the nature of day-to-day functions and become better able to articulate goals. Only after I have completed my research will I seek an internship or entry-level employment in the field.

In advance, thank you for your time.

Sincerely,

Hiram E. Now

P.S.   A copy of my resume is enclosed to quickly inform you of my background. It is not meant to solicit job search consideration.

HIRAM E. NOW

Correspondence Comments

✏   Request for information conversation clearly noted early in letter.

✏   Notes typical questions to reinforce nature of meeting.

✏   Encloses resume, yet notes for information exchange only.

HIRAM E. NOW
31 Lincoln Street #9 • San Francisco, California 94777 • (415) 323-9888

November 16, 1993

Mr. Al Adman
Advertising Inc.
298 Post Street, Suite 450
San Francisco, CA 99965

Dear Mr. Adman:

I am seeking an internship which will allow me to use and further develop my promotional event planning skills and allow me to learn as much as I can about advertising. I would be so grateful if you, or one of your staff, could give me 10 to 15 minutes of your time to discuss whether I could serve Advertising Inc. within these capacities.

As you can see from my resume, I possess a variety of generalist skills, but I now wish to fine tune them to apply to my chosen field of interest. Through the internship, by working on projects in client services or related areas, I hope, I will enhance my chances to land my first full-time job in the field. Only after I have completed the internship will I seek entry-level employment. My desires to find a position of this kind are so strong that I would be willing to volunteer my time for three days a week for a three to four month period.

Again, I am seeking an internship with Advertising Inc., and I look forward to discussing this possibility with you or a member of your staff. I will call soon to discuss your reactions to my request and, I hope, to arrange a time when we can meet.

In advance, thank you for your time.

Sincerely,

Hiram E. Now

HIRAM E. NOW

Correspondence Comments

- ✉ Letter of inquiry requesting consideration for an internship.
- ✉ Cites motivations and defines "internship."
- ✉ Briefly refers to resume and reinforces desire for in-person discussion.

HIRAM E. NOW

31 Lincoln Street #9 • San Francisco, California 94777 • (415) 323-9888

December 29, 1993

Mr. Al Adman
Advertising Inc.
298 Post Street, Suite 450
San Francisco, CA 99965

Dear Mr. Adman:

First, thank you so much for your support of my candidacy for an internship with Advertising Inc. Your willingness to share information about the firm, about the field, and about the functions served by an intern is very much appreciated.

Second, it is with mixed feelings that I inform you that I have accepted an intern position with U.R. Competitors, Inc. This organization offered me the opportunity to immediately work within account services and media planning areas; something I very much wanted. The fact that your firm only had Summer Internships allowed me to make this decision quite easily. Although I was very impressed with Advertising Inc., I felt the sooner I received "hands on" experience the better.

I would of course like to continue our communications regarding a Summer Internship or, perhaps, a full-time entry-level position. When I complete my internship with U.R. Competitors in May I would like to transition quickly into another situation.

Again, you were most helpful and your consideration was very much appreciated. Please, let's keep in touch.

Sincerely,

Hiram E. Now

P.S   Enclosed is an updated version of my resume with the new internship noted. The description is now brief, but I look forward to expanding it as I actually perform in these capacities. I do hope I'll have a chance to share these experiences with you someday.

HIRAM E. NOW

Correspondence Comments

☞   Letter requesting termination of consideration (should be done immediately after accepting offer).

☞   Defines new "internship," yet identifies potential future contacts.

☞   Includes resume and reinforces desire for continued contact.

Dawn Daley

232 New Hampshire Avenue • Oakland, CA 94433 • (510) 898-6587

October 13, 1992

Mr. Albert Reece
Superflight, Inc.
76 Embarcadero Avenue
Palo Alto, CA 94331

Mr. Reece:

I sincerely hope that you haven't filled the public relations position at Superflight, Inc., because I would very much like to be considered for the job. I read of the opening this morning in the Businesswire newsletter and I feel that my prior experience in sports marketing and media relations would allow me to work with you to achieve all of the goals stated in the posting.

Currently I am involved in wine industry public relations, working in an agency which has several wine and beer clients. I have enhanced my knowledge of how to handle industry specific issues and, more importantly, expanded my achievement oriented view of what is necessary in public relations. While I enjoy the challenges of my position, and believe I have contributed much to my clients' efforts, I have fond memories of my experiences in sports promotions and marketing. I now sincerely wish to re-enter this specialized area where I have had past success.

As noted on my resume, I worked as a press liaison for the first San Rafael Cycling Classic and as an intern for GoSport Communications, an event and sports marketing firm.   There I worked effectively with the media to garner publicity for GoSport's corporate ski racing series, "The Ski Classic." It is within this environment that I learned how to promote, publicize, and generate public interest in sports products and events. Enclosed are copies of some of the materials I developed for GoSport as well as other clients.   know I perform as well for Superflight, Inc. as I have in all of my employment settings.

I will call to confirm receipt of this note and, I hope, to arrange an interview. While a resume and cover letter can be effective, and I did think a great deal about what is cited under the Qualifications and Accomplishments section of the resume, written materials can do only so much. A meeting will allow you to get to know more about me and allow us to brainstorm ideas regarding how to market your products and promote related activities. Thank you for your consideration.

My current situation necessitates that our communications remain confidential. Of course, should we reach the stage when you require references, I would be happy to provide them.

Best regards,

Dawn Daley

DAWN DALEY

Correspondence Comments

☞ Letter of application written some weeks after ad appeared.
☞ Notes present situation, but focuses on most related past experience.
☞ Notes current circumstances and requests confidentiality.
☞ Identifies phone call as her next step after clearly requesting an interview.

GINA JOBYET
3333 Twin Tree Avenue • Stockton, CA 95211 • (209) 444-9449

October 20, 1992

Jacob Stevens
W.A. Laboratories
222 East Ridge Road
Folsom, CA 94337

Dear Mr. Stevens:

I understand that University of the Pacific Career Services forwarded you a copy of my resume. I hope my attempts to reach you by phone reveal that I am very interested in discussing opportunities with W.A. Laboratories. Also, as the enclosed revised version of my resume reflects, pharmaceutical sales is a strong goal.

I thought a great deal about what to include on the Qualifications and Capabilities section of this document and I believe I have summarized my greatest assets. So, I will not elaborate with a lengthy cover note because a resume and letter can only do so much. It is through an interview (in person or by phone) that I can better share my qualifications with you. I do look forward to hearing from you regarding my request for an interview. I will continue to call to discuss your reactions.

Sincerely,

Gina Jobyet

GINA JOBYET

Correspondence Comments

☞ Letter following resume referral.
☞ Briefly, yet strongly, cites goal, refers to Qualifications and Capabilities section, and requests meeting.
☞ Note date of initial correspondence.

GINA JOBYET
3333 Twin Tree Avenue • Stockton, CA 95211 • (209) 444-9449

January 11, 1993

Jacob Stevens
W.A. Laboratories
222 East Ridge Road
Folsom, CA 94337

Dear Mr. Stevens:

As per past phone messages and correspondence, I remain very interested in getting together to discuss my qualifications for a sales position with W.A. Laboratories. I've just returned from a meeting of pharmaceutical sale professionals where I heard that you might still be seeking candidates for positions in the Northern California area. You may recall that I did try to reach you over the phone on numerous occasions after my initial correspondence, but it has been a while since my last attempt. My interest in the field and, most importantly, in your firm, remain strong. It is only through an interview that I can present my motivations and qualifications to you effectively.

I look forward to our meeting soon.

Sincerely,

Gina Jobyet

P.S. Enclosed is another copy of my resume to quickly remind you of my background.

GINA JOBYET

Correspondence Comments

- ✏ Letter following original unsuccessful inquiry after several months.
- ✏ Reinforces continued interest and notes enclosed resume.
- ✏ Note date of this correspondence.

GINA JOBYET
3333 Twin Tree Avenue • Stockton, CA 95211 • (209) 444-9449

January 24, 1993

Jacob Stevens
W.A. Laboratories
222 East Ridge Road
Folsom, CA 94337

Dear Mr. Stevens:

It was great finally meeting you. As you know by now, I am a person who believes in persistence and positive thinking. As a seasoned sales professional I learned never to give up when you want something. Thank you so much for the opportunity to share with you my desires and, most importantly, qualifications to become a sales representative with W.A. Laboratories. I do want to join your sales team and look forward to hearing regarding your deliberations soon.

For me, it was well worth the wait. Again, thank you for your time and consideration.

Sincerely,

Gina Jobyet

GINA JOBYET

Correspondence Comments

- Thank-you note for long-awaited interview.
- Brief, to the point, subtly reinforcing qualifications for sales and clearly stating desire for offer.
- Note date of this correspondence.

GINA JOBYET
3333 Twin Tree Avenue • Stockton, CA 95211 • (209) 444-9449

___

February 5, 1993

Jacob Stevens
W. A. Laboratories
222 East Ridge Road
Folsom, CA 94337

Dear Jake:

It is with great pleasure that I formally accept your offer to join W. A. Laboratories as a Sales Representative. The base salary and bonus structure outlined in your letter is exactly what we discussed and I hope to succeed well beyond stated goals. Medical and other benefit information is yet to be received, but I anticipate all will be acceptable. If I have any questions or concerns, I'll certainly give you a call.

I understand that I will begin formal training on March 3rd and that William Truly of your corporate headquarters will soon contact me to make all arrangements.

I trust you now agree that it was worth the wait for both of us.

Sincerely,

Gina Jobyet

GINA JOBYET

Correspondence Comments

✏ Acceptance letter finalizing and documenting a prolonged, but successful effort!

✏ Compare date of this correspondence with original note. Persistence, patience, and continued communications, did pay off.

Professor William Referral
University of the Pacific
Stockton, CA 95211

July 23, 1993

Joyce Hiremeplease
Senior Analyst
Brad & Dunstreet
1238 Mission Way
Concord, CA 97665

Dear Joyce:

First, thank you for your continued interest in recruiting UOP students for Business Analyst positions with Brad & Dunstreet. It's always rewarding to know that an alum wants to give back to the school by offering others the opportunity to begin meaningful careers. I understand that all is going very well. Congratulations on your recent promotion.

Second, I am writing to introduce a student who I believe would make a wonderful candidate for one of your analyst positions. Larry Ladd has been in two of my finance courses and has performed very well. More importantly, when he and I recently had discussions regarding career interests, he stated the desire to use analytical as well as marketing talents. When he shared his resume with me (a copy for you is attached) and discussed his concern over missing on-campus recruiting, I encouraged him to contact you directly by phone. I hope this was appropriate.

Not many students take the initiative to speak with faculty about goals and aspirations. You may recall that you were one of the few who did just that. Well, Larry has followed in your footsteps, doing the same. If all goes well, he may follow you to Brad & Dunstreet.

Let me know if you need any additional information on Larry or other candidates. Give me a call soon.

Thanks,

Bill Referral

LANCELOT (LARRY) LADD

Correspondence Comments

- Letter of introduction written by faculty member (could have been by family member, friend, or past employer) at the request of candidate.
- Helps ease the process and often ensures first interview.

DATE:	AUGUST 10, 1993
TO:	JOYCE HIREMEPLEASE
	BRAD & DUNSTREET
FAX:	(510) 834-5667
FROM:	LANCELOT (LARRY) LADD
FAX:	(209) 946-2649
PHONE:	(209) 964-3387

As we discussed, I am sorry that we didn't have a chance to meet when you interviewed on campus last March. After reading literature on your firm and discussing my goals with Dr. Referral, I am very enthusiastic about how well my abilities match the qualifications stated as required of the Business Analyst position. After reading my resume I hope you conclude that I have developed and used skills required to succeed with Brad & Dunstreet.

My undergraduate studies combined coursework in economics, policy, and business. Whether working on a project, a paper, or simply contributing to an in-class discussion, I used abilities to understand concepts, to go beyond the obvious in order to find an answer through various research methods. I am very confident of my ability to use library and interview skills in order to research companies, markets, or topics. Basically, I am a driven investigator. I can transform my research into written or verbal presentations. I am very comfortable with quantitative problem solving, having successfully completed classes and an internship that required a lot of research and utilized basic market research techniques.

In addition, I have overseas experience. I studied Marketing at Grenoble, France at the Ecole Supérieure des Affaires de Grenoble in the second year of the Maîtrise de Sciences de Gestion, during the 1990-91 school year. There, I took classes with French students and became integrated into the French culture. Classes thoroughly explored French Marketing concepts and how the French view Advertising.

While in France, I had the opportunity to do an internship with the Alliance Universitaire de Grenoble (AUG). Basically, I undertook actions designed to expand the AUG's market base and tailor services to specific populations. I interviewed people to assess views regarding what AUG offers student and corporate members, and, ultimately, analyzed information to develop recommendations to increase membership, enhance interest in the organization, and most importantly, improve services.

Most recently, not yet appearing on my resume, I have had the opportunity to work as a Summer Community Representative for Pacific Gas and Electric in Stockton. Whether assessing customer needs, using French skills to interact with members of the Southeast Asian business community, meeting with PG&E's Marketing Director, or handling the concerns of a customer, I use my research, analytical, and communication skills to their fullest.

I have a broad educational background which includes international relations, business, and liberal arts coursework. I can speak, read, and write French fluently. I can type 60 WPM, answer phones, meet deadlines on time, handle stressful situations while maintaining a positive attitude, and manage time and tasks in order to complete projects efficiently. I am optimistic, adaptable, dependable, patient, determined and a hard worker. I like challenges and meeting new people. While I don't wish to sound "perfect," I am so enthusiastic about the chance to work for Brad & Dunstreet that I wanted to be sure that all my qualifications are made known to you.

I would very much like to share my background with you personally. I will call to discuss the possibility of arranging an interview. Because I wanted to begin the process as quickly as possible, I faxed this note and my resume. Originals will follow soon by mail. Thank you for your consideration.

LANCELOT (LARRY) LADD

Correspondence Comments

- ✉ Fax communiqué, following a faculty referral to an on-campus recruiting organization.
- ✉ Lengthy, but well written and achievement oriented.

DATE: SEPTEMBER 21, 1993
TO: BILL JULY
             REGIONAL MANAGER
             BRAD & DUNSTREET
FAX: (510) 834-5667
FROM: LANCELOT (LARRY) LADD
FAX: (209) 946-2649
PHONE: (209) 964-3387

My visit this afternoon was most enjoyable and informative. I do hope that I presented to you my qualifications and motivations for seeking an Analyst position with Brad & Dunstreet. Having met you, as well as a number of your colleagues, and having learned first-hand about the nature of the job and of the environment where I would work, I am even more enthusiastic about the prospect of working for Brad & Dunstreet.

I do want to work at B&D and I look forward to hearing from you regarding your decision.

Again, I appreciate the opportunity we had to meet and I do hope that I will someday join you as a member of the B&D team. Also, enclosed is a copy of my updated resume which details my summer position with PG&E.

Thank you.

LANCELOT (LARRY) LADD

Correspondence Comments

- ✏ Fax thank-you note to highest ranking interviewer for off-campus screening interviews.
- ✏ Highlights request for the offer by using italics and placement as single line.
- ✏ Encloses updated copy of resume.

DATE: SEPTEMBER 21, 1993
TO: JOYCE HIREMEPLEASE
BRAD & DUNSTREET
FAX: (510) 834-5667
FROM: LANCELOT (LARRY) LADD
FAX: (209) 946-2649
PHONE: (209) 964-3387

It's over! I do hope that I did well during my interviews, because the more I think about it the more I want to work at B&D. Quite honestly, I didn't feel as optimistic after I finished my interview this afternoon as I did when we met last week. It's really hard to tell how well I did. Each interviewer has a different style. All I know is that I answered the questions honestly and to the best of my ability. Please convey my thanks to Jane, Sue, and Brad. I have already faxed Bill a personalized thank-you note (copy attached).

As I have stated in a number of ways, I do want to work at B&D and I believe I have the skills and capabilities to succeed. At this stage, any support you can give my candidacy would be most appreciated.

Thank you so much. Whatever the outcome of the deliberation process, I did enjoy meeting you and appreciate your assistance with my job search efforts.

LANCELOT (LARRY) LADD

Correspondence Comments

✎ Fax thank-you note to coordinator of interviews and alumni contact.
✎ Also reinforces desire to get an offer and request support for candidacy.
✎ Asks for centralized coordinator to thank others.

TO:	**WILLIAM U. INTERVIEWME**
E-MAIL ID:	**WUI 3456**
FROM:	**I.M. UNIQUE**
DATE:	**01-20-1993**
TIME:	**9:23 PM**

I.M. UNIQUE
777 Bonn Drive
Stockton, CA 95244
(209) 454-9732

William U. Interviewme
Employment Supervisor
Klose of California
334 Market Street
San Francisco, CA 94225

Mr. Interviewme:

First, I trust you won't be surprised to receive an E-mail message. I contacted your office this morning and they said it would be an appropriate way to reach you. Originals of this note and my resume will be forwarded soon by mail.

Now, please allow me to introduce myself and request that you review the accompanying resume. My background in production within the apparel and textile industry, coupled with past merchandising experience motivates me to actively pursue positions with Klose of California.

As noted on my resume, most recently I was with *International Design's D. Ecollection* division as a Textiles Developer and Buyer. Through this position I learned about the present state of the industry and about future trends and developments. The nature of D. Ecollection gave me special insights into new production strategies and technologies. Most importantly, I was actively involved in the development of an environmentally friendly textile from initial fiber purchasing to weaving or knitting and, ultimately, to the dyed and finished product.

Prior, I managed and operated a European designer apparel boutique where I gained experience in retailing as well as design and production. Along with handling all store and buying line operations, I was actively involved in supplementing core men's and women's designer collections with a private label product line. When developing this private label collection, I personally researched design trend and color, constructed flat patterns on computer aided design (CAD) systems, sourced fabric, trim, and production, and developed and implemented a complete marketing image for the end product. This private label experience allowed me to gain considerable exposure to innovations in textiles and apparel construction in the United States and abroad in Europe and Asia.

As you can see, I am aware of the importance of having a broad-based, multidimensional, and, yes, multinational perspective if one is to be successful in the apparel and textile industry. I am now seeking consideration for a production-focused position with Klose and, ideally, an interview. I will call soon concerning your reactions to my request and to discuss appropriate next steps. Thank you for your consideration.

Of course, you can contact me in care of the above address or phone or through TELnet E-Mail User ID IMQ234

I.M. UNIQUE

Correspondence Comments

- ✉ E-Mail letter of inquiry.
- ✉ Also reinforces desire to get an offer and request support for candidacy.
- ✉ Asks for centralized coordinator to thank others.

HILLARY T. ECHNICAL

3345 West Stadium Apartment 23B • Stockton, CA 95222
Home: (209) 956-5173 • Messages: (209) 946-9865

March 5, 1993

Ms. Sue Pervisor
Project Manager
Hewlett Packard Company
88987 Foothill Canyon Drive
Roseville, CA 98654

Dear Ms. Pervisor:

My six month co-op assignment with Hewlett Packard allowed me to experience and learn the HP approach to business. I was thoroughly impressed with the degree of expertise of my co-workers, with HP's commitment to innovation, and with the dedication and hard work involved in bringing to market products that meet HP's high standards. I hope you learned of the skills and dedication I can bring to a work environment.

I am now seeking consideration for entry level positions at Hewlett Packard. As you may recall, I will be receiving my B.S. in Electrical Engineering with a minor in Computer Science in May of 1993 from the University of the Pacific. I want to express my strong interests in returning to Hewlett Packard and working with you and your team. I am sure that given the chance I can make significant contributions to your efforts.

Enclosed is a copy of my resume to support this formal request for employment consideration. Of course, I will complete any application materials necessary. Please let me know of the steps I should follow.

I will call soon to confirm receipt of this letter, to discuss next steps, and, I hope, to arrange an interview. In the meantime, if you need to contact me, my phone numbers appear above and my E-mail address is "hte@uop.cs.uop.edu". Thank you for taking time out of your busy schedule to read my letter.

Sincerely yours,

Hillary T. Echnical

HILLARY T. ECHNICAL

Correspondence Comments

- Letter of inquiry to previous co-op supervisor.
- Reminds reader of experience with organization and seeks consideration for full-time position.
- Identifies e-mail as communication option.

**THE JOB SEARCH CORRESPONDENCE QUOTIENT STUDY
TIPS FOR THE RETEST (ACTION STEPS TO TAKE)**

✎ Find an appealing posted opportunity. Review *Cover Letter Guidelines* which follow, draft a letter of application and use the *Correspondence Quotient Quiz* to assess its quality. Then, have a friend, family member, or, ideally, a career services professional critique it. Now, send it! Don't let geographic issues stop you from completing this activity. The location of the job isn't as important as what it involves and, most critically, developing writing skills required to solicit and obtain an interview. Simply, find a posting and write a cover letter now!

✎ Review all samples in this section. Select two you believe are "weak." These are letters you, for any reason, judge as less effective than others. Make corrections and use appropriate Quotient Quizzes to see if you've improved the communiqué. I'm sure you did and, more importantly, you've practiced an important skill.

✎ Review five samples of correspondence appearing in other publications (some noted below). Use the appropriate *Correspondence Quotient Quiz* to assess the quality of these letters and make improvements. This will enhance your writing skills. As with almost anything, practice will make perfect. Your correspondence should be as perfect as your resume.

**THE JOB SEARCH CORRESPONDENCE QUOTIENT
HELPFUL RESOURCES (PEOPLE, PLACES, AND THINGS)**

✔ Without being too redundant (right!), college and university career service professionals regularly critique job search correspondence and provide advice regarding appropriate follow-up actions. Don't ever feel as if you are conducting job search solo. There is always someone else you can (and should) talk to about your efforts. Counselors at community agencies and services that require reasonable hourly rates are also available to serve as correspondence critiquers and job search coaches.

✔ Books you may want to examine include: Beatty/*175 High-Impact*

Cover Letters, Wiley, 1992; *200 Letters for Job Seekers,* Ten Speed Press, 1990; *Cover Letters that Knock 'Em Dead,* Bob Adams, 1992; and *Dynamic Cover Letters*, Ten Speed Press, 1990. Again, avoid the temptation to copy correspondence. Review these publications to complete the above exercise and, whenever possible, to inspire you.

✔ College Communication and English profs can provide some guidance, but don't be frustrated if they seem more concerned about usage and grammar. Any reactions can serve to facilitate honing your skills and using better documents. Again, you are not alone!

THE JOB SEARCH CORRESPONDENCE QUOTIENT STUDY SKILLS SUMMARY

✏ Reinforced importance of quality written communications and displayed various quality samples.
✏ Highlighted diversity of types of communiqués.
✏ Introduced new issues associated with fax and e-mail.

Cover Letter Guidelines

Right Writer's Tips

☞ Whenever possible call to confirm spelling and title of person who will receive letter.
☞ If you cannot identify a person or you are told to address it to "Personnel," don't use a "Dear Sir/Madam" or "To Whom It May Concern" salutation. Simply begin the letter without one.
☞ Opening paragraph (first sentence if possible) states why you are writing.
☞ In a "letter of application," cite position for which you are applying and note how you learned of it.
☞ In a "letter of inquiry," cite functional areas or, if possible, the particular area of interest. If you can identify actual job titles (pRe-search can uncover them), do so.
☞ In a "letter of introduction," requesting an information conversation, clearly outline what you expect from the reader (i.e., "15 to 30 minutes to learn about your career background and obtain a bit of advice").
☞ Notes confirming arrangements are brief, yet thorough, projecting enthusiasm for the upcoming meeting.
☞ If referred by a former employer, alumni, or person with "clout," mention that person's name early in the letter and note that he or

she suggested you write. Always send a copy of any letter to the person cited. You can follow up with a phone call to this person and ask for additional help obtaining an interview.

☞ Middle paragraphs (two or three brief ones) draw attention to your resume and highlight specific skills relevant to the potential employer. For users of the perfect format, request that the reader review your Summary of Qualifications (or similar) section. It's okay to simply "copy and paste" a well-written qualifications section or strongly encourage the reader use it as the basis of your candidacy.

☞ Show you know what it takes to be successful, that you researched qualifications required to perform specific tasks, and that you possess capabilities needed to succeed within the firm and the job function. Don't just "qualifications drop," noting broad and generalized qualities. Specifically connect skills and abilities (as well as "potential" if that's all you can do) to tasks you can perform.

☞ Be focused, directing attention to specific entries on the resume that illustrate traits you possess, and show that you have a sense of career direction. The more you show that you know about the field you wish to enter, the job you wish to have, and the company you wish to work for, the better. Don't be afraid of "limiting" yourself. Present one or two options. You can follow up to expand consideration.

☞ Readers should be excited about your sense of focus, about your background and qualifications, and about your writing style.

☞ Final paragraph states what you will do next, including "call to arrange an interview at your convenience," "contact you to confirm receipt of this letter and discuss steps I should follow" or "call to discuss your reactions to my request."

☞ Don't forget to sign the letter!

☞ "Enclosure," indicating that your resume or additional materials are enclosed, can appear after your signature, but isn't really necessary if you stated such in the body of the letter.

☞ Type *all* correspondence, even brief thank-you notes.

☞ Write whatever letter is appropriate. It's not as hard as you think. *Do it now!*

CHAPTER 7

Interview Readiness Indicator

This is a two-part fill-in-the-blank and short-essay exam. Provide desired information as briefly, yet thoroughly as possible. Answers will be judged based upon content and ability to express ideas clearly and concisely.

PART A: Assume you are preparing for an interview you will have in the next 48 hours. Review your resume (you should have one by now) and insert the requested information.

JOB TITLE

Enter name of a job.

Note title of posted position, one you will actually interview for, or simply one you have read about and identified as a job search target.

ACTIVE JOB DESCRIPTION

*Describe position in as much detail as possible,
but using as many verbs as you can.*

*This may involve "translating" a posting or recruiting
description into more active terms, but they must be
your words.*

THREE KEY POINTS

**Cite three key points that make you qualified for
this job.**

Don't overgeneralize, using terms like "I like to work
with people" or " I have "management skills."

Clearly define points that make you the strongest
possible candidate by using statements like:

"I've already had two sales-related jobs and succeeded
in each case."

"Marketing courses provided knowledge required to
learn concepts and achieve in this advertising-
oriented position."

"Research methods class and project developed and
nurtured questionnaire writing, data collecting, data
analysis, and report-writing skills required to perform
within this role."

1.

2.

3.

THREE ANECDOTES

Note three anecdotes that illustrate your capabilities to do this job.

Make sure the stories support the three key points cited earlier, describing skills you used to achieve a goal.

Describe actively how you once sold an idea or a product, when you completed a difficult research project, or anything that projects skills and achievements.

Note when you were the STAR . . . describing Situation, Tasks, Activities, and Results.

1. Situation

   Tasks

   Activities

   Results

2. Situation

   Tasks

   Activities

   Results

3. Situation

   Tasks

   Activities

   Results

THREE QUESTIONS

List three questions you would ask the interviewer if you could.

These can be general job- or field-related inquiries, but they must reflect a sincere interest in the field and job function.

If the title noted is of an actual posting for a real organization, questions can be function- and firm-related.

1.

2.

3.

PART B: Review the following three interview scenarios. Imagine yourself in the situations described. Then, note how you would answer the questions posed and handle the circumstances described. Your answers should be brief, yet thorough and descriptive. Don't be afraid to state your views. Your first impressions are fine; don't analyze too much.

SCENARIO I: CASUAL AND CREATIVE

Your arrive for your interview 15 minutes early, dressed in business attire. While you conduct some last minute reading and preparation a casually dressed person, clad in a sweater and jeans, introduces himself as the interviewer and says: "Let's go for a walk and get to know one another." During your one-hour stroll around the grounds, sprinkled with some guided tour information, the recruiter asks you some nontraditional questions:

Tell me about yourself.
What makes you tick?
Sell me this pencil.
What one word best describes you?
Who is your best friend and how would he or she describe you?
Would anyone be surprised to hear that you are interviewing here for the job we're discussing? Who and why?

After the walking interview you are unexpectedly invited to lunch with the recruiter and someone introduced as "one of the people you would work with if we offer you the job." Lunch seems more casual than the interview (if possible) and all you talk about is sports, hobbies, and current events. Your two hosts are having beer and wine with the meal. You're offered a drink. After the meal the two say "good-bye" and tell you "we'll be in touch."

SCENARIO II: TRADITIONAL, TYPICAL, AND TOO SHORT

The third of your on-campus interviews goes almost too well and is definitely too short. Everything starts as expected, with the recruiter greeting you in the waiting area and taking you to one of the career services' interview rooms. It's 10 A.M., so both you and the interviewer seem ready to go and alert. It begins with the five questions on your list of typical recruiting inquiries:

Why do you want this job?
What made you choose your major?
What are your greatest strengths and weaknesses?
What are your greatest accomplishments and what roles did you play?
Is your grade point average a true reflection of your academic abilities and success potential?

Your answers are brief, but good. Surprisingly, after 15 minutes, the recruiter stands, shakes your hand and says: "Thank you. You'll hear one way or another within two weeks. Make sure you complete an application and leave it at the front desk before the end of the day." You leave with some curious feelings and don't quite know how to deal with the situation, because this is one of the key companies you've interviewed with. You really want to receive a callback and, ideally, an offer, but don't know what to do.

SCENARIO III: STRESSED TO THE MAX

At the end of a rather lengthy day of interviews, you meet with a senior manager who doesn't seem to like you, or anyone else for that matter. You were very encouraged because you had reached the second phase of the interview process. After responding to a posting and completing an initial screening, you were invited back for a series of meetings. Several morning sessions went quite well. You finished a writing test and a personality inventory with little pressure or anxiety. Lunch with a human resources representative went as expected, casual yet informative. Then, after waiting in the reception area for over 30 minutes, you have your fourth session, with a senior manager to whom your potential immediate supervisor reports. He is harried and curt, making some strong statements and asking some rather pointed questions:

> *I don't know what I'm looking for, but you don't seem to have all of the experience I want. Why should I hire you?*
> *What makes you think you can handle a job that requires so many different talents and persuasive skills?*
> *You didn't seem to excel in the classroom. What makes you so sure you'll do well on the job?*
> *Why don't you want to stay with your current (or previous) employer or why don't they want to you?*
> *Why didn't you major in business? Couldn't you handle it?*
> *Didn't you have concerns about working with those you've already met?*

You handle the stressful hour as well as you can and, relieved to be done, meet briefly with the human resources rep, ask a few quick questions, and leave for home to complain about the "jerk" to your significant other.

INTERVIEW READINESS INDICATOR ANSWER KEY AND SCENARIO ANALYSES

Only you can provide answers to Part A. If you can't, additional pRe-search is in order. This exercise is in truth one of the best preinterview prep devices you can use. It simply asks you to develop brief study notes for the verbal exam that is an interview. It's easiest to complete when you have a particular on- or off-campus interview scheduled, but it can be completed as a hypothetical exercise. The hardest part could be describing the job, but that's why it's a great exercise. If you can't describe a job, it's very difficult to successfully interview for a job!

While many, many books (a few very good) have examined this aspect of job search, interviewing isn't that complicated to understand or prepare for. A few basic tips for most soon-to-be and recent college grads:

○ **Dress so dress isn't an issue!**
Yes, everyone has an opinion about what's "hot" and what's "not" for interviewing this season, but don't get caught up in that hype. Simply, for men and women, conservative well-pressed suits in solid colors or (very) subtle patterns. When selecting an interview outfit (definitely purchase at least one new outfit for your job search campaign) if you ask yourself whether your skirt is too short, it most likely is. If you have any concerns about your tie being too "loud," it most likely is. If you have doubts, err on the side of being too conservative. You want your words, not your clothes to be what an interviewer remembers. Honestly, after you've made a positive first visual impression (in about ten seconds), your attire shouldn't be an issue. You don't ever want him or her to think: "does he ever polish his shoes," "doesn't he realize that his button (or fly) is open," " can't he tie a tie at his age," or any similar judgmental unspoken inquiry. When clothes are not an issue, you're fine! Naked is never acceptable!!!

○ **Stay focused on the job you are interviewing for!**
Students are regularly told to conduct research prior to an interview, and they do, but they don't really find out the true nature of the job. They spend too much time reading annual reports, looking for current events articles about the company, and locating alumni who work there. While these are all admirable research efforts, a phone call to the recruiting contact to ask some basic questions is an often

overlooked, yet very simple, first step. If you cannot obtain information regarding the job prior to the interview, you must ask about it during the first five minutes of your exchange. It will be awkward, but you must identify the job title and functional responsibilities early if you are to be successful projecting qualifications later. I can't tell how often students tried to "bluff" their way through a session when I was a recruiter. It was sad to be with someone who had talents but couldn't connect them to the position in question, because they didn't know what it was. When responding it is appropriate to begin with "Thinking about the job. . . ." Don't make this statement before *each* answer, but definitely think it!

○ **Cite by example and connect skills to job roles!**
Don't offer interviewers generalized skill statements (especially "I like to work with people") and expect that a connection will be made to your ability to perform job responsibilities. You must do that. Always be prepared to tell when you used particular skills to achieve specific goals. Whenever possible, without being overbearing, connect your talents to those required of the position. Don't hope that appropriate examples will arise spontaneously from your memory during an interview. Think about your employment, academic, and extracurricular achievements and write them down. Actually, it isn't a bad idea to review self-assessment exercises and be prepared to cite your five greatest skills, interests, and values.

○ **Refer to your resume!**
The one thing you definitely have in common with the interviewer is this document. Use phrases like "as you see on my resume" regularly during the session. This will allow him or her to mark (mentally or physically) the item and provide you a shared point of reference. Always read your resume before an interview. The interviewer will. Know why you put something on it and what you learned from each experience cited.

○ **Ask questions throughout, not just at the end when invited to do so!**
Interviewers often end sessions with "Do you have any questions?" You should! A lack of questions is interpreted as a lack of interest. Always have questions prepared to ask. But you can also ask them throughout the exchange. The best interviews are two-way conversations, not just question-and-answer sessions. If a question asked by a recruiter stimulates an inquiry, go for it. Ask about whether your skills match those required of the job after you've identified your greatest strengths. Ask whether case studies are ever used in training

after you've explained the courses you enjoyed most. Curiosity is always perceived positively. If questions addressed earlier will help you later, ask them. Always inquire regarding next steps and when you might hear. This will lessen anxiety associated with waiting and allow for some strategic planning.

○ **State "I want this job!"**
Recruiters do judge candidates' interest in the job. Make it easy. Say you want the job. Show a confident, yet appropriate, goal-directed attitude.

○ **Practice, practice, practice!**
Thinking about the consequences of your actions and how important an interview is won't make you more prepared or less anxious. Actions speak louder than words. Rehearsal, not memorizing answers, will magnify the volume and meaning of words you speak in the interview.

Now we'll analyze each scenario and address approaches to interviewing circumstances and questions.

SCENARIO I: CASUAL AND CREATIVE

☐ Don't be "thrown" by interview setting or interviewer style. Casual or formal doesn't matter. If you feel comfortable, take off your suit jacket or blazer and show that you "fit in." Or, simply, be yourself! Feel confident that everyone knows candidates dress up. Enjoy the fact that if you get an offer and eventually work in this environment, you'll wear jeans and a sweater and conduct business over brisk walks.

☐ Open-ended questions are not designed to trick you. Often, they are used as "ice-breakers" to relax candidates. Ironically, these inquiries tend to make them more nervous.

☐ Always keep in mind that you are "interviewing for a job with a company," not just "with a company." If you focus your thoughts and, ultimately, responses, on your skills to perform job-related tasks, you'll do great! Remember, you are interviewing for a job, a particular functional role, with specific responsibilities. Even answers to open-ended inquires can begin with "Thinking about why I'm here and the position I would like to have. . . ."

"Tell Me About Yourself."

There is no magical answer to this question, nor is it used to put a candidate off guard. In most cases it is asked to start things off casually, with as little pressure as possible. You can respond by focusing on why you are seeking the particular position. Begin with a phrase similar to the one above, or "Let me tell you about why I am so excited about being considered for a sales position with this firm." If the interviewer wants you to be more personal he or she will say so, reacting with "No, tell me what you like to do in your free time. What is your favorite hobby?" Interviewers will let you know if they want additional information. You can ask "Do you want me to tell you about my professional background or about my personal interests?" No matter the approach, speak freely and without hesitation. Relax, it's just a first question!

"What makes you tick?"

Another open-ended beauty! Again, the best approach involves staying functionally focused. Begin the answer with "What turns me on about this industry . . . and I'm most excited when I. . . ." Refer to past experiences when you have achieved something significant and received external as well as internal rewards. If you had completed Part A of this activity before the meeting (you should before each interview), you would have had three anecdotes ready to tell. Also, state "As noted on my resume. . . ." This will serve as a reference point and motivate the interviewer to circle or highlight the example. Show emotion. Be proud and enthusiastic, without being obnoxious. Follow your response with an inquiry, "How would I learn whether I'm doing a good job? Are there formal and informal feedback mechanisms; tangible and intangible rewards?" You don't have to wait for the interviewer to ask if you have any questions; just ask on. An interview is a two-way conversation, not an "I'll ask the questions and you give the answers" interrogation. Interviewers prefer exchanges.

"Sell me this pencil."

A typical question used on candidates considered for sales positions. The pencil may be a "notebook," or a "calculator," or anything handy, but your strategy remains the same. Don't just sell the pencil. Talk the interviewer through the sales process and relate it to the particular item. "First, I'll determine the customer's needs and uses for the product *(Please tell me when you use pencils and what you've liked or disliked about pencils you've used in the past)*. Second, I'll pinpoint what particular qualities, including cost, are most attractive to the customer by noting as many as I can think of and asking for responses. Then, I'll ask the customer to identify any I've missed *(So, as I note a particular quality of pencils in general could you tell me whether it is important or irrelevant to you).* Third, I'll realistically present the technical capabilities as well as limitations of the product, matching each to presented needs and quality priorities *(Now that you've told me how you use pencils, what you like about some and dislike about others, and what you think is important in a writing implement, let me tell you about this particular brand)."*

You may not wish to precede each statement with an analysis regarding the sales technique used, but don't be afraid to do so. Any interviewer who asks this question wants to see your sales style and how willing you are to be "in the spotlight." It is a bit of a personality assessment in addition to an interview question. Salespersons shouldn't be shy or easily embarrassed. Go along with it and have fun!

"What one word best describes you?"

Like all open-ended and quasi-creative questions, this one doesn't have one "correct" response, but several "good" ones. Don't think too much about you, but spontaneously a great deal about the job. Your answer should be "A word that could best describe the person holding the job I want is. . . ," with the first portion of this statement remaining silent and only the adjective spoken. Also, be prepared for the follow-up "why?" Connect elaboration to past achievements. Begin with "Because I once . . . ," or "I have always . . ." when clarifying your answer. Again, keep in mind that you are interviewing for a job with a company, not just with a company. Don't present "free-floating" qualities, skills, or adjectives. Anchor them firmly in the job description in question. Whenever possible give your answer and associate it to your capacity to perform job-related tasks. You are not going through psychoanalysis and the questioner really doesn't want to know about your deepest, darkest, or highest and brightest, philosophies of life. Stay focused.

"Who is your best friend and how would he or she describe you?"

Who your friend is and how this person would describe you isn't really the question. Answer this one as if it were "If you had this job, how would someone who knows you well assess your potential?" Or, think of the question as "I want to know more about your personality and whether it is suited for this job. How would you *honestly* characterize yourself?" As with the previous question, don't get too psychoanalytical. Frame your response with a sense of the qualities needed to succeed on the job. This is a chance to show that you know yourself, that you know the job, and that you can visualize yourself being fulfilled in the job and with the company (wearing jeans on occasion).

> *"Would anyone be surprised to hear that you are interviewing here for the job we're discussing? Who and why?"*

This is either another creative inquiry about your sense of focus or it could be an attempt to learn about your current employment circumstances. "Are you interviewing for a position very different from the one you hold? Are you breaking out of a typical career path? Would someone judge you as different from our corporate culture? Would your present employer (if you have one) be upset? Is it okay to contact someone regarding your background?" could all be questions behind this inquiry. Whatever way you interpret it, show the interviewer that you know what you want. No one will be surprised to hear that you are interviewing for a position that matches your skills and ambitions. This can be an opportunity to present references and a chance to reinforce research done prior to the interview. "In fact, I spoke to a few people in the industry about my plans and they encouraged me to go for it" may be a good way to begin your response. If you do wish to keep your interview confidential, not allowing your current employment to be negatively impacted, this is the time to say so. Otherwise, an interviewer may feel it is okay to contact a current employer.

○ Informal meetings, especially meals, are most often used to "get to know" a candidate. Let your "social self" shine, but remain business-like, as if lunching with a client or customer. Remember, people hire people who are qualified and whom they like, not just people who are qualified. Talk about whatever they want.

○ Don't push the conversation toward business, although you can try to do so once and see what happens. Be likable, yet professional. Enjoy meeting someone new, someone who has a job you would like. Enjoy the meal and conversation, especially if this behavior will be expected if you get the job.

○ Don't drink, unless you're interviewing for a position with a brewery, vineyard, or spirit distributor! It's just not a good idea. You won't be judged negatively if you just say no to a drink over lunch.

○ No matter the setting, whether walking through a tree-lined corporate campus or at lunch, what you say and how you behave will be judged. Don't be paranoid, but don't be too open or loose. Never put others down or be controversial.

○ Always project a positive attitude. Close an interview with an "I want this job" statement.

○ Also, always ask "When might I hear and what might next steps involve?" You don't want to anxiously await word without a sense of when it might arrive. Also, you can plan for follow-up actions.

○ A thank-you note can, and should, state that you want the job. It can seek clarification regarding next steps, but it's best to do so during an interview.

SCENARIO II: TRADITIONAL, TYPICAL, AND TOO SHORT

☐ On-campus interviews are best thought of as screening sessions, when recruiters meet with a great many candidates in order to identify those with greatest "potential." They are not intended to be lengthy, although they can seem that way to an anxious student; 25 to 30 minutes is the norm.

☐ Brief interviews should not be interpreted as failures or successes. It's quality of time spent with a recruiter, not quantity of time that counts.

☐ Use a thank-you note, personally delivered before the recruiter leaves campus, to express your sincere and enthusiastic desire to receive a callback. These "office or site visits" are when actual decisions are made. They regularly last an entire day and involve more than one interview, so you'll definitely not complain about these sessions being too short.

"Why do you want this job?"

Wow! A great opportunity to show commitment to a field and function, and, perhaps, a firm. Expressing focus early, beginning with a brief summary of skills (referring to this section of your perfect resume) is ideal. Answer what you can do for the job, not what it can do for you! Show that you have done homework and realistically understand the nature of the position. If not, present applicable skills and then seek clarification regarding responsibilities of the job. You can always connect the two later. "I'm interested in this position because of the skills I would use and because it will allow me to interact in settings that will allow me to succeed" might be a good lead statement. Show you know yourself as well as the job. Don't dwell too much on the fact that "you will teach me" or "the training program is ideal." The recruiter knows that. He or she doesn't know whether you can learn what they will teach or that you have the capabilities to successfully achieve beyond training. If you don't know a lot about the job, follow your general skills presentation with questions about the exact responsibilities. "Am I correct in assuming these skills would be used? What others would be important and how would I develop them?" are appropriate early interview inquiries.

"What made you choose your major?"

If your major is directly related, great! If not, don't become defensive. First tell the interviewer a bit about how you made the decision. Later, connect what you have learned to what will be expected of you on the job. No matter your major, you have developed particular skills that are applicable. The least of these are: the ability to learn large amounts of information quickly, yet accurately; good research and writing skills; and ease in making presentations and asking individuals for specific information. Don't dwell on this question unless the interviewer does. It isn't really critical in most cases.

"What are your greatest strengths and weaknesses?"

This is the most often asked question, yet the one that still causes the most anxiety. Simply answer "My greatest strengths for the job include. . . ." Do not present a generalized discussion of strengths or weaknesses. The best way to handle a weakness is to note one skill that is desirable, but you have not yet fully developed. Show that you realistically know what you have to work on. You can inquire regarding how you can strengthen these areas. Don't say your weakness is perfectionism! That's the most often stated answer and, as my daughter would say, " it is bogus." Use this opportunity to clearly and concisely present greatest strengths for the job and cite an area that could use some improvement. Don't dwell on the weakness or offer in-depth analysis why you didn't get around to taking an accounting (or any other) course. Show that you know what is required to do the job and that you have the quantitative aptitude to quickly learn accounting, or any other subject for that matter.

What are your greatest accomplishments and what roles did you play?

If I had a dollar each time a recruiter said "We want the best of the best. Campus leaders. Achievers," I would be able to give this book away instead of charging for it (just kidding). Honestly, there are only so many officeholders and so many people with GPAs in the top 10 percent. But, everyone gets a job if they work hard enough at it. Everyone has stories to tell about when they worked hard to reach a personal or group goal. Even if it was the time you didn't go skiing to spend the entire weekend studying for a final that you aced! That's a goal-directed story. Be prepared to tell a lot of these. Don't worry if you weren't the president of your club or group. You've achieved as a member of a class project team or as someone who has made good decisions and worked hard to reach your academic goals. As always, don't just cite achievements, present the skills you used to make things happen. If you can connect these skills to job requirements, fine, but don't push everything as job related. You may want to write down a list of achievements prior to interviewing.

Is your grade point average a true reflection of your academic abilities and success potential?

You knew it would be asked sooner or later. Leaving it off of your resume doesn't make the issue disappear. If your GPA is good, be proud and tell the recruiter "yes." If it isn't so good, be analytical and tell the recruiter which courses you did better in and why. Don't ever get defensive or apologetic. Prior to interviews, review your transcripts and calculate a major GPA and a GPA for Junior and Senior years. Don't hide anything or be deceptive. "I don't really know" is not acceptable. Everyone knows their grades. Be prepared to say "no" to the question, but be able to say when you did achieve in the classroom. It's not enough to say "I worked all through school and I would have had better grades if I had more free time to study." You want the interviewer to know that you were able to earn some A's and B's in spite of challenges you faced.

○ Don't overanalyze on-campus sessions. Fifteen minutes may be enough if you're clearly a strong candidate. Always do your best and follow up appropriately. Request reconsideration if you receive a "ding" letter.

○ Applications must be completed. Don't brush off an application because you don't want to take the time or because you think you don't have a chance with the company. For many organizations, an application is required to "formalize" a candidacy. If it's not done, you don't exist.

○ On-campus recruiting is not how most grads get jobs. It is convenient and a great way to get the metaphorical ball rolling, but it isn't the only way to reach job search goals. Most, if not all, college students should develop and implement a "self-recruiting strategy." Take the steps required to conduct an effective proactive search. They are outlined earlier and will be reviewed at the end of the book.

SCENARIO III: STRESSED TO THE MAX

☐ You'll eventually meet all kinds of interviewers, including "stressers." Some use this technique to determine if you can thrive within a stressful work setting. Others don't intend to use the approach, but they are just "stress inducers" (not really jerks).

☐ Almost assuredly, during a day-long callback or on-site visit you'll have one of these nightmare sessions. Day-long efforts, particularly those that involve testing, several interviews, and lunch can be anxiety provoking and tiring even without a stress interview. Keep your energy level and enthusiasm high throughout. When waiting, make notes about earlier sessions or draft thank-you notes. Do something to defuse the anger that naturally arises when anticipating a delayed interview.

☐ Don't ever blow your cool with anyone at any time! Remain poised and alert with administrative assistants as well as interviewers. Don't back away from responding to stressful interview questions, but don't be argumentative.

☐ Be consistent throughout your day. Think about earlier responses. Rephrase them and elaborate upon information cited. Use examples to support your claims. Project realistic knowledge of strengths as well as weaknesses. Don't try to convince the interviewer he or she is "wrong." Simply, and not so subtly, provide as much information as you can to support your claim that you can do the job.

"I don't know what I'm looking for, but you don't seem to have all of the experience I want. Why should I hire you?"

No matter the preface, "Why should I hire you?" is the basis of almost all interview inquiries. This is the ideal opportunity to highlight the job-specific skills you possess and, of course, to ask the interviewer what he or she is really looking for. If completed early in the session, subsequent answers can be linked to the interviewer's criteria listing. Don't argue about experience or try to convince someone that it doesn't matter. Cite as many achievements as you can and, if appropriate, note that you've spoken with some very successful young salespersons and that you really do know what would be required to achieve goals. Don't compare yourself to unknown competitors for the job. Hypothetical comparisons with "those with more experience" or "internal candidates" could prove difficult and ineffective. Focus on yourself. Refer to your resume when making points. This written document is tangible proof of your capabilities.

> *What makes you think you can handle a job that requires so many different talents and persuasive skills?*

Retell anecdotes used earlier. You don't have to think up new ones. In fact, each session should have the same themes and illustrations. Repetition in this circumstance is very reinforcing. Prove by example that you have what it takes. Tell about how you once sold a pencil to an interviewer and share your approaches to persuasive sales. If the job requires different talents and sales skills, show that you are multitalented and persuasive. Again, cite as many achievements as you can. Be proud and show enthusiasm for past accomplishments. Show that you are a goal-driven person.

> *You didn't seem to excel in the classroom. What makes you so sure you'll do well on the job?*

Typically this arises if you left GPA off of your resume. As noted earlier, if it isn't so good, be analytical and tell the recruiter which courses you did better in and why. Don't be defensive or apologetic. Cite major GPA and a GPA for Junior and Senior years if above 3.0. Use "letters" instead of numerical references. For some reason GPAs seem low if they aren't above 3.5, but letter grades sound better. Think about it. Which sounds better "B minus" or "2.8?" Don't hide anything or be deceptive. Again, it's not enough to say "I worked all through school and I would have had better grades if I had more free time to study." Tell the interviewer that you were able to pull some A's and B's. If you have a few years of experience and left GPA off because it wasn't appropriate, say so. Be ready to cite what it was (if good) and focus your response on your work-related report cards, performance reviews, or bonuses. The interviewer wants to know what motivates you to achieve, whether you work to gain specific recognition.

> *Why don't you want to stay with your current (or previous) employer or why don't they want you?*

When discussing why you want the job, don't identify negatives about your current or previous employer. Focus on all of the things that are attractive about the position in question. State "this is what I really want to do now" and realistically analyze how serving in these capacities is the logical next career step. If you want, project beyond the current position to future responsibilities and rewards, but stay focused on why the job "fits." This question can also be perceived and addressed as: "Is there something about your current situation I should know?" While most like to hire people who already have jobs and are cautious when considering unemployed candidates, all are curious about why you would leave your current situation. Again, focus on what the new firm and function can offer, not on any negatives regarding past or present circumstances. If you are unemployed, concisely tell current status and reasons behind your not having a job. Being laid-off isn't so bad if you are prepared to tell what you learned from the experience and if you can show how it motivated you to seek this position. If you want your interviewing activities to be confidential so as not to jeopardize current employment, say so. People bold enough to conduct stress interviews may be bold enough to contact a current employer. State "If you wish to make my offer contingent upon a positive reference from my current employer, fine. Make the offer first, then I'll be happy to have you contact my employer." Or, inform the interviewer that "references from persons who are aware of my abilities are available if you wish."

Why didn't you major in business? Couldn't you handle it?

Don't let this one get you defensive either. All interviewers know that academic majors don't equate with career success. If posed in a nicer style, this question would be "Why did you select your major and do you feel a lack of business courses could hamper your performance?" Focus on your ability to learn applicable information, not on your academic major. Tell about a circumstance when you were required to incorporate a business concept or better, a business skill into your daily responsibilities. Don't dwell on how hard it was to get business classes at your school or on who was allowed to major in what. Project a confidence in your capacity to learn. Proudly tell of lessons you learned in the "real world."

Didn't you have concerns about working with those you've already met?

Don't say anything negative about anyone you met during the day-long session, even if tempted to do so. They will, if all goes well, be the people you work with. Always, especially during stress-filled interviews, remain positive and upbeat.

○ Even if you don't really want to, write thank-you notes to everyone you met, including the stresser. State that you want the job and that you would welcome further discussions if required. Show that you weren't ruffled. Fax, hand deliver, or express mail for immediate delivery.

○ Don't complain too much to too many, although it is okay to vent with a significant other. Don't make subtle comments to others. Wait until you have received an offer to share your uneasiness and investigate the situation. You never know when feedback finds its way to persons making employment decisions.

○ Post-offer analysis is critical when you've experienced a stress interview! After an offer is received, arrange another visit. Speak with everyone you met earlier. Diplomatically share your stressful experience. Solicit information regarding whether stress inducement is the person's everyday style or whether he or she merely uses it as an interview technique. Seek from the stresser positive indications that you will be welcomed and that he or she believes you are right for the job.

INTERVIEW READINESS INDICATOR STUDY TIPS FOR THE RETEST (ACTION STEPS TO TAKE)

✎ Complete the *Do-it-With-a-Friend Roleplay Interview* exercise (later in the chapter) at least twice. Practice doesn't really make perfect, but it will make you pretty darn close to it. It brings to short-term memory all of the information you want to have at the tip of your tongue.

✎ Using information available at a college career services office, contact three recruiters and ask their favorite three interview questions. Now you will have a total of nine questions to think about and, if you really want to improve, use them in your next attempt at the *Do-it-With-a-Friend* exercise.

✎ Review the list of most common on-campus questions and note the three you find most "confusing" or "anxiety provoking." Discuss them with a career services professional. Examine different ap-

proaches and how you feel most comfortable addressing the particular inquiries. Also, use these three questions during your next
version of *Do-it-With-a-Friend.*

✎   Complete Part A of this assessment each time you have an interview!
Enter the exact job and note three key points, three anecdotes, and
three questions on the back of a copy of your resume. Remember,
this exercise creates study notes for the open-book verbal exam that
is an interview. Take these notes into the interview with you, but be
very subtle when you refer to your notes. You want to be "natural,"
not prepackaged or programmed. You do want to be "dressed for
success," metaphorically and literally; confident and prepared. After
appropriate preparation you'll never feel naked!!!

INTERVIEW READINESS INDICATOR HELPFUL RESOURCES (PEOPLE, PLACES, AND THINGS)

✔   You guessed it! College and university career services facilities offer
both live and videotaped roleplay. Locate and use these services.
Roleplaying is the very best way to diminish interview anxiety and
enhance interview effectiveness.

✔   Books you may want to examine include: *101 Great Answers to the
Toughest Interview Questions*, Career Press, 1991; *Sweaty Palms:
The Neglected Art of Being Interviewed*, Ten Speed Press, 1990;
Knock Em' Dead: The Ultimate Job Seeker's Handbook, Bob Adams,
1993; and *Successful Interviewing for College Seniors*, VGM Career
Horizons, 1992. While you might read contrasting views and,
perhaps, contradictory recommendations, reading about interviewing can be helpful. Remember, don't memorize answers or try to
develop a "technique" designed to make all interviews a game with
winners and losers. Interviews are very special conversations with a
particular purpose (getting an offer). They are not games. Practice,
not necessarily reading, will improve your interview skills.

✔   Camcorders have made it convenient to tape roleplay efforts. Even if
you do it alone, complete the *Do-it-With-a-Friend* exercise, video-
tape your responses, and study the playback. As mentioned earlier,
don't worry about your head position or count your "uh's." The
bigger picture, what you are saying and how focused you are, is most
important.

Do-it-With-a-Friend Roleplay Interview

Have a friend (or family member), acting as an interviewer, ask the following questions and judge your responses via the criteria listed. Before the interview "set the scene," determining the organization and position you are interviewing for. After completing the exercise with these questions, have your friend replace them with others and repeat it.

QUESTIONS	RESPONSES	YES	NO
What are your job-related goals?	• realistic goals, clearly defined	___	___
	• too general	___	___
	• too specific	___	___
What background and qualifications do you have to enable you to succeed in this kind of job, with our organization?	• cited examples	___	___
	• referred to resume	___	___
	• demonstrated understanding of required skills and abilities	___	___
What are your most significant accomplishments in work or school?	• demonstrated analytical abilities	___	___
	• related events to employment goal	___	___
What did you like most and least about previous work experiences	• communicated ideas clearly	___	___
	• demonstrated analytical abilities	___	___
	• elaborated on resume information	___	___
	• related past to position in question	___	___
Why should I hire you?	• provided direction to open-ended question	___	___
	• was enthusiastic and assertive	___	___
	• summarized qualifications well	___	___
	• cited demonstrated use of skills	___	___

OVERALL EVALUATION AND COMMENTS
Did the candidate give clear and concise answers?
Did the candidate demonstrate effective body language and eye contact?
What might the candidate do to improve?

OVERALL EVALUATION AND COMMENTS
Did the candidate give clear and concise answers?
Did the candidate demonstrate effective body language and eye contact?
What might the candidate do to improve?

Interview Evaluation Form

This is a composite of forms interviewers use to judge candidates. Now that you know what they are looking for, you can prepare appropriately. You can also use it to evaluate your roleplay interview performance.

COMMUNICATION SKILLS
States ideas clearly

10	1
outstanding	poor

Uses interesting and varied word choices

10	1
outstanding	poor

Speaks in complete and organized sentences

10	1
outstanding	poor

Has good eye contact

10	1
outstanding	poor

QUALIFICATIONS
Has necessary degree/academic requirements

10	1
outstanding	poor

Has relevant work experience

10	1
outstanding	poor

GPA/Professional accomplishments

10	1
outstanding	poor

INTERPERSONAL EFFECTIVENESS
Relaxed and friendly

10	1
outstanding	poor

Social mannerisms pleasant and appropriate

10	1
outstanding	poor

Handles variety of questions without becoming rattled

10	1
outstanding	poor

PREPARATION FOR INTERVIEW
Researched employer and position

10	1
outstanding	poor

Asked pertinent and relevant questions

10	1
outstanding	poor

SUMMARY COMMENTS AND RECOMMENDATIONS:

SELF CONFIDENCE
Sells sell well

10	1
outstanding	poor

Adequately and sincerely inquisitive

10	1
outstanding	poor

Outgoing and confidence of abilities

10	1
outstanding	poor

DIRECTION
Has well-defined goals

10	1
outstanding	poor

Demonstrates goal analysis is ongoing

10	1
outstanding	poor

SOCIABILITY
Enthusiastic

10	1
outstanding	poor

High energy level

10	1
outstanding	poor

Personality creates positive impression

10	1
outstanding	poor

Presents appropriate and positive image

10	1
outstanding	poor

OVERALL EVALUATION
Overall performance verbal

10	1
outstanding	poor

Overall performance behavioral

10	1
outstanding	poor

Most Common On-campus Interview Questions

The following is a list of typical questions originally compiled by Dr. Frank Endicott of Northwestern University. Do not memorize answers. The questions will make you aware of your qualifications and how you can present them to an interviewer. There are no "right" answers. Interviewers do not look for specific answers to particular questions. They are interested in how you respond and qualities projected via responses.

1. What are your long-range and short-range goals and objectives, when and why did you establish these goals, and how are you prepared to achieve them?
2. What specific goals, other than those related to your occupation, do you have for the next ten years?
3. What do you see yourself doing five years from now?
4. What do you really want to do in life?
5. What are your long-range career objectives?
6. How do you plan to achieve your career goals?
7. What are the most important rewards you expect in your career?
8. What do you expect to be earning in five years?
9. Why did you choose the career for which you are preparing?
10. Which is more important to you, the money or the type of job?
11. What do you consider to be your greatest strengths and weaknesses?
12. How would you describe yourself?
13. How do you think a friend or a professor who knows you well would describe you?
14. What motivates you to put forth the greatest effort?
15. How has your education prepared you for a career?
16. Why should I hire you?
17. What qualifications do you have that make you think you will be successful?
18. How do you determine or evaluate success?
19. What do you think it takes to be successful in a company like ours?
20. In what ways do you think you can make a contribution to our company?
21. What qualities should a successful manager possess?
22. Describe the relationship that should exist between a supervisor and subordinates?
23. What two or three accomplishments have given you the most satisfaction? Why?
24. Describe your most rewarding college experience.
25. If you were hiring a graduate for this position, what qualities would you look for?
26. Why did you select your college or university?
27. What led you to choose your field of major study?
28. What academic subjects did you like best? Least?
29. Do you enjoy doing independent research?
30. If you could do so, would you plan your academic study differently?

31. What changes would you make in your college or university?
32. Do you think that your grades are a good indication of your academic achievement?
33. What have you learned from participation in extracurricular activities?
34. Do you have plans for continued study? Graduate students: Why did you pursue an advanced degree?
35. In what kind of work environment are you most comfortable?
36. How do you work under pressure?
37. In what part-time or summer job have you been most interested? Why?
38. How would you describe the ideal job for you following graduation?
39. Why did you decide to seek a position with this company?
40. What do you know about our company?
41. What two or three things are most important to you in your job?
42. Are you seeking employment in a company of a certain size? Why?
43. What criteria are you using to evaluate the company for which you hope to work?
44. Do you have a geographic preference?
45. Will you relocate? Does relocation bother you?
46. Are you willing to travel?
47. Are you willing to spend at least six months as a trainee?
48. Why do you think you might like to live in the community in which our company is located?
49. What major problem have you encountered and how did you deal with it?
50. What have you learned from your mistakes?

There are questions interviewers should *not* ask because of Equal Employment Opportunity regulations. You still should be prepared to respond appropriately. These questions involve information about: marital status, family plans or number of children, child care, physical data, criminal record (unless security clearance is involved), religion, race, ownership of home, spouse's occupation, and maiden name. Consult with a counselor for specific advice regarding these inquiries.

INTERVIEW READINESS INDICATOR
STUDY SKILLS SUMMARY

- Assessed readiness for employment interviews.
- Presented scenarios with analyses following.
- Noted practice techniques and guidelines.
- Demystified the process of interviewing.

CHAPTER 8

Phone, Fax, and Voice Mail Etiquette Exam

The basic premise of this book is that college students and grads have the ability to transform study skills into effective job search skills with a few simple motivational and subtle behavioral modifications. While this is true (or I wouldn't have written the book), some critical skills are really not developed or practiced in the classroom or academic settings.

Phone skills, while a part of everyone's college survival repertoire, are most frequently used and nurtured in social or extracurricular contexts. You regularly call to arrange group or personal "meetings" (I hear the phrase "date" is not "campus correct"); with social calls very difficult for most. You occasionally call faculty members with questions or to make appointments; yet many confess this seems very awkward. You all too frequently (yet easily) call home for more money! Wouldn't it be great if you perceived job search–related calls to be as easy as the ones you make to mom and dad? They can be if you spend as much time planning and practicing as you do when you really, really want a parent to say "yes" to a special request for funds. Seriously, you've had years of practice asking for things from parents and relatively little, if any, practice asking for job search consideration.

Fax skills, because this technical capability has only recently become publicly accessible, are possessed by few. How many have used these magic boxes to send facsimile copies anywhere? Probably not as many as you think, but the number is growing daily. I encourage job seekers to use this resource more and more. While I don't recommend buying one (yet), I do recommend you locate a fax you can send and receive from, and learn how to use this device.

Voice mail (or phone message) skills have become increasingly a part of everyone's business and personal lives. Who can you call without the potential of "leaving a message at the beep?" We now feel comfortable calling friends at unusual hours, confident that "the machine will get it," and we feel comfortable leaving home when expecting important calls, because "the machine will get it." But we still think that business calls can only be made from 9 A.M. to 5 P.M. I would suggest you contact employers *whenever* you find the time in your busy schedule. It really is chronologically and psychologically demanding to have academic, extracurricular, and job search responsibilities.

Because of limited natural development, it is critical to consiously and conscienciously nurture the above mentioned capabilities. Ironically, they are often ignored by career services professionals. Perhaps because behaviors associated with these skill areas are, to say the least, "awkward for those who are not assertive," counselors do not feel comfortable training job seekers to take appropriate action. Well not this Job Search Coach and not this book! Reviewing the *Phone, Fax, and Voice Mail Etiquette Exam,* on page 185 and subsequent information will serve as a good start to learning these most vital of job search skills.

Information is not presented as "techniques" (tricks used to overcome obstacles), but as response-able actions to take when responding to job search circumstances. You must be the most effective communicator possible if you are to be the most effective job seeker you can be. Avoiding seemingly awkward actions, those that make you feel uncomfortable, means you might be avoiding success! The more you use the phone, fax, or voice mail, the more comfortable you will feel.

This exercise assesses your knowledge of Phone, Fax, and Voice Mail etiquette and rates your comfort with potential actions. Review each statement. Check whether you believe the action suggested is best charactarized as a "Don't" or a "Do." If you think it is something that should be done regularly (a "Do"), note how comfortable you are with undertaking that action.

		DON'T	DO	No Problem!	Maybe ?	No Way!
				COMFORT SCALE		
P H O N E	☎ Call even when a posting states "no calls."	❑	❑	❑	❑	❑
	☎ When making first calls, use another name and say you're writing a college paper to avoid looking foolish or uninformed.	❑	❑	❑	❑	❑
	☎ Keep calling until you speak with your "target person" or the "key decision maker."	❑	❑	❑	❑	❑
	☎ Call early in the morning to improve chances of getting through to the desired person.	❑	❑	❑	❑	❑
	☎ Whenever possible, conduct a quick information conversation.	❑	❑	❑	❑	❑
	☎ Have a resume and copies of all related correspondence in front of you when calling.	❑	❑	❑	❑	❑
	☎ Call prior to sending cover letters and resumes to identify proper person(s).	❑	❑	❑	❑	❑
	☎ Follow up all correspondence with calls.	❑	❑	❑	❑	❑
	☎ Prepare a script or outline prior to calling.	❑	❑	❑	❑	❑
	☎ Ask whomever you speak with if you can arrange a meeting with your targeted contact.	❑	❑	❑	❑	❑
	☎ Wait by your phone for at least two hours after leaving a mesage with a receptionist.	❑	❑	❑	❑	❑
F A X	✆ Fax all resumes no matter the circumstance.	❑	❑	❑	❑	❑
	✆ Fax when responding to all postings.	❑	❑	❑	❑	❑
	✆ After faxing a resume and cover letter ("fax cover page"), send original in mail.	❑	❑	❑	❑	❑
	✆ Fax polite notes when you are having trouble reaching someone by phone.	❑	❑	❑	❑	❑
	✆ Fax all thank-you notes.	❑	❑	❑	❑	❑
	✆ Use cute fax covers to get attention.	❑	❑	❑	❑	❑
	✆ Fax messages over and over again until you get a phone response.	❑	❑	❑	❑	❑
	✆ Fax late at night for better rates and so it will be on recipient's desk in the morning.	❑	❑	❑	❑	❑
V O I C E M A I L	✉ Use funny messages on your answering machine to show creativity.	❑	❑	❑	❑	❑
	✉ Call after hours, in case someone is working late and in order to leave a message.	❑	❑	❑	❑	❑
	✉ Provide three-to-five minute summary of your resume when leaving initial message.	❑	❑	❑	❑	❑
	✉ Follow messages with fax notes.	❑	❑	❑	❑	❑
	✉ Wait by the phone after leaving a message.	❑	❑	❑	❑	❑
	✉ Leave your name and phone number even if you don't expect a return call.	❑	❑	❑	❑	❑
	✉ Identify your next action ("call later today") and what you would like recipient to do ("please call between noon and 1 P.M.").	❑	❑	❑	❑	❑

Review the answer key to determine how well you did.

PHONE, FAX, AND VOICE MAIL ETIQUIETTE EXAM
ANNOTATED ANSWER KEY

☎ **Call even when a posting states "no calls."**

Don't follow up with a call if a posting states "no calls," but do mail or fax two quick follow-up notes two and five days after sending initial corre- spondence. In this way you reinforce interest and, because you include a copy of the original letter and resume with each follow-up note, you gain additional reviews of your credentials. This approach has proven very successful with so-called "blind ads" that typically appear in classified sections. Also, you can call ahead to confirm fax numbers or determine whom to address a letter to, but keep the call very direct and brief.

☎ **When making first calls, use another name and say you're writing a college paper to avoid looking foolish or uninformed.**

Don't ever use a false name or in any way try to deceive a potential employer. It's okay to be uninformed at first and ask basic questions. Don't be embarrassed. Asking clear and direct questions, no matter how simple, is always appropriate, by telephone or in person. It is a great idea to combine academic projects with job search–related research, but you should never lie when seeking information. If you are conducting academic research, say so. If not, state that you are "research- ing prospective employers and would like some basic information."

☎ **Keep calling until you speak with your "target person" or the "key decision maker."**

Don't be a pest. It is okay to follow up with a brief fax or mailed note, but don't be too pushy. Assertive follow up is critical, but you can take "no" for an answer and still take appropriate next steps. You can communicate with more than one person in a particular organization, but don't get carried away. Be direct, inquisitive, and polite, and know why you are calling. If conducting initial cold calls to confirm whom you should write to, you don't need to speak with your target person. If following up initial correspondence, someone other than a targeted person may be able to help.

☎ **Call early in the morning to improve chances of getting through to the desired person.**

Do call early, as well as late. Most organizations have voice mail or message systems, so you can conduct your phone work whenever you have time. Yes, it is best to call during standard business hours, and many suggest that earlier is ideal. You might get someone before daily events have piled up and you will have the rest of the day to call back or receive a return call (8 to 9:30 A.M. seems a best bet). Of course, a quick fax note might facilitate the process.

☎ **Whenever possible, conduct a quick information conversation.**

Do take opportunities to learn about the background of people you speak with. Preface inquiries with "I hope you don't think me too pushy, but can I ask you some quick questions about your background and about your experiences with the company?" Ask simple questions like, "How long have you worked for the company?" "What are the nature of entry-level jobs in a particular area?" and "What exactly should I do if I want my resume reviewed by the right person?" Be brief and appreciative. A few quick answers, followed by a thank-you note, can begin an effective relationship. If you sense it appropriate, you can ask to arrange a more formal 15-to-30-minute information conversation.

☎ **Have a resume and copies of all related correspondence in front of you when calling.**

Do have your thoughts as well as previous communiqués organized. If you are lucky, or proficient, enough to get through to a targeted person, you should be able to concisely refer to previous actions and to your background. Because a brief employment interview may occur, it's always best to have your resume and correspondence available.

☎ **Call prior to sending cover letters and resumes to identify proper person(s).**

Do call to identify proper persons. It's easy to get the name and address, as well as fax number from a receptionist. Just be prepared and ask for exactly what you want . Don't beat around the proverbial bush. Also, don't expect to conduct a cold call employment interview. You may have the opportunity to say a few things about your background, but you won't be given more than a few minutes.

☎ **Follow up all correspondence with calls.**

Do follow all correspondence with calls and, just as important, all calls with correspondence or fax messages. Alternating communication techniques, and taking appropriate time between communiqués, will lessen the chances of your appearing too pushy.

☎ **Prepare a script or outline prior to calling.**

Do use them to ease anxiety and organize thoughts. Write down your questions before calls or in-person meetings. Phone communiqués and interviews are open-book tests. You can look at your notes!

☎ **Ask whomever you speak with if you can arrange a meeting with your targeted contact.**

Do ask for an interview. Who knows? You might just get what you want. Face-to-face communication is your ultimate goal. Ask if it is possible to set up an employment interview or an information conversation.

☎ **Wait by your phone for at least two hours after leaving a message with a receptionist.**

Don't wait, unless you said you would. Have a message machine attached to your phone so you can return calls. Waiting doesn't accomplish anything.

✆ **Fax all resumes no matter the circumstance.**

Don't fax all resumes, but do feel comfortable faxing most. Don't worry about it not appearing "pretty" or showing the quality of paper used. Note that originals will follow later by mail. A faxed resume and cover note appears almost immediately at someone's office and soon thereafter on his or her desk. You can conduct phone follow up on the same day without wondering "did it get there?"

✆ **Fax when responding to all postings.**

Do fax whenever you can identify a fax number. Send a brief note and your resume immediately, but follow with a lengthier cover letter and resume by mail. Receiving a mailed communiqué does ensure that someone will review your materials for a second time. As with almost all job search efforts, don't expect one communication to be enough and don't think one way alone will be magic. If you fax, you follow with a letter, then a call.

✆ **After faxing a resume and cover letter ("fax cover page"), send original in mail.**

Do just that! Isn't that what I said in the previous comment? Show reviewers that you know what's correct, that your resume is on appropriate paper, and give them a chance to give you a second look.

✆ **Fax polite notes when you are having trouble reaching someone by phone.**

Do follow up with difficult-to-reach persons using fax notes. They'll be received immediately and they might stimulate a response. Don't get carried away. Once you've faxed and called again, be patient. Give the person a reasonable chance to respond. If you still have trouble after about a week, write and mail a note clearly describing your purposes, then be very patient. Of course, enclose a copy of your resume.

✆ **Fax all thank-you notes.**

Do so if you want to impact the process quickly and effectively. Hand delivering notes or using express mail also works, but faxing can be more convenient. Remember to state you want the job or, at the very least, that you want to take next steps.

✆ **Use cute fax covers to get attention.**

Don't do it unless you are very confident that it won't offend anyone. I know many companies use them and I even have one with a caricature of my handsome profile, but it is always best to be conservative (no political implications intended, Rush). Cute may get you in trouble.

✆ **Fax messages over and over again until you get a phone response.**

Don't. *Don't. Don't. Don't. Don't. Being a pest never pays. Being a pest never pays. Being a pest never pays. It's obnoxious. See what I mean?*

✆ **Fax late at night for better rates and so it will be on recipient's desk in the morning.**

Do *fax whenever it is convenient and save money if you can. It is a good idea to follow up late-night faxes with phone calls between 8 and 9 A.M. You might get to speak with someone before the demands of the day have begun. Again, this is not a "technique," it is just another approach you might use.*

✉ **Use funny messages on your answering machine to show creativity.**

Don't *ever risk turning anyone off. In fact, you should change your message now if it is a bit too creative.*

✉ **Call after hours, in case someone is working late and in order to leave a message.**

Do *call whenever you have time, even if it is after 5 P.M. Most people stay well beyond the traditional 9 to 5 timeframe and you might get to speak with someone important. Also, in most cases a voice mail message can be left. Don't ever put off a follow-up call, even if you think it's too late to call. Give it a try. Also a fax follow up noting why you were calling could be very effective.*

✉ **Provide three-to-five-minute summary of your resume when leaving initial message.**

Don't *make it that long. Briefly describe why you are calling and remind the person of your background ("I'm the UOP student with the experience in real estate"). Make your intentions clear, stating what you want to happen next. Note that you will call again or ask (politely) for the person to return your call.*

✉ **Follow messages with fax notes.**

Do *just that! Didn't I already suggest you do so? This can be a powerful way of reminding someone of your background via your resume and the brief, yet direct message.*

✉ **Wait by the phone after leaving a message.**

Don't *wait, unless you have cover letters to write or other job search tasks to complete at home. You should have your own message* *machine. This is a must job search support device. Also, there are always more important things to do than wait.*

☒ **Leave your name and phone number even if you don't expect a return call.**

Do so even if you don't think they will call back. It's the polite thing to do. I hate to hear silence when I 'm retrieving voice mail messages. You never know, especially if you do follow with another call and eventually with a mailed or faxed note. You may receive that return call.

☒ **Identify your next action ("call later today") and what you would like recipient to do ("please call between noon and 1 P.M.").**

Do so, definitely! A vague message doesn't get results. In any form of communication, you must identify what you would like to happen or, better, what you will do next. You can control only your actions. Keep communicating and keep working toward your job search goals.

Even if you did well on this exam, correctly identifying do's and don'ts, you must feel comfortable undertaking the actions involved. Saying it's right doesn't make it so. It's easy for me to write that you should call, but many find the phone an uncomfortable communication device. In this case, as in many others, practice does indeed make perfect, so you should discuss which skills you would like to enhance with a career services professional or with a friend. Roleplaying phone conversations can be fun, and it definitely improves your phone skills. The telephone and fax are perhaps the most underutilized job search devices. Don't think that written communiqués are enough. They aren't!

More and more students and alumni are inquiring regarding the use of e-mail as a communication option. At present it isn't as commonplace as the fax machine, but many hi-tech firms do employ modem-accessible message systems. If you know how to use these, do so. Some telenet systems also have job postings through "electronic bulletin boards." In truth, any approach to sending or receiving job search messages can prove valuable. Don't be afraid to boldly go where no job seeker has gone before (thanks to Star Trek for that metaphorical reference).

PHONE, FAX, AND VOICE MAIL ETIQUETTE EXAM
STUDY TIPS FOR THE RETEST (ACTION STEPS TO TAKE)

✎ Review the *Start Now Script Samples* on the following pages to prepare a telephone script for use when calling an employer. Use copies of the template on page 192 to plan an actual call to a potential employer.

✎ Locate a fax machine you can use (for a fee or for free). Establishments like Kinko's typically offer fax services. College offices (career services and others) allow you to use a fax on occasion. Also, if a relative or friend ever asks "Is there anything I can do to help?," respond with an inquiry regarding whether you can use a fax machine in their office. Be inquisitive and creative, yet appreciative, but find a fax.

✎ Roleplay several phone calls with a friend or counselor. The more you practice, the better. Ask your partner to act as friendly or as challenging as possible. The more diverse your roleplay circumstances the better prepared you will be for real situations.

PHONE, FAX, AND VOICE MAIL ETIQUETTE EXAM
HELPFUL RESOURCES (PEOPLE, PLACES, AND THINGS)

✔ Anyone willing to practice with you or provide fax accessibility is a wonderful resource. Use them!

✔ Books you may want to examine include: *The Perfect Follow-up Method to Get the Job,* Wiley, 1992; and *Guerrilla Tactics in the New Job Market,* Bantam, 1991.

SCRIPT SAMPLE: BLANK TEMPLATE

Use a copy of this document when creating your own phone scripts or outlines.

Say "hello" and acknowledge (and note) the name of the person you are speaking with.	
Tell why you are calling and whom you wish to speak with. **T**ell about previous communications if a follow-up call.	
Assess status of application or consideration process. Assertively focus on identifying appropriate next steps.	
Request an appointment for an employment interview or information conversation. **R**equest a suggestion for next steps or for a referral.	
Thank the person you are speaking with and confirm spelling of all names, addresses, phone and fax numbers.	
Never be impolite, impatient, or pushy. You can always call back or send mail or fax note later if you don't get results.	
On-target conversations get the very best results, so stay focused and know what you want.	
Whenever possible ask to arrange a telephone or in-person employment interview or information conversation, or ask to speak with someone "who can tell me a bit about entry-level jobs." **W**rite and mail or fax a thank-you note.	

START NOW

While your scripts will contain notes concerning what you would like to say, the following samples identify potential responses of people you might speak with. Every call may not go as positively as these, nor as negatively as you might think, so keep using and developing your phone skills. Once you have written scripts, you should roleplay conversations with a friend or counselor. Writing something down is very different from saying it. Don't appear to a listener as if you are reading your script. Your conversation should be as natural as possible (given that you will be nervous).

SCRIPT SAMPLE II: INITIAL COLD CALL

S	**S**ay "hello" and acknowledge (and note) the name of the person you are speaking with.	○ Hello, my name is Ivana B. Astar. Whom am I speaking with? ❑ *Teri. May I help you?* ○ Yes, Teri, your last name please? Thank you.
T	**T**ell why you are calling and whom you wish to speak with. **T**ell about previous communications if a follow-up call.	○ I understand that your organization offers a wonderful executive training program. Is that right? Well, I would like to speak with someone to learn a bit more about it and confirm to whom I should send my resume. ❑ *We do have an ETP, but someone in personnel will have to speak with you about it. I'll forward you there.* ○ Before you do, is there anyone specifically I should ask for? ❑ *No, whoever answers should be able to help.*
A	**A**ssess status of application or consideration process. Assertively focus on identifying appropriate next steps.	○ Hello. My name is Ivana B. Astar. I'm about to graduate from University of the Pacific and I am very, very interested in a retailing career. Is someone available to answer a few questions about your training program? Also, I would like to confirm whom I should send my resume to and what steps I should take. ❑ *No one is available now, but I can send you some materials.* ○ I'm sorry for being so impolite. I forgot to ask your name. Oh, Jordan. Written materials would be great. Would it be possible to pick them up?. ❑ *I guess it would be okay.*
R	**R**equest an appointment for an employment interview or information conversation. **R**equest a suggestion for next steps or for a referral.	○ When I stop by do you think it would be appropriate to have an information conversation with someone in your office? I have a few questions about the program and I do want to learn exactly what steps I should take. ❑ *It depends on who's around when you stop by.* ○ Well, you've been great. Before I hang up, is there a particular person to whom I should address my correspondence?
T	**T**hank the person you are speaking with and confirm spelling of all names, addresses, phone and fax numbers.	○ Does Ms. Meta Decision have a fax number and do you think it would be okay to send her a brief fax note and my resume? Thanks so much. You were very, very helpful.
N	**N**ever be impolite, impatient, or pushy. You can always call back or send mail or fax note later if you don't get results.	*Ivana handled this conversation perfectly. She was pleasant with both persons and maintained a positive tone.*
O	**O**n-target conversations get the very best results, so stay focused and know what you want.	*Ivana stayed very much on target. She asked for what she wanted and got as much information as was available given the circumstances.*
W	**W**henever possible ask to arrange a telephone or in-person employment interview or information conversation, or ask to speak with someone "who can tell me a bit about entry-level jobs." **W**rite and mail or fax a thank-you note.	*Ivana asked for all appropriate options. She didn't ask Jordan for more information about the program because she planned on visiting the office. A thank-you note to Jordan and a brief letter of introduction to Ms. Decision will be faxed prior to the visit to pick up materials. This will be followed by a more detailed cover letter.*

SCRIPT SAMPLE III: FIRST FOLLOW UP

Say "hello" and acknowledge (and note) the name of the person you are speaking with.	○ Hello, my name is Justin Timetohire. Whom am I speaking with? ❏ Mary. May I help you? ○ Yes, Mary, your last name please? Thank you.
Tell why you are calling and whom you wish to speak with. **T**ell about previous communications if a follow-up call.	○ Mary, is Mr. Yuri Mean Recruiter available? ❏ Let me see if he's available. Why are you calling? ○ I recently wrote Mr. Recruiter and I want to confirm that he received my letter and clarify what I should do next. ❏ Let me forward you to his assistant.
Assess status of application or consideration process. **A**ssertively focus on identifying appropriate next steps.	❏ Mr. Recruiter's office, this is Billy, may I help you? ○ Billy, my name is Justin Timetohire and I recently wrote Mr. Recruiter regarding a sales position. Could I speak with him about the status of my candidacy? ❏ Yes we did receive the letter. I'll see if Mr. Recruiter is available. He'll speak with you, please hold.
Request an appointment for an employment interview or information conversation. **R**equest a suggestion for next steps or for a referral.	❏ Yuri Mean Recruiter here. Who are you and what do you want? ○ Hello, Mr. Recruiter, this is Justin Timetohire. I'm the UOP Senior who worked for Shoesource as a salesperson, and I wanted to follow up on a letter I recently wrote regarding a sales position with your firm. I would very much like to meet with you to discuss my qualifications. Would that be possible? ❏ I'm not sure yet who I'll invite in for interviews, but your resume is still under consideration. Please be patient for a week or so. ○ I understand. I really do want to meet with you or one of your staff. Is there any way to arrange even a preliminary interview now? I've got all Thursday and all morning on Friday free. ❏ No. That's not appropriate. I understand how enthusiastic you are, but let's wait until I've had a little more time to review all of the resumes and letters. You might be one of those called in. ○ I hope so. Before I hear, is there anything I should do, perhaps speak with a salesperson to learn more about the position? ❏ No, just be patient. Thank you.
Thank the person you are speaking with and confirm spelling of all names, addresses, phone and fax numbers.	○ Mr. Recruiter, thank you very much. I do hope I have a chance to meet with you sometime soon, because I really do want to interview for the sales position. If you would give me just 15 minutes, it would be appreciated. If I haven't heard by the end of next week would it be all-right to call Billy?
Never be impolite, impatient, or pushy. You can always call back or send mail or fax note later if you don't get results.	*This conversation went fairly well, so there was no chance for any "friction," but receptionists are often very good gatekeepers and can be curt with job seekers. You don't want to spar with anyone, so maintain a polite demeanor.*
On-target conversations get the very best results, so stay focused and know what you want.	*Justin stayed pretty much on target. While he didn't overview his background in detail, he did cite a bit about his sales experience. He wanted to schedule an interview, but only confirmed that he was still in the running. That's okay for a first follow up.*
Whenever possible ask to arrange a telephone or in-person employment interview or information conversation, or ask to speak with someone "who can tell me a bit about entry-level jobs." **W**rite and mail or fax a thank-you note.	*Justin did ask if it would be appropriate to conduct an information conversation. He also asked if he could contact a salesperson to discuss the nature of the job. He didn't receive permission, so if Justin has any contact with employees of this firm he must be very, very diplomatic. Justin will of course follow up with a fax note to Mr. Recruiter and, perhaps, to Billy. Assistants often have a great deal to do with who gets an interview. He will also ask a previous employer to fax a very brief letter of recommendation urging that an interview be granted. Justin's call showed Mr. Recruiter some important qualities and sales potential. Follow-up actions and, eventually, an interview will result in success.*

SCRIPT SAMPLE IV: SUBSEQUENT FOLLOW UP

S	**S**ay "hello" and acknowledge (and note) the name of the person you are speaking with.	○ Hello, my name is Hiram E. Now. I met with Mr. Recruiter last week and I want to speak with him about the status of my candidacy. ❏ *I'll forward you to his office. Please hold.*
T	**T**ell why you are calling and whom you wish to speak with. **T**ell about previous communications if a follow-up call.	○ Hello, I'm Hiram E. Now. I interviewed with Mr. Recruiter last week at UOP and I want to speak with him about the status of my candidacy. ❏ *He's not available now. I'm sorry.* ○ Maybe you can help me. Is there any way of finding out how well I did and if I will be invited back for additional interviews? I really want to work for your company.
A	**A**ssess status of application or consideration process. Assertively focus on identifying appropriate next steps.	❏ *No, I can't give you that information.* ○ Oh, I'm being impolite. Your name is? Suzie, do you know when Mr. Recruiter would be available? Should I call back or should I just fax him a quick note? His fax number please?
R	**R**equest an appointment for an employment interview or information conversation. **R**equest a suggestion for next steps or for a referral.	❏ *You can try both. I'll leave him a message you called.* ○ Thank you so much. You've been great. I don't want to be a pest, but I am very eager to hear and I do so much want to get an offer. Do you have any suggestions regarding what I could do to enhance my chances?
T	**T**hank the person you are speaking with and confirm spelling of all names, addresses, phone and fax numbers.	❏ *It seems like your doing everything right to me.* ○ Thanks again. You're very nice. I hope I have a chance to meet you someday.
N	**N**ever be impolite, impatient, or pushy. You can always call back or send mail or fax note later if you don't get results.	*No problem here. All went well.*
O	**O**n-target conversations get the very best results, so stay focused and know what you want.	*While Hiram didn't speak with his targeted person, he did accomplish something. Mr. Recruiter's Receptionist knows of his enthusiasm and his desire for feedback.*
W	**W**henever possible ask to arrange a telephone or in-person employment interview or information conversation, or ask to speak with someone "who can tell me a bit about entry-level jobs." **W**rite and mail or fax a thank-you note.	*Hiram didn't get the name of the first person who answered, but he did get the name of the most important person. Of course, he will fax a nice note to Suzie (even without knowing her last name) and one to Mr. Recruiter. Hiram did all that was appropriate. Subsequent calls might involve arranging a callback interview or, if necessary, following up a rejection letter. Whatever, he now feels comfortable speaking with Suzie.*

PHONE, FAX, AND VOICE MAIL ETIQUETTE EXAM STUDY SKILLS SUMMARY

- ✇ Presented humorous, yet informative do's and don'ts.
- ✇ Illustrated "phone scripts" for practice communications and to prepare for typical interactions.
- ✇ Addressed issues regarding voice mail, fax, and e-mail.

CHAPTER 9

Mr. Recruiter's Tell it All Test

We compiled the 13 most commonly asked (and unlucky) questions regarding college recruiting and sought the advice and guidance of the world's most famous (or infamous, yet honest) on campus interviewer, Mr. Yuri Mean Recruiter. Circle answers you believe *best* identify Mr. Recruiter's responses.

1. How do you determine which schools you recruit at?

(a) If we have a VP who graduated from there, or if the son or daughter of a board member, major shareholder, or senior manager goes there, we go there!

(b) If the school has a reputation for a particular major that we believe matches our needs, we go there!

(c) If the school has a general reputation for excellence, it's ranked in someone's "top ten," or it requires very high SAT scores for admissions (if I couldn't get in), we go there!

(d) If for some reason, we have a lot of alumni employees from the school and they ask me to go there, we go there!

(e) If students and alums have bothered me with letters and calls for two years, and I hire at least one per year, we go there!

(f) All of the above

2. Why do you prescreen resumes?

(a) We want our recent hires to feel "involved" in the process, so we let them screen resumes and identify their friends!

(b) We want to appear "selective," even if it's not the case, to gain a better reputation and attract the best of the best!

(c) We want to maximize our time on campus, only interviewing those that match our "profile" and seem to fit!

(d) We want candidates to think about opportunities and write cover letters (show us analytical abilities and writing skills) before interviews!

(e) We really don't know why we do it, we just do it!

(f) All of the above

3. Do you ever consider candidates and hire from nontargeted schools?

(a) If they have a GPA above 3.5 or they have been referred by someone with "clout" (someone I fear), I'll consider them, but I may not interview them.

(b) If they have really done their homework and express specific goals well, and they are persistent and patient, I'll consider them and, maybe, interview them.

(c) If I have high targets (seeking large numbers of new hires) and if they are willing to travel to my office or meet me on a campus where I have scheduled recruiting, I'll consider and interview them.

(d) If I have low targets, not really, unless it's after recruiting season and I need to fill a hole.

(e) All of the above

4. Can a candidate ever really overcome a poor GPA?

(a) Are you kidding? HA!

(b) If he or she is the son or daughter of a board member, major shareholder, or senior manager, definitely "yes," otherwise definitely "maybe!"

(c) If he or she can get an interview, I'll consider other factors and listen to his or her explanation, but it better be good!

(d) It depends on the position I'm considering a person for—for some jobs, yes, for others definitely "no!"

(e) All of the above

5. What is the real purpose of information sessions, on-campus interviews, and callbacks?

(a) Information sessions and on-campus interviews are really "promotional" and "PR"-oriented ways to keep our name in the minds of students year after year. Callbacks are, if anyone ever is invited back, when we really decide who to hire.

(b)   Information sessions are my chance to sell the company and answer stupid questions students have. On-campus interviews are simply screening sessions where I get to guess who might fit. Callbacks are when persons who really know what candidates might do on the job get to make decisions regarding who is qualified and who to hire.

(c)   Information sessions give me a chance to show off recent hires and take career services people to dinner. On-campus interviews are for assessing talent and ranking potential candidates. Callbacks are when I bring back candidates who match our hiring needs.

(d)   All of the above

6.   **Are Career Fairs of any value to you or the job seeking student?**

(a)   Not if I expect to find time to conduct "real interviews."

(b)   Not if candidates think that I'll invite someone back just because they left me a resume (especially one without an objective) and had a firm handshake!

(c)   Only if I think of them as good ways to get out the word regarding anticipated openings and students think of them as ways to informally meet me and learn as much about my company as is possible in five minutes.

(d)   Only if candidates follow up, follow up, and follow up.

(e)   All of the above

7.   **Do you ever use "search firms" to recruit recent grads?**

(a)   Rarely, because they cost so much (fees can be as high as 25–30 percent of first year's salary), but they are persistent , so I do on occasion.

(b)   Usually for some of the very difficult to fill spots, particularly the technical ones.

(c)   Only if I'm trying to fill 101 sales positions that don't seem attractive to most college grads.

(d)   All of the above

8.   **Do you ever use "resume databases" to locate recent grads?**

(a)   Didn't I answer this question? Oh, it's the very same as with "search firms." Rarely, because they cost so much.

(b)   If I ever do, it's for some of the very difficult to fill spots, particularly technical ones.

(c) Only if I'm trying to fill 101 sales positions which don't seem attractive to most college grads.

(d) If I do, I use the free ones offered by professional associations, because the others ask for ridiculous fees.

(e) All of the above

9. **When is it too late to look for a job?**

(a) The day after I leave your campus!

(b) While it's never too late, chances for consideration and, ultimately, for an interview diminish as the season goes on.

(c) It gets more and more difficult as you get closer to graduation, but things improve throughout the summer and I do regularly hire in the fall.

(d) Why? If you don't have a job as of a certain date will you go to grad school or join a monastic order?

(e) All of the above

10. **Do "contacts" really help?**

(a) Yes, if you need glasses but you're too vain to wear them. HA! Seriously, as noted in answers to earlier questions, they can help a great deal, but you have to let me know who they are.

(b) Contacts can get you an interview (especially if I know the person has good judgment or a great deal of power), but they can't get you a job.

(c) Contacts aren't as effective if they call me and say "I don't know what this kid wants, but please read the resume and think about where he or she might fit."

(d) Contacts can be most effective if you've discussed goals with them and they (or you) can clearly state what positions are of greatest interest and if they clearly request that I interview you.

(e) All of the above

11. **If rejected after a campus interview, is there any hope of working for your company?**

(a) Little, but you know the old saying, "nothing ventured, nothing gained."

(b) It's a long shot, but I do hire (usually in the summer) about one or two people each season whom I rejected on campus.

(c) If the candidate can show me a great deal of focus and goal-directedness (usually through correspondence, phone conversations, and with a well-written specific letter of recommendation).

(d) Once rejected, it's even more important to be able to cite appropriate job preferences and then, just maybe. . . .

(e) All of the above

12. What are you *really* looking for?

(a) Candidates as smart and bright and good looking as I am!

(b) Candidates who know what they want to do and why they can do it successfully!

(c) Candidates who match specific needs, not just "good" people.

(d) It depends on my needs in any given year or during any given time period . . . I really can't say!

(e) All of the above

13. How did you get your job and do you like it?

(a) I started in sales and didn't do a very good job, so they promoted me to this position. Yes!

(b) I started in the exact position I recruit most grads into and when I had the choice to manage a department or become a recruiter, I selected recruiting. Yes, but all of the travel does get to me. It isn't as much fun as one might think.

(c) I don't really know. After a few years in a general management track, I was given a choice to continue on the traditional path, which required a move to some god-forsaken city, or become a recruiter. I guess so.

(d) It was something of a promotion, but it's got a lot more accountability and headaches than I thought it would. Not really, I want to get into college career services!

(e) All of the above

**MR. RECRUITER'S TELL IT ALL
TEST ANSWER KEY**

You guessed it! The correct answer is *All of the above*! Every statement in the test was an answer given by our illustrious guest lecturer. Don't be too upset if you had a few incorrect responses. You simply tried too hard to find the very, very best answer. Like my wife says when asked why she married me: "I knew I had found Mr. Right, but I didn't know I found Mr. right all of the time." Mr. Recruiter is right all of the time. He couldn't give false information. Everything he said was on target and worthy of your consideration.

While the information is presented in a humorous format, it is realistic and informative. On-campus recruiting is an important part of many job search efforts, but students can not depend on it for success. Many fields, like advertising, public relations, publishing, and human services, are not traditional on-campus recruiters. Those that do visit schools are usually large enough, structured enough, and predictable enough to target a need for a large number of potential employees in specific areas (i.e., sales, engineering, accounting). Where firms recruit is as much a function of subjectivity as it is of objectivity, so you should not limit your efforts to those who visit your school. While on campus recruiting is a valuable and very convenient way to begin a job search, it often is not the way most efforts continue. Only about 20 to 25 percent of those who participate in this process receive offers. Most college grads must go beyond on-campus recruiting. They develop and implement effective self-initiated search efforts, with job search typically requiring three to six months of postgraduation activities.

MR. RECRUITER'S TELL IT ALL TEST STUDY TIPS FOR THE RETEST (ACTION STEPS TO TAKE)

✎ Mr. Recruiter was nice (and verbose) enough to provide some additional words of wisdom. His list of don'ts (he is rather negative) appearing later should help you when preparing for on-campus interviewing.

✎ Visit your school's career services facility to learn as much as you can about past, present, and future recruiting activities. Don't just look at materials and schedules. Speak at length with a professional so you can learn about procedures, policies, and preparation steps. If at all possible, meet informally with the "Recruiting Coordinator." This person usually isn't considered a "counselor," but he or she knows as much (if not more) than anyone. Plan ahead. The worst thing you can do is jump headlong into recruiting without having completed self-assessment, goal setting, or interview preparation.

While recruiting is not the way most college grads find employment, it should never be thought of as a "hit-or-miss" proposition.

✎ Use formal or informal alumni networks to locate and speak with recent graduates regarding their recruiting experiences. Don't be turned off by horror stories, which tend to be exaggerated for dramatic purposes. Learn via the 20/20 hindsight what these people possess.

Mr. Recruiter's List of Don'ts

☞ **Don't research a company ... too much!**
First research the job you'll be interviewing for. If it is not clearly described in recruiting literature, ask a career services person for help. Speaking with someone who currently holds the position is ideal. Call me! When I'm in a good mood, I'll refer candidates to appropriate people. If not, my assistant will describe the job I'm recruiting for and, maybe, give you the name of someone to speak with. If you can do this before I see you on campus, I'm very, very impressed.

☞ **Don't just look at this year's schedule.**
Review lists of organizations that participated in previous seasons. Contact recruiters by phone and mail. Identify the nature of entry-level options and where the firm may be recruiting this year. Offer to meet at a mutually convenient site (another school) or at corporate headquarters. Or, if enough students contact the recruiter, he or she may decide to revive the relationship with your school and conduct on-campus interviews.

☞ **Don't interview for practice, although you should interview for the "experience."**
Practice interviewing is for career services people to do, not for on-campus interviewers. You're wasting your time and the recruiter's if you use an interview for practice. But, you don't have to "love" a company and the job to sign up for an initial screening interview. Have the experience even if you just have a bit of interest.

☞ **Don't wait for specialized firms to recruit, but take advantage of those that visit campus.**
Most on-campus recruiting programs include many sales-oriented firms, insurance companies, financial service organizations, and retailers. Students stereotype and don't sign up for these organizations. If you are at all interested in one, interview with several. Sometimes you can be surprised! You could end up getting an offer from, and working for, an organization that at first didn't appeal to you. Don't wait for ad agencies, PR firms, or not-for-profits. You'll recruit them, not vice versa.

☞ **Don't ever be afraid to call recruiters and ask for information on their firm and for details regarding the positions they will be holding interviews for.**
While you may not actually speak with one, an attempt will be worth the effort. Administrative assistants, often called "Recruit-

ing Coordinators," will be better able to answer any questions you have. Preinterview research doesn't have to take place covertly in some dark library. Call to learn what you need to know.

☞ **Don't assume career fairs are ways to get the attention of recruiters and set up interviews, but attend as many as possible.** They can involve traveling to a nearby city, but they can be very valuable. Remember, job search really begins the day after an event, with your initial follow-up actions. These cattle calls are not really for meeting and greeting recruiters and impressing someone enough to get an interview. They are for you to gain enough first-hand and in-depth information to write the very best cover letter and, then, request an interview. In fact, some of my helpful hints regarding career fairs appears in the Appendix of this publication.

☞ **Don't forget search firms.**
While search firms don't find jobs for people, but people for jobs (postings from clients), they can be effective. Be focused when communicating with these organizations. They often receive postings that will not appear anywhere else. They can "connect" you with a client who has hired grads for specific positions in the past. Also, many specialty firms (accounting, advertising, legal) can help those seeking positions in hard-to-break-into fields. I do use them once in a while.

☞ **Don't limit yourself to the recruiting schedule of your school.**
All of you have friends that attend other schools (I know. I've interviewed them), so ask them for copies of their schedules. Don't be a pest, or silly enough to assume that you can participate in another institution's recruiting program, but you can write letters to recruiters and request that they see you during "free" (HA!) time when visiting a particular campus. After they say "yes," you conveniently arrange to visit your friend and coincidentally bring your interview attire with you.

☞ **Don't ever tell me you want to be a "manager" or your goal is "management training."**
I'm sorry to report of the demise of the "generalist generation." Awhile ago, General Mills, General Foods, General Dynamics, General Motors, General Electric (almost any firm with "general" in its title), and many others hired grads for "General Management Training Programs." It was then okay to say "I want to be a 'general manager.' " What was once thought of as an ideal objective, is now inappropriate to cite for most firms. General Management is not really a career field. It might not even be a job function. It is truly a way one is viewed (or trained) after entry into a specific job in certain firms. I implore you to be prepared to cite functional goals, including: administration, communications, engineering and technical services, finance, human resources, information systems, marketing, operations, or sales. Also, don't tell me you "want to work with people." Who doesn't?

☞ **Don't limit job search efforts to on-campus recruiting, unless there's a perfect match.**
They are very convenient and, occasionally, productive, but on-campus efforts are not the way most grads find jobs. In fact, our data indicates only 20 percent find employment this way. You

must develop and mount a "self-recruiting" campaign, involving a great deal of goal-directed research, initial contacts, and follow up.

MR. RECRUITER'S TELL IT ALL TEST HELPFUL RESOURCES (PEOPLE, PLACES, AND THINGS)

✔ You guessed it again! College and university career services facilities are the locations for on-campus recruiting. Examine all information available through your school and local offices. The most important information includes the names, addresses, phone and fax numbers of recruiters and descriptions of why they recruit on campus. Yes, corporate literature, available at most facilities, can be valuable, but nothing is as effective as direct communication to recruiters. Don't forget about college grad–oriented career day or job fairs. These activities can prove valuable.

✔ Books you may want to examine include: *The Elements of Job Hunting*, Bob Adams, 1991; *Career Planning Today*, Kendall/Hunt, 1990; *Hot Tips, Sneaky Tricks & Last-Ditch Tactics: An Insider's Guide to Getting Your First Corporate Job*, Wiley, 1989; and *The Directory of Executive Recruiters*, Kennedy Publications.

✔ The College Placement Council, an association whose members include career services and college recruiting professionals, annually publishes directories and job search guides targeted to college Seniors. Most schools receive and distribute these publications free. If yours does not, try another institution or contact CPC directly in Bethlehem, Pennsylvania. Use the CPC's membership directory to identify college relations professionals as well as career services people who can help. Remember, a mass mailing is not effective, so your first efforts should be some pRe-search phone calls, followed by targeted mailed or faxed correspondence.

✔ Seasonal and annual magazines to locate and read include *Careers and 'the College Grad*, Bob Adams; and *Managing Your Career*, National Business Employment Weekly. These periodicals, as well as special editions of most major newspapers, contain helpful hints, identify (via ads) employers seeking candidates, and often profile various career fields and functions.

MR. RECRUITER'S TELL IT ALL TEST STUDY SKILLS SUMMARY

- Via "multiple-guess" format, identified basic and little-known issues regarding recruiting.
- Presented recruiter's perspective to educate and motivate readers.
- Covered issues associated with use of search firms.
- Reinforced need for patient yet persistent communications with recruiters.

CHAPTER 10

Job Search
Secrets Quiz

Note your reactions to statements below. These were once secrets revealed to only a select few, but anyone who has read this book carefully should now find them all too familiar. Check whether you agree or disagree with each statement or whether you're not quite sure.

	STRONGLY AGREE Yes! Yes! Yes!	AGREE Yes. I know. But . . .	NOT SURE Maybe. But, isn't . . .	STRONGLY DISAGREE No Way! Keep it a secret!!!
If I can describe a job, I can get that job.	○	○	○	○
Goal setting is critical to my job search success.	○	○	○	○
My descriptions cannot simply include adjectives like "a good, well-paying, people-oriented, secure job."	○	○	○	○
They must include nouns and verbs, like "a consumer product sales job where I call on grocery stores."	○	○	○	○
If I've met someone with a job I want, I can get a similar job.	○	○	○	○
Information conversations are the best way to identify goals and begin effective networking.	○	○	○	○
I won't just read about jobs, I'll meet people who have jobs of interest.	○	○	○	○

	STRONGLY AGREE Yes! Yes! Yes!	AGREE Yes. I know. But . . .	NOT SURE Maybe. But, isn't . . .	STRONGLY DISAGREE No Way! Keep it a secret!!!
I know job search is a communications process, not an applications or correspondence process.	○	○	○	○
I won't simply "apply" for jobs, but communicate my goals verbally and in writing to as many people as I can.	○	○	○	○
I will follow up all leads and initial contacts, seeking to meet face-to-face whenever possible.	○	○	○	○
I will use phone calls, letters, faxes, and voice mail and, ultimately, interviews as effective job search tools.	○	○	○	○
Job search is simple, if not necessarily easy, and can be outlined in easy-to-follow steps.	○	○	○	○
There are actually two types of job search.	○	○	○	○
I will conduct a reactive search by reacting to postings, want-ads, and recruiting activities.	○	○	○	○
I will conduct a proactive search by being goal-directed, networking, and contacting organizations related to my field of interest.	○	○	○	○
I will not limit myself to reactive efforts.	○	○	○	○
Search firms won't find me jobs, but they might represent a firm with selective and hard-to-find postings.	○	○	○	○
I know search firms seek and receive postings from employers, then source to identify candidates, so I will be focused.	○	○	○	○
I know they screen to determine which candidates will interview with client firms that posted positions, so I'll be assertive.	○	○	○	○
Fees should be paid by client firms, not me.	○	○	○	○
Resumes and cover letters won't get me jobs; I'll get a job.	○	○	○	○
No matter how great, job search tools are only as effective as my follow-up efforts.	○	○	○	○
There is a "perfect" format I can effectively use forever.	○	○	○	○
Job search success often comes in follow-up stages and frequently after rejections.	○	○	○	○
I won't fool myself into thinking I'm doing job search by sending out a great many resumes.	○	○	○	○

	STRONGLY AGREE Yes! Yes! Yes!	AGREE Yes. I know. But . . .	NOT SURE Maybe. But, isn't . . .	STRONGLY DISAGREE No Way! Keep it a secret!!!
I'll respond to rejections by seeking additional consideration or, at least, information conversations.	○	○	○	○
The more people I talk to about their jobs, the more likely I'll find mine.	○	○	○	○
I'll ask "What do you do?"	○	○	○	○
I'll ask "What was your first job in this field like and what advice do you have regarding entry-level options?"	○	○	○	○
I'll ask "Are there books or magazines I should read or association meetings I should attend to learn more?"	○	○	○	○
I'll ask "Can you tell me two others whom I can talk to about their careers?"	○	○	○	○
An interview is simply a conversation with a purpose.	○	○	○	○
I'll read my resume and cover letter and bring copies to every interview.	○	○	○	○
I'll have three key points to make written down on back of my resume.	○	○	○	○
I'll have three anecdotes to tell written down on the back of my resume.	○	○	○	○
I'll have three questions to ask written on the back of my resume.	○	○	○	○
Job search takes three to six (really six to nine) months, so I'll sign-up for a course or two.	○	○	○	○
I'll develop reality-based strategies and seek "meaningful" options.	○	○	○	○
I'll take a class or two (through a community college or seminar series).	○	○	○	○
I know that increased knowledge and a fine-tuned career vocabulary can overcome a lack of experience.	○	○	○	○
Reference Librarians are the most underutilized, and best, job search support persons.	○	○	○	○
If I ask for an obscure listing of potential employers in a given city, a reference librarian will probably find it.	○	○	○	○
I'll learn about database search programs to identify and research potential employers and prepare for interviews.	○	○	○	○
I'll find a job search support person willing to identify a next resource when I need it the most.	○	○	○	○
It's easier to find a job when I have a job, so I'll work (or volunteer) somewhere while looking.	○	○	○	○

	STRONGLY AGREE Yes! Yes! Yes!	AGREE Yes. I know. But . . .	NOT SURE Maybe. But, isn't . . .	STRONGLY DISAGREE No Way! Keep it a secret!!!
I'll take a part-time or volunteer position while my search continues.	O	O	O	O
Job search can successfully be done while I work if I plan properly.	O	O	O	O
Employers don't like to hire "unemployed" people, they like to hire people who are "working" or volunteering.	O	O	O	O
Hard workers work hard and busy people are not too busy to get results.	O	O	O	O
Those who are looking for "anything," often find "nothing."	O	O	O	O
An inability to say what I want to do and where is the most common reason for prolonged job search. Being "open" limits me to posted options (ads, search firms, career fairs).	O	O	O	O
Networking is not just using people I know; it's getting to know new people.	O	O	O	O
Networking is simply telling people my "job search story" and my goals, and asking for assistance and guidance.	O	O	O	O
Writing, calling or faxing "special" persons I might consider "famous" or "hard to reach" is a great idea.	O	O	O	O
I'll contact my alma mater and *all* local colleges and universities regarding career services.	O	O	O	O

Now, tally all of your responses and note results here:

	STRONGLY AGREE Yes! Yes ! Yes!	AGREE Yes. I know. But . . .	NOT SURE Maybe. But, isn't . . .	STRONGLY DISAGREE No Way! Keep it a secret!!!
TOTALS				

You ***must*** receive a combined Strongly Agree and Agree score of 50 or above. If not, please retake the *Job Search Survival Quiz* and then reread sections associated with Not Sure or Strongly Disagree responses.

This final assessment is offered as a summary presentation of all issues appearing in this publication. The answers should appear obvious. If not, you may wish to review particular chapters. This device is meant to motivate as well as review. It can be viewed as guidelines for job search actions.

I hope you enjoyed this book and I encourage you to take actions with a positive and optimistic attitude. You've all passed with flying colors. In truth, the self-paced test that is job search has no failures. Some take a bit longer, but eventually everyone receives the highest grade possible. You will find a meaningful first, or next, job! Remember, job search is really a never-ending course. I'm sure you will take these tests more than once in your vocational lifetime. To remind you of the basics, we'll revisit some specific guidelines for the last time:

Successful job seekers:

☆   Review, and document in writing, knowledge of self and knowledge of career fields and job options.

☆   Synthesize knowledge of self and information pertaining to careers and job functions in order to set tentative research goals (worthy of more inquiry) and job search goals (targeted for job search actions).

☆   Verify information regarding research and job search goals, fine-tuning job search goals, identifying and researching in greater detail potential employers, and developing job search strategies.

☆   Prepare to express information effectively via written (resumes, cover letter, fax messages, and follow-up letters) and verbal (telephone calls, informational and employment interviews, and voice mail messages) communications.

To be successful, you will:

☞   **Write thorough descriptions of jobs you want on 3x5 index cards.** State geographic and functional goals—what you want to do and where—on paper and, whenever asked. Remember, goal setting involves self-assessment (clarification of skills, values, and interests) and, most importantly, pRe-search of career fields and job functions. Introspection is not enough! You must be able to cite goals, even if they are only exploratory in nature.

☞   **Develop a distribution copy of your resume, with at least one version citing an objective.** Resumes can be "multipurpose" (without an objective) or "targeted" (with an objective citing goals), but you should develop at least one targeted version. Resumes and all job search correspondence must project goals and qualifications. Cover letters and follow-up notes communicate goals and qualifications and identify desired next steps (i.e., interviews) . Writing skills must be fine-tuned and applied to these special projects.

☞ **Identify the names, addresses, and phone and fax numbers of at least 25 potential employers.**
Use directories and other resources to develop a list of employers to contact. Then, don't do a mass mailing. Call first, identify whom to communicate with, begin research on the nature of the firm and learn as much as you can about how the job you want fits into the operations of this organization. Don't research the firm too much and ignore the function.

☞ **Network! Network! Network!**
Share pRe-search and job search goals and resumes (in person or via letters) with friends, family members, faculty, business associates, past employers, and, of course, alumni of your school. Meet someone who has (or had) a job you would like. Ask for exactly what you want, not simply for "help." If you want an information conversation, ask for it. If you want the names of firms (and contact person) that hire within functions of interest, ask for them. Identify how your network member can help. Don't simply make a vague request for assistance. Be honest, inquisitive, and appreciative, not pushy or obnoxious.

☞ **Respond to posted opportunities with confidence.**
Use the best resumes, cover letters, and follow-up strategies. Locate and use job postings, such as want-ads, employment agencies, job fairs, and on-campus recruiting programs. Identify whether professional associations have field-specific newsletter and posting mechanisms. Use search firms to uncover hidden postings, but be assertive and don't wait for these services to find you a job. Yes, also use resume data banks, but don't depend on them.

☞ **Conduct a thorough proactive, goal-directed campaign.**
Inform as many people as possible, as often as possible, about job search goals. Don't wait for postings to appear. Contact persons on your potential employer listing and members of your network on a regular basis. Get involved in professional groups. Do internships, volunteer projects, or take classes while seeking a full-time position.

☞ **Locate and use college or other career services professionals.**
There are a great many career counselors and job search coaches available. Contact your alma mater and local schools, as well as private services. Ask others (including reference librarians) for guidance. You're not alone!

☞ **Follow up all initial contacts and even negative responses.**
Communicate consistently, persistently, yet appropriately with potential employers until an interview (by phone or in person) is given. Use phone, letter, voice mail, or fax communiqués.

☞ **Interview confidently and effectively, with little if any physical or psychological symptoms.**
Communicate your motivations and, most importantly, qualifications to do a job during initial and follow-up interviews.

☞ **Receive, analyze, and accept or decline offers.**
Conduct post-offer analysis and determine whether to say "yes" or "no." While difficult to do (emotionally and financially), rejecting an offer may be the right thing in certain circumstances.

JOB SEARCH SECRETS QUIZ STUDY SKILLS SUMMARY

- Assessed whether concepts presented were internalized.
- Overviewed and summarized important information.
- Addressed some special issues not covered in other quizzes.
- Motivated readers to suggest that others buy and use this book.

Appendix:
Tips Not Tests

No book is complete without an appendix. This is where authors or editors (depending on who had the last word in a constructively critical discussion) put valuable information that didn't fit anywhere else. The following are tips for special populations. Placing information in this section is not an indicator of its value. In this case, last is definitely not least important (my final reference to a home-spun homily).

TIPS FOR RECENT COLLEGE GRADS

Whether you graduated this spring or a few years ago, these suggestions should prove valuable for job seeking alumni:

Be focused and stay focused. If you cannot express your goals, meet or speak with a career services counselor. Do some "telecounseling" if you have moved far from campus. You should be able to state two or three functional goals (job titles and fields of interest) as well as geographic goals (cities where you will actively seek employment). Those who are "open to anything, anywhere" often find nothing, nowhere and unintentionally prolong job search. Remain upbeat and optimistic, even during the tough times. Job search traditionally takes three to six months beyond graduation, but it is not unusual for it to take longer. If you graduated in June, or if you just began your efforts to locate a new position, stay energetic and enthusiastic.

Respond to posted openings, but don't depend upon them for success. Identify posting sources—newspaper want-ads, professional association newsletters, search firms, and, yes, college career services offices. Respond well, via dynamic cover letters and resumes, while uncovering hidden opportunities. Visit your school's or local career services facilities to learn about posting mechanisms and how to effectively contact potential employers. Scan all newspapers (in a library if you don't want to buy them). Contact search firms and inquire regarding the nature of postings (client companies) they source for. These organizations are often underutilized or misused by recent grads. Spending time learning about what they can and can not do can pay off now, or a few years later. Also, many hire recent grads into challenging positions that combine the roles of salesperson, account manager, and recruiter. Identify professional associations and employers who post openings in newsletters (or internal listings) or via hotlines. Don't depend upon reactive methods, but don't ignore them either.

Job search is a communications process, not an application or correspondence process. While you will occasionally "apply" for posted jobs or for openings you hear about, you should frequently communicate goals directly to potential employers and to members of your job search network (faculty, friends, family). Success does not come from the quantity of resumes sent, but the quality of your efforts to communicate goals and to follow up all communications persistently and patiently.

Update your resume six to eight weeks after graduation (or after first job search efforts). It's always good to have a "fresh" and newly "sharpened" job search tool. A new resume is a good excuse to contact someone you haven't communicated with in a while.

Become actively involved in professional associations. Join (even if it costs money), attend meetings, volunteer to help with an event or with the newsletter (you have the time). Do whatever you can to increase your opportunities to interact with professionals in fields of interest. When you have a job, you're too busy. When you're looking for a job, you're to embarrassed. Overcome the awkwardness and get involved! Follow up all contacts with a cover letter and, ultimately, with an information conversation or employment interview.

Take courses related to fields of interest, volunteer, or consider "postgraduation internships." Courses build additional skills and illustrate an eagerness to be qualified for your goals. By taking one course or attending a seminar you expand your network and could be granted access to career services of other schools. Employers are impressed by candidates who aren't simply "looking." Those who volunteer to work in their field, investing time and energy for the ultimate payoff, become strong candidates. Whether formal "internship," "part-time jobs" or informal "apprenticeships," these can be springboards to permanent employment. Every job seeker can "give" three days a week to a firm involved in an area of interest. Job search is not "a full-time job" that doesn't allow for constructive alternatives. Also, many locate "transition positions," jobs required to earn rent and student loan money. Don't be afraid to take a "for the money" job. A well-motivated and well-organized job seeker will make time to find the professional opportunity he or she deserves.

Review and follow all of the guidelines that have been presented in this book!

MR. RECRUITER'S TIPS FOR GETTING THE MOST FROM A CAREER FAIR

IF YOU ARE USING THE CAREER FAIR FOR CAREER EXPLORATION . . .

1. Greet a recruiter by saying "hello" and shaking hands. Introduce yourself and identify your status, saying something like *"I'm just beginning to explore career options. I'm very interested in the fields of sales and retailing. Could I ask you a few questions about sales and, if appropriate, about your background and general views regarding the field?"*

2. Questions can include: *"I read that your organization offers opportunities in sales. Do they require any special skills or experiences? What abilities do you believe contribute most to success in sales? Do you know of sales opportunities in your organization?"* Be inquisitive.

3. Thank the representative for his or her time, collect literature, and continue on to another table. The more people you talk to, the better. If time permits, review materials collected, think about your conversations, and return to particular representatives for continued discussions.

4. You should write thank-you notes. Collect business cards or jot down names of those you speak with. Follow up can set the scene for informational interviews and, ultimately, for job search consideration. Also, visit your career services office to discuss your experience and set strategy.

IF YOU ARE USING THE CAREER FAIR FOR JOB SEARCH . . .

1. Introduce yourself, making eye contact and shaking hands. Offer a copy of your resume and give a bit of background, including major, date of graduation, and state your interest in an entry-level, intern, or summer position.

2. Ask a few questions pertinent to your goals, like: *"What entry-level, intern, or summer sales- and marketing-related opportunities are available with your organization? What are the qualifications you seek in candidates for these positions? When you interview candidates do you focus on particular skills and experiences? Who are the most successful recent hires? Do you have alumni of my school working for your organization? What is the best way of expressing my interest? Whom should I write to or call?"*

3. Listen carefully to the representative's responses and to his or her discussions with others. Don't be afraid to express goals. You might think that the more "open" the better, but in truth, the more "focused" your discussions, the better. Be sure to clarify appropriate steps to follow if you are interested in being considered for opportunities within your fields of interest.

4. Always leave a quality copy of your resume. If you are only somewhat focused, be inquisitive and enthusiastic. Remember, this is simply an introductory meeting. The more information you gain, the more effective your follow-up communications. Identify the best

way to communicate in the future and with whom you should communicate. If you are *very* focused, provide enough insight into your candidacy to ensure a more formal screening interview. You may ask *"can I call soon to arrange a more formal interview?"*

5. Thank the representative for his or her time, collect literature, and continue on to another table. The more people you talk to, the better. If time permits, review material collected, think about your conversations, and return to particular representatives for continued discussions. Definitely stop by a bit later to say "good-bye" to those representing firms that offer opportunities you really like.

6. You *must* write thank-you notes. Collect business cards or jot down the names of individuals you speak with. Follow up *will* set the scene for future exchanges and, ultimately, for formal interviews. Also, visit your career services office to discuss your experience and set strategy.

Career Fairs (a.k.a. Job Fairs and Career Days) are sponsored by schools, professional associations, local radio and television stations, public agencies, or private firms who do so for profit. Attend as many as you can. They are advertised in newspapers or through career services office ads. Don't mistakenly assume that giving out resumes and briefly speaking with a great many recruiters is effective. Remember, job search begins the day after a career fair. Your follow-up activities are critical.

TIPS FOR INSTRUCTORS, CAREER COUNSELORS, AND JOB SEARCH COACHES

This book was designed for use by career services professionals as well as job seekers. I hope you found the information motivational and informative. Each assessment can be used to develop 30-to-45-minute miniworkshops or 60-to-90-minute seminars. They can also be portions of larger job search skills courses.

For a 45–60-minute miniworkshop . . .

➡ Allow five to ten minutes for participants to complete the assessment. Of course, give appropriate credit when using any photocopied materials.

➡ Take three "open" questions from the group, addressing issues of particular importance.

➡ Cover what you judge are the three most significant questions appearing in the answer key. Elaborate upon content appearing in the text, yet focusing on these key issues.

➡ Choose a next step outlined in the Study Tips section of the appropriate chapter or identify one of your own. Via a prepared handout, clearly outline this next step and resources to use. These can be those noted in the Helpful Resources section, or they can be those of your making (i.e., your school's resume-writing guide). Make sure this step is clear and that all participants are aware of what is expected. Schedule individual follow-up sessions now if at all possible.

➡ Answer one more "open" question. Then, suggest that participants review the entire answer key to cover any remaining questions and, if you feel comfortable, suggest they locate and use the complete text.

For a 60–90-minute seminar. . .

➡ Allow five to ten minutes for participants to complete the assessment. Of course, give appropriate credit when using any photocopied materials.

➡ Take five "open" questions from the group, addressing issues of particular importance.

➡ Cover what you judge are the three most significant questions appearing in the answer key. Elaborate upon content appearing in the text, yet focusing on these key issues.

➡ Choose a next step outlined in the Study Tips section or identify one of your own. Via a prepared handout, clearly outline this next step and resources to use. These can be those noted in the Helpful Resources section, or they can be those of your making (i.e., your school's resume writing guide). If time permits, brainstorm ways to complete this activity or, using some of the resources noted, actually begin the effort. After, schedule individual follow-up sessions if at all possible.

➡ Answer three more "open" questions or cover three more from the answer key. Then, suggest that participants review the entire answer key to cover any remaining questions and, if you feel comfortable, suggest they locate and use the complete text.

For a job search skills course . . .

➡ Simply use the text as you would any for a particular course. Cover material chapter by chapter, or use selected sections for appropriate topic-related sessions. If you wish, invite the author in for your initial meeting or for any other class.

Seriously, please accept the offer appearing earlier and rein-forced here. I would very much enjoy spending a few hours or a few days on your campus conducting any of the above events. To make arrangements contact me through University of the Pacific Career Services, McConchie Hall, 235 W. Stadium, Stockton, CA 95204, (209) 946-2361

TIPS FOR U.S. STUDENTS SEEKING OVERSEAS JOBS

Many students ask about ways to locate postgraduation employment overseas. While this is not an easy goal to obtain, it is an easy question to answer. Basically, there are three ways to find an overseas job:

✈ **First, pay your own way to the city, country, or region of interest to look for your job.**
Yes, you do have to get over there (wherever "there" is), investing your own (or mom and dad's) funds into your dream. Prior to doing so you complete pRe-search required to familiarize yourself with the laws and regulations associated with U.S. citizens working in this nation; you identify as many U.S. firms with offices in this nation as you can; you prepare two versions of your resume (one in English and one in the native language of your targeted destination); and you develop as long a listing of family, friends, and alumni who live in this country as is possible. Fax or mail letters to all on your "hit list," outlining your desire to stay once your "vacation" is completed and asking for advice and guidance. When you arrive you spend at least three to six weeks (ideally three months, minimum) enjoying yourself and seeking employment. You follow up with all preidentified leads

and establish and act upon new ones. Once there, find a reason for staying. It may not be a professional position, and often it might involve teaching English as a second language, childcare, or physical labor, but you will find employment for about a year. If in that time you network well, you might locate a more professional position and actually begin that most mystical of all goals, "an international career." This approach has proven about 70 to 80 percent effective (based upon reports of job seekers who returned unsuccessful and those who stayed). The potential for success depends upon the targeted country or region.

✦ **Second, apply for and participate in a formal internship, study-abroad, or work-abroad program.**

Yes, this approach also requires investing funds to achieve your dream, but it can be successful. Many have already studied abroad, but some have not. As a graduate you still apply for summer and semester-long programs. Research and identify those that match geopolitical and subject-specific interests. Once identified, application procedures are relatively easy. Formal programs have step-by-step guidelines, with corresponding paperwork. These can be simply study-abroad programs, or they might involve an internship or a "workcamp"-like component. Whatever the case, the more established the program, the easier to identify and, ultimately participate in. It's getting mom and dad to pay for it that may be difficult. You can use funds raised from a summer job to do the trick. Prior to shipping out on one of these programs you undertake all of the pRe-search outlined above. When you are overseas as a student or intern, conduct efforts described in the first approach and find something to extend your visit long enough to find a more professional opportunity. This approach has also been proven about 50 to 60 percent effective.

✦ **Third, apply for employment with U.S. firms with "international" and overseas operations.**

This is the most often tried, most frustrating, and least effective approach. If you think about it realistically, how many companies are willing to hire recent grads and send them immediately overseas? No matter how fluent you are in a particular language, home nationals speak their native tongue, and perhaps English, a bit better. Don't naively present yourself as possessing the skills to be a "cultural liaison," simply because you've spent some time overseas and do speak a second, or even a third language "fluently." This approach is successful in only 5 to 10 percent of the cases, with most having unusual circumstances like dual citizenship or strong "contacts."

If you are going to implement this strategy, utilize the approaches outlined earlier, including bilingual resumes. Be prepared to state functional goals. Do you want to sell a product? Do you want to guide a group of tourists? Do you want to conduct market research? State your goals clearly, concisely, and as often as you can. While you may not receive an overseas assignment, you may locate an organization that could offer an "international flavor" at first and, ultimately, overseas responsibilities. "International careers" are, as you might suspect from the tone of this piece, difficult to obtain yet desired by increasing numbers of college grads. It may not make you feel better to know that these options do exist within governmental agencies, not-for-profit organizations, and corporate entities, but you must "grow into" these positions rather than "apply for" them upon graduation. Don't give up. Think about Washington D.C. as the most likely city in the United States to find an appropriate first summer internship; then a job. Follow the above two strategies as best bets. Think about graduate study abroad. But don't give up.

A few resources that could prove valuable include: *How to Get a Job In Europe,* Surrey Books 1991; *Work, Study, and Travel Abroad: The Whole World Handbook,* Council on International Educational Exchange Annually; *International Careers,* Bob Adams 1990; *International Jobs,* Addison-Wesley 1989; and *International Jobs and Careers,* Impact Publications 1990. Also, almost every county you can imagine has a United States–linked Chamber of Commerce. Use the International Chamber of Commerce Directory, contact the CofC in the nearest major city, or contact the nearest consulate to identify leads regarding companies expanding business with particular countries.

JOB SEARCH SURVIVAL QUIZ FOR INTERNATIONAL STUDENTS SEEKING HOME COUNTRY EMPLOYMENT

This is a quick and easy assessment of your Job Search Survival Rating. Answer the questions by checking the appropriate boxes, tabulate your score as instructed, and match your results with the comments that follow.

		Yes	No
(1)	Do you have a distribution-ready copy of your resume or vita within arm's reach?	[ ]	[ ]
(2)	Does your home country have a "special" approach to resumes and vitae and do you have samples?	[ ]	[ ]
(3)	Have you visited or spoken with your school's career services office in the past three weeks?	[ ]	[ ]
(4)	Have you communicated with any appropriate business or trade associations (i.e., California Council for International Trade or California State World Trade Commission) in the past two weeks?	[ ]	[ ]
(5)	Have you contacted your home country's consul, tourist and trade office, or chamber of commerce in New York, San Francisco, Los Angeles, District of Columbia, or any major U.S. city within the past week?	[ ]	[ ]
(6)	Do you have a "before I leave" and "after I arrive home" list of job search–related tasks?	[ ]	[ ]
(7)	Have you recently written a friend or family member outlining job search plans and travel calendar?	[ ]	[ ]
(8)	Have you recently contacted U.S.–based organizations that do business in your home country?	[ ]	[ ]
(9)	Can you write thorough descriptions of the jobs you want on 3x5 index cards?	[ ]	[ ]
(10)	Can you write the names of three books or magazines pertinent to your field(s) of interest?	[ ]	[ ]
(11)	Have you recently solicited the help of a reference librarian for a job search–related task?	[ ]	[ ]
(12)	Has anyone ever looked puzzled and confused when you describe your ideal job?	[ ]	[ ]
(13)	Can you cite the name, address, and phone and fax numbers of at least ten potential employers?	[ ]	[ ]
(14)	Have your parents, spouse, or significant other promised to support you forever?	[ ]	[ ]
(15)	Have you won the million-dollar lottery at any time in your life?	[ ]	[ ]

For questions 1–13 score 5 points for each "yes" and zero for each "no." Add your total scores for these 13 questions.

A score of 50–65 indicates that you will not only survive, but you will thrive because you have taken important first steps. You are very familiar with helpful resources and can be confident that you will be successful. You are intuitively aware of the nature of job search.

A score of 40–50 indicates that you may have taken some critical first steps, but don't quite know what to do next. You may need to discuss your goals more carefully with a career services counselor or another job search support person and develop a clearer strategy. You may need to finish your resume or make some decisions as to how to identify potential employers and how to follow up initial contacts, but basically you are on the right track.

A score below 40 indicates that either you have a unique strategy or that you have yet to take steps in the right direction.

If you answered "yes" to question 14 or 15, ignore your Job Search Survival Rating, because you obviously don't need a job and if you wanted to find one (just to keep from being too bored), you could depend upon luck, rather than on your own efforts.

Seriously, this quiz was written to educate as well as motivate. Unless you think you are a very lucky person, you should act upon the ideas presented throughout this book. Every reader should be prepared to take a critical job search step within a week after completing this quiz. Don't wait. Take action. Don't depend on luck. Utilize skill and intelligence. Also, the laws and regulations associated with international students seeking postgraduation employment in this country are complex and subject to ever-changing interpretations. Become very familiar with these regulations should you seek "practical training" or other experiences. First contact your school's international student advisor, as well as the local office of immigration and naturalization.

Index